Getting Out

A Step-by-Step Guide to Selling a Business or Professional Practice

Getting Out

A Step-by-Step Guide to Selling a Business or Professional Practice

Lawrence W. Tuller

LIBERTY HALL
PRESS™

This publication is designed to provide accurate and authoritative information in regard to the subject matter covered. It is sold with the understanding that the publisher is not engaged in rendering legal, accounting or other professional service. If legal advice or other expert assistance is required, the services of a competent professional person should be sought.

—from a declaration of principles jointly adopted by a committee of the American Bar Association and a committee of publishers.

LIBERTY HALL PRESS books are published by LIBERTY HALL PRESS, an imprint of TAB BOOKS. Its trademark, consisting of the words "LIBERTY HALL PRESS" and the portrayal of Benjamin Franklin, is registered in the United States Patent and Trademark Office.

First Edition
First Printing

©1990 by TAB BOOKS
Printed in the United States of America

Library of Congress Cataloging-in-Publication Data

Tuller, Lawrence W.
    Getting out : a step-by-step guide to selling a business or
professional service / by Lawrence W. Tuller.
        p.   cm.
    ISBN 0-8306-8063-2
    1. Business enterprises, Sale of.   I. Title.
HD1393.25.T85   1990
658.1'6—dc20   89-29882
                                                                                   CIP

TAB BOOKS offers software for sale.
For information and a catalog, please contact:

TAB Software Department
Blue Ridge Summit, PA 17294-0850

Questions regarding the content of this book
should be addressed to:

Reader Inquiry Branch
TAB BOOKS
Blue Ridge Summit, PA 17294-0214

Acquisitions Editor: David J. Conti
Book Editor: Lori Flaherty
Production: Katherine Brown
Series Design: Jaclyn J. Boone

This book is dedicated to Susan,
whose deep faith in the basic goodness of people
and to Charles,
whose personal strength and courage,
kept their father from conceding defeat,
and with heartfelt gratitude to Barbara,
whose unyielding support and encouragement
during thirty years of soul-wrenching experiences
always provided inspiration and courage.

Contents

Acknowledgments

MORE THAN 60 PEOPLE HAVE CONTRIBUTED THEIR PERSONAL EXPERIENCES TO THIS book. It would be impossible to express my gratitude to each of them individually. In fact, many prefer to remain anonymous. Some, however, cannot go unnoticed: John Irwin and Roman Fedirka for their patient critique of the technical sections; Donald A. Bordlemay for proving that such a book needed to be written; David J. Conti for invaluable editorial assistance; and finally, my agent Michael Snell without whose unwavering faith, guidance, and encouragement this book would never have been published.

Introduction

NO MATTER HOW MUCH YOU LOVE YOUR BUSINESS, OR HATE IT AS THE CASE may be, there comes a time when it's right to get out, either voluntarily or otherwise. The day will arrive when it's time to climb new mountains, reap well–earned retirement benefits, or perhaps to pass the torch. The business you've nurtured through years of anguish and toil—your baby—will have to be cast aside, disposed of, sold. Perhaps failing health, financial difficulties, a divorce settlement, or maybe just plain boredom has led you to the decision. Whatever the reason, it's time to get out and do something else with your life.

But how? It might take years to find an appropriate buyer. Cash requirements, tax laws, estate planning, family considerations, and economics all influence how and when to put a company on the market. The options seem unlimited. And all this at the same time you're spending 12 hours a day running the business!

Not only does selling a business or practice require an enormous amount of time and energy, it creates potentially severe psychological trauma. Fear, anguish, self-doubt, possibly even despair, can grip you just at the time you need strength and composure. We've all been taught that failure is somehow un-American. But until now, you probably haven't realized that people often equate getting out of your own business with quitting, and in our society, quitting is tantamount to failure. Employees are hurt, friends regard you as a defeated opportunist, and family members become distant.

Further, once the sale becomes final, a vacuum remains. What to do now? Retire to the golf course for a dull life of par fours? Cruise the Mediterranean? Fight grub worms in the garden? Or seek a new career, something to offer a change in life style; make a contribution to society; or realize a dream there was never time nor resources to pursue? Whatever the choice, it's necessary to forget the sale and go forward with your life. This book addresses three key questions:

1. What are the mechanics of actually selling a business or professional practice, at the right time, for the best price?

2. What steps can be taken to mitigate the psychological trauma of getting out?

3. What options are available once the sale is completed?

There is nothing perfunctory about getting out of a business, whether it is sold on the open market, to a partner, or to a successor. It is a human experience with profound effects on the owner, family members, employees, and customers. A humanistic approach must be used to reduce the hardship and hurt to others, while maximizing the financial gain to the seller. Too many business books have been written by those who have never experienced the agony of selling their own business—lawyers, business brokers, consultants, corporate castoffs—that treat a private business sale with the same cold, mechanical approach practiced by corporations. This book doesn't. Having been through the wars several times, I have tried to convey the need for a caring, compassionate attitude to everyone associated with the business, including advisors, bankers, employees, and of course, the buyer, as the secret to a successful sale.

This book is written for the private business owner or professional practitioner who decides it's time to get out. Business advisors will also find the book valuable in structuring deals for their clients. The size or type of business notwithstanding, the same principles, problems, and opportunities apply to selling the local hardware store or a manufacturing company, a business doing $50,000 a year or $50 million, one with 500 employees or none. Practitioners of law, medicine, accounting, consulting, or any other profession, regardless of size of the practice or number of employees, face the same challenges as any business owner, but the techniques of selling differ. Entrepreneurs and professionals at all levels will learn how to dispose of their business in the shortest time, at the best price, how to cope with the psychological trauma to themselves, employees, and customers, and how to structure a meaningful life after the sale.

More than 65 entrepreneurs and professionals have contributed their true experiences to this book. Most prefer to remain anonymous for confidentiality reasons, and I have respected their privacy by avoiding surnames in some cases and merely referring to them as clients in others. A few have graciously allowed the use of their full names and they are included with their stories.

This book is structured into five parts. The first six chapters reveal the critical aspects involved in the preliminary process of getting the business ready, including timing the sale, planning for the minimum tax bite, valuing the company, cleaning up loose ends, and preparing an offering prospectus.

Chapters 7 through 11 disclose proven methods for selling a company to outsiders—open market, merger, or public stock offering - and to insiders—employees (using an ESOP), a successor, or a partner. In addition, these chapters provide tips and guidelines for financing the sale, as well as legal matters you will need to attend to.

Owners of financially troubled companies will find Chapter 12 useful in learning how to sell a company by using Chapter 11 of the Bankruptcy Code.

Chapter 13 is directed specifically to professional practitioners—lawyers, doctors, accountants, dentists, consultants—and includes tips and special techniques for selling either a share of a professional partnership or a complete practice.

The final two chapters provide a program for coping with the psychological trauma of getting out of a business and some options for beginning a new life after the sale.

Although every situation has some unique characteristics, common threads run through all business sales. True case histories and anecdotes used throughout the book illustrate how others have met the challenge and won. If someone else has uncovered the answer, there's no need to reinvent the wheel.

The adventurous road of entrepreneurship must end eventually. Closing the door on one chapter of your life and opening a new door for the next, can be an exciting and rewarding experience, provided you don't jam your finger or bump your head. Adhering to the recommendations in this book, I'm sure you won't. Enjoy and Godspeed!

1

The Dilemma

Deciding When and How to Get Out

DURING THE PAST DECADE, THE NUMBER OF BUSINESSES SOLD, TRANSFERRED, or liquidated have more than doubled the number of start-ups. Are you ready to join the growing ranks of entrepreneurs who have decided they've had enough? Are you ready to trade the stress and anxiety of owning a business or professional practice for a new, less demanding career, or even a new life–style?

"I've had enough. I want out—now—and don't try to talk me out of it." The telephone lines burned with Roger's fervor and his voice shook with uncontrolled emotion. Could this frantic man be the same person I counseled six years earlier when he was buying a business? Then, he couldn't move fast enough to join the ranks of budding entrepreneurs and now he wanted out? "Calm down Roger. You sound like the world is coming to an end."

"I don't care what it sounds like," he retorted, "I've had it with this business and I want to get out, with no strings attached."

During lunch that next Thursday Roger dropped the bomb. "Sorry to bring you into this mess, Larry, but I have to do something and you're the only one I could think of I can trust to be discreet. First, the business isn't doing too well. I've lost some key employees, the union is threatening a strike, and customer orders have dropped off. Second, my wife wants a divorce. She owns 50 percent of the stock, and she's threatening to take half of the business as part of the settlement. Third, I've been putting in 60 hour weeks for the past year, and I'm getting tired. In fact, my blood pressure has skyrocketed and my doctor has told me to slow down or face a possible stroke. Finally, but probably most important, who wants to keep making ball bearings the rest of his life? This was an exciting challenge when I first took over, but now it's just drudgery."

"Whew! You sound like you've really had it," I countered. "But what are you going to do once you get out? Have you thought of that? You're a bit young to retire?"

"I don't really care what I do. Almost anything is better than this mess. Maybe I'll buy a boat and sail around the world. To be honest though, I'll have to admit I am frightened at the prospect of no income. And I hate the idea of being a quitter."

Can all or any part of this story apply to you? If you can relate to Roger's dilemma, then read on, because that's what this book is all about: getting out when you've had enough, and getting out of a business is a lot more difficult than getting in. Much like a marriage, it's easier getting to the altar than breaking the contract.

THE ALTERNATIVES

There are three ways of getting out of your business:

1. Give it away.
2. Close the doors and sell its assets.
3. Sell the whole company.

Giving the business away is probably the easiest. If you own a card or gift shop maybe you can donate it to a museum or church and take a big tax deduction. A print shop might be useful to a social services organization. Or perhaps giving your business to a son or daughter, wife, or other relative willing and able to run it might be part of your estate plan to save taxes when you die. The latter alternative to selling has long been recognized as a way to provide for continuity of the business and save taxes at the same time. But first there must be an able recipient, and you must be willing to forego the cash.

These are very specific cases, however, and really beyond the scope of this book. There are often more feasible ways of building an estate. Readers interested in exploring such a possibility should consult with a qualified accountant or lawyer who specializes in estate planning before proceeding too far down that road. Most business owners and professional practitioners, however, find that giving the business away is not really a viable alternative.

The second option, closing the doors and selling the business assets, is increasing in popularity as a viable alternative to selling the company as a going concern. It is particularly attractive for a business in financial trouble or one that is so unique it precludes a market of potential Buyers. Although for most businesses, liquidation entails more risks than benefits. Chapter 12 explores some of the mechanics and personal risks in liquidating a business.

More than likely, you're probably better off selling the company as a going business rather than donating or liquidating it, and therefore, most of this book deals with the three areas of greatest concern to a Seller:

- What are the mechanics of selling a business?
- How can you grapple with the psychological impact of leaving?
- Where do you turn after the sale to continue living a productive life?

There are a number of ways to sell a business, and there are specific tools available to enhance the possibility of a successful sale for each method. Some of the major questions raised by any Seller are:

- How do I prepare the business for sale?
- What price should I ask?
- When should I begin looking for a Buyer?
- Where will I find a Buyer?
- Who can help me sell it?
- What impact will the sale have on my family?
- What will I do with my time after the sale is completed?

Accurate and timely answers to these questions determine the success or failure of a sale. It might come as a surprise, but there are more failures in selling than there are successes. Many businesses can be on the market for years without finding a viable Buyer, and when one finally does show up, he expects a giveaway. There's no easy way out. Selling a business is one of the most difficult, time consuming, and psychologically depressing actions you will ever be called upon to take.

Buying or starting a business is fun. Oh yes, there are sleepless nights worrying about financing, increasing sales, personnel problems, and customer complaints. But regardless of these difficulties, building a business is productive, it's fun. It's a challenge which, if met successfully, will yield many years of fruitful experiences. The American Dream fulfilled; a job worth doing.

Selling a business, however, can only be described as a pain. You face the same difficult situations as in starting or buying, but now it's no longer fun, because you know it's the end of the dream. Depressing and psychologically draining, anyone who has actually sold a business will vouch that it is far more difficult than buying.

Most business owners believe that the asset they own—their company— is the hottest property around, and they can't imagine why everyone else doesn't agree with them. Unfortunately, most don't. Outsiders quickly spot worn equipment, competitor advantages, personnel incompetence, and faulty marketing strategies.

Yes, a number of entrepreneurs and would-be entrepreneurs are always searching for a company to buy, but the number of viable Buyers shrinks dramatically when the time comes for you to sell.

Disposing of a business, at a fair price and terms, and in a reasonable period of time, differs from selling a house or a piece of land. The market of Buyers is small no matter how glamorous the business might be (and the less glamorous, the smaller the market). The transaction can be extremely complicated and time consuming; not as simple as doing a title search for a house closing. Financing can be a nightmare. Almost any bank in the country wants to place real estate mortgage loans; but how many will gamble on loaning money to buy a business? Not very many, and the names and faces of those who are willing to participate keep changing so fast that sources available yesterday are gone today.

But before we get to the mechanics of how to sell a business, the reasons for getting out must be examined. The reasons for selling determine the timing or when you can sell, the structure or method of sale, and to some extent, your life–style after it's over. Your reasons for selling also influence your feelings about leaving. Failure myths and fears of the future must be dispelled before the sale can be satisfactorily culminated.

THE REASONS

Several years ago, or perhaps many, you either started your business from scratch, purchased it, or inherited it. Otherwise, you wouldn't be reading this book. You've made a decent living from the business. Financed a college education for your kids, invested in a few pieces of growth real estate, and still managed to put away something for those retirement years. Several of the new people you have met over the years have turned into very good friends. Increasing profitability and a strong growth record have caused the business to appreciate in value and you have genuinely enjoyed your stint as an entrepreneur. Why would you ever want to leave? Well, there could be a number of reasons:

- You might just be restless.
- You want to retire.
- You see an economic downturn coming.
- You want to maximize your investment return.
- You need cash.

· You're in bad health.

· Maybe you didn't even want the business in the first place.

In most cases, when an owner seriously considers getting out, there are many reasons prompting the decision. Seldom can he point a finger to one specific reason and say, "That's it! That's why I'm getting out!" It would make the selling process a lot easier if he could, because he could then structure a deal to serve that specific purpose. Nothing in business is simple, however, and the reasons for getting out are usually so varied and complex that true motivations become difficult to define. Of course, if an owner dies, the reason for getting out is clear, but that's the exception rather than the rule.

You Need a Challenge

Restlessness is one of the marks of an entrepreneur. The challenge in making an acquisition or starting a business comes from conquering new horizons and solving new problems. Real joy comes from accomplishing the impossible. Climb the mountain because it's there. Sail the rough waters to meet the challenge of the sea. Bring a new product to market in the face of stiff competition. Buy a company with someone else's money. But don't ask a genuine entrepreneur to sit behind a desk and administer a going business, at least not for very long. He'll be bored silly. This is probably the most dominant reason for selling a business.

In the companion book in this series, *Buying In* the most common reason for buying a business is that nothing else will satisfy the restless spirit and driving ambition for self accomplishment. That need for constant challenge is both the blessing and the bane of entrepreneurs. Without such an overpowering ambition, no sane person would ever venture down the lonely, failure–ridden acquisition trail or risk everything to start a business from scratch. This same drive to accomplish individual acts of risk–taking, however, causes the entrepreneur to become restless with administrative routine until he eventually begins looking for a way to get out. He must push forward; he must continue to push the limits of his ability to conquer.

A close friend of mine for many years was fired by his corporate employer after many years of faithful service. He was approaching 50 and couldn't face dragging out his resumé again. Bob had always wanted to try his hand at running his own business and now the opportunity presented itself. Following my acquisition guidelines, he acquired a small electronics manufacturing company. Success followed success and by the time he turned 56, most of his debt was liquidated and Bob was living quite comfortably.

One day he asked me to find a Buyer for his business. I was astounded that he would think of moving on at his age. "Are you sure, Bob?," I asked, although I knew him well enough to know that he was very sure.

"Yep, I've had enough of this desk job. I've accomplished everything I set out to do and the business is really humming along now. There's a great management team on board and we've introduced several new product lines over the past three years. There isn't anything left for me to sink my teeth into Larry, and I'm certainly not ready to vegetate yet. So see if you can't get me out of this grind and get me some cash so I can try something else."

His wife was looking forward to retirement, but Bob wasn't! He wanted to do it all again! Just when his wife, family, and friends thought he had finally achieved his lifelong goal of having his own business and should be ready to settle down and reap the benefits, he found the urge to venture out again into uncharted waters in search of something new and different to do. Such is a true entrepreneur! By the way, Bob's second acquisition turned out equally well.

If you want out because you're bored, chances are good your business is doing well with no major problems. If that's so, the smoothest road to selling it is probably through the open market. You already know how to buy a company, and many of the same techniques can be applied to selling. If the company was salable at one time, most likely it still is. Some important variations, however, are looked at in the remaining chapters.

Time to Hang it Up

Unfortunately, we all run out of gas sooner or later. It's especially unfortunate when you've been active in the business for years, only to realize that there is no one to take over now. Somehow, you must find a way to dispose of your company before you retire. With no children or family members to take over, and a wife who doesn't have the interest or ability to run the business, you better start looking to the outside market place.

You'll need to begin planning for the transfer well in advance of anticipated retirement. Estate planning, tax laws, and retirement income must be carefully weighed. It could very well be that the form of transfer or the timing of it will be crucial in providing your retirement nest egg. Unlike the corporate employee who participates in a well–established retirement plan, stock purchase program, or extended medical benefits, you can't enjoy the luxury of someone else providing for your retirement income and security. You have to do it the same way you purchased or started the business, on your own.

Certainly, there are self–employed retirement plans: IRAs, Keogh Plans, brokerage house retirement funds, and life insurance annuity programs. Unless you began contributing to these plans early in your career, however, they probably won't provide enough income to meet your needs after retirement, especially if you purchased or started a business later in life. You must now face up to living your twilight years without a sufficient source of income unless you can sell the business for either a large cash nest egg or a steady stream of monthly payments, or find some other way to make a living.

Many of us can recount personal examples of friends who seemed to have sufficient income during their working years only to find that when reaching retirement age, they have nothing to fall back on except the value of their business. If you are past 50, begin planning and providing for the retirement years now, before it's too late.

Planning for the succession of ownership is also crucial to peace of mind. If you have a son or daughter coming along who has both the desire and the ability to run the business, that's terrific. If not, maybe you can bring in a partner or hire an employee to train as a successor, and then sell your business to him. This route carries with it a separate set of complexities, however. Dealing with partnerships and succession is addressed in Chapter 8.

Regardless of who your successor might be, it's still necessary to proceed with a well–defined retirement program well in advance of your getting out. Chapter 15 can help you establish such a plan. It also illustrates some possibilities for a new career after you sell.

A Downturn is Coming

Few people have the ability to predict the future. Natural optimism often blinds the entrepreneur to the reality of the marketplace until it's too late to react. Because business failures are rapidly approaching the number of business start-ups, it is necessary to constantly reassess the future of your business and take corrective measures if you see trouble brewing on the horizon. Reggie S. recognized a downturn coming in his industry but couldn't face up to getting out before it was too late.

Reggie started his construction business 12 years before we met. Starting from scratch with seed money raised from friends, over the years he was eminently successful in building a profitable, growing company. The international market for his construction specialty was booming in the seventies and early eighties and jobs came faster than he could handle. Successfully completing more than 40 overseas jobs, and recently booking several new Middle East contracts, it seemed desirable to increase the office staff and begin a program to develop more sophisticated financial control systems. That's when I came into the picture.

Disaster was looming on the horizon, however. Shortly after completing his Middle East projects, the world market demand for Reggie's specialty collapsed. New marketing programs failed to generate new orders. With developing nations completing the first building phase of national infrastructures, Reggie could not keep his volume up and the business began to deteriorate. Forced to layoff most of the same people he had hired two years earlier, it became clear to this dynamic businessman that something had to be done: either sell, merge, buy another profitable business, or something else.

Reggie was middle age and, although not ready to retire, wanted to have more leisure time for his hobbies. Consequently, after a few unsuccessful attempts at overseas acquisitions, he finally decided to sell what he had and retire to the ski slopes. As with most entrepreneurs, he was impatient and wanted immediate results, but with the business already suffering a scarcity of orders, his financial statements were dismal and a quick Buyer did not materialize.

Eventually, Reggie shifted his market from international to domestic projects with vastly reduced personnel, liquidated his existing company and, essentially, began all over again on a much smaller scale. Today, he has realized his goal of a retirement in the mountains. Without the large cash reserve, however, he might have captured preparing for the sale of his construction company before the collapsing market forced his hand.

The solution to Reggie's getting out problem could very well have been a merger with another construction company. Had he recognized the approaching demise of the overseas market early enough, his company would have been an attractive addition for a larger domestic contractor trying to establish an international presence. Although seldom considered by entrepreneurs, a well planned merger can be a viable way to get out and, in some cases, the only way, which is described in Chapter 7.

The Investment Game

Although most entrepreneurs are in business to satisfy their urge for power or personal freedom, there are also many who buy or start a business as an investment strategy. These people intend from the beginning to sell the company at the appropriate time and maximize their return. In fact, some individuals have become so adept at this form of speculation that it has become almost as commonplace as investing in the stock market only a good deal more risky. Perhaps you are one of these new breed of investor entrepreneurs.

When you're ready to get out, timing the sale becomes crucial. If you're ready but the market isn't, you've lost the gamble, just as in the stock market. If price earnings ratios are below book value, you'll never make your expected gain on the sale. In fact, there might not be any takers at all. The longer a company stays on the market, the more it will deteriorate in value. So if you purchased your company as a speculative investment and the market isn't right to sell, hold onto it because eventually the market will turn. In the meantime, act like an entrepreneur instead of an investor.

At one time I tried this form of investing, but just once! I saw the opportunity to buy a small machine shop at a very low price. In fact, the Seller was so eager to get out he priced the company at below liquidation value and was even willing to carry Buyer paper for 80 percent of the purchase price. I couldn't go wrong. It was an industry I knew, in a convenient location, with a good management team, and the economic cycle was right. I closed the deal quickly with no outside financing and kept the General Manager in place to run the company. We rode the economic curve up and earnings skyrocketed for two years.

Applying my favorite economic yardsticks, I forecasted a downturn in the market in about six months, so I put the business up for sale knowing I could peddle it before the slide began. How wrong could I be! Not only couldn't I find a Buyer quickly, but the market turned down almost overnight. There I was with a company on the skids, owing over $1.5 million to the original Seller, and because of severe reductions in the defense budget, it looked like the market recovery wouldn't begin for at least another three years. I had gambled on my ability to forecast the economic curve and lost miserably. Finally, I agreed to a management buy out through an Employee Stock Ownership Plan and was lucky to net enough cash to pay off the original Seller. But by gambling on such a risky investment strategy, I lost all of my original investment plus valuable time and effort.

To play the game of buying and selling businesses the way you would play the stock market seems inordinately risky. Yet people do it all of the time. In fact, several investment bankers built their financial fortunes by just such a strategy. But it's too risky for me.

Wise stock brokers will always advise their customer to, "Never invest more money in the market than you can afford to lose." I advise clients interested in the business investing game of an even stronger caveat: **Don't play the business investing game unless you can afford to lose at least twice what you have invested and possibly more.**

You Must Have Cash

There are times when the need for personal liquidity overshadows all other criteria. This happens to entrepreneurs as well as anyone else. College costs, medical bills, a new house, a bad stock investment, and many other reasons might create a liquidity need. If cash cannot be raised any other way, selling your business might be the only alternative.

Unfortunately, the increasing trend in divorce suits to award the spouse a share of the assets of a business can create a very real need to raise cash. Many entrepreneurs, and particularly those who are in their first business, feel some emotional need to give their spouse a share of the business, ranging from a token number of shares to 50 percent, sometimes more! While I'm sure this promotes goodwill in the marriage, it can cause a nightmare when one files for divorce. Increasingly, divorce settlements force business assets to be split up, and for an operating business that can be a deathblow. Because of the impracticality of splitting business assets, a court decision usually calls for a cash settlement in lieu of business assets. Consequently, the only way to raise cash is by selling the business.

A client was recently sued by his wife for divorce. She owned 50 percent of the stock in his small printing company but never played an active role. The court awarded a fifty-fifty split of all assets between the two parties and, since his wife had no interest or ability to help manage the print shop, the court directed my client to pay her share of the business in cash.

To make matters worse, with no written agreement between them for valuing the business in the event of a separation, the court, in its infinite wisdom, assigned a value to the business assets significantly in excess of the market. My client had no choice but to sell the company to raise whatever cash he could.

As I searched for a Buyer, it became clear that the court–assigned value was not going to be realized. The business finally sold for about half of the assigned value and all of the proceeds of the sale went to my client's wife. He ended up with nothing. No cash and no business.

If you are in a business partnership with your spouse, no matter what the proportionate shares are, be sure to have your lawyer execute a definitive agreement to value the business and provide for the cross-purchase of stock in the unlikely event of a divorce. I know you love your spouse, but this is only good business. Who can predict what tomorrow might bring?

Unfortunately, when you sell a company to raise cash, it often becomes a forced sale, without regard to fair market value. You need cash fast and, unless you are lucky, will probably not get a fair price. Also, by requiring a full cash deal you lose the advantage of using deferred payment terms to attract Buyers. This limits the market and most often means you'll wind up with significantly less cash than the business is worth. Sometimes there isn't any choice, however, thus creating an attractive acquisition market for quick–buck artists and charlatans (and there are plenty playing the business investing game). If one of these unscrupulous Buyers takes over, it's almost certain he'll have little regard for the welfare of employees or customers. If you value your employees and customers and there is any other way to raise cash or if you can delay the sale until a legitimate Buyer comes along, by all means do so.

In some cases, selling stock to the public (an IPO) can be an alternative way to raise cash. With the right market and business circumstances, this method can solve two problems at once: raise needed cash and still provide an avenue to get out of the business completely, but at an appropriate time. An IPO is tricky and expensive, but as pointed out in Chapter 7, it can be the answer to your cash needs for an otherwise unsellable business.

The Doctor Says STOP

Occasionally, even a young entrepreneur will find himself in bad health and unable to continue running his business effectively. Cancer, a stroke, or other serious ailments can force him to make a choice between selling his business or hiring a manager to run it for him. Some owners solve the problem by bringing in a partner to run the business. This probably means giving up an equity share of the business, but it also means that you can continue to play a role in your company (albeit, not as the boss) and still provide for complete succession.

You Didn't Want it in the First Place

What happens if you inherit a business you don't want or are not qualified to operate? This happens with increasing frequency in family–owned businesses where the owner suddenly dies, willing the business to his wife, son, daughter, or someone else without affording the individual any previous training in the business. The following true story happened when John L., who had very different personal characteristics and management skills than his father, inherited the business.

On his father's unexpected death, John, 32–years–old, inherited a small chain of electronics distribution outlets. His father had started the business many years before and managed it profitably. Most of the employees were of long tenure and liked and admired "the ol' man." He practiced what I like to call merciful management and made a genuine effort to understand and help with the personal and business problems of every employee wherever he could. He was well respected in the community as a caring businessman and earned a reputation with competitors, customers, and vendors for being honest and loyal. He always made an honest effort to understand the other person's concerns in a business transaction.

When John inherited the company, everyone expected him to continue in his father's footsteps. John did not inherit the sensitivities and perceptions of his father, however. He wasn't a bad businessman. He understood the products and markets and had a certain flair in the marketing area. He wasn't afraid to put in the requisite hours on the job either. But he was not a good manager of people and, after a while, employees began leaving the company, customers became disenchanted, and the company began to lose market share.

Four years into his reign, John saw profits slipping drastically and sales lagging behind industry standards. Recognizing something was wrong, he came to me for assistance. "I don't know what the problem is. We've taken on several new product lines, the industry seems to be booming and I've tried to carry on as my father would have done, but I just don't have an interest in the business.

The employees haven't been helpful either. I've replaced nearly all supervisory personnel, but even that hasn't helped."

Here was a classic case of how a contrast in management styles can, and often does, change the entire complexion of a business. Whereas the company was his father's whole life and whose management practices reflected an honest, caring attitude, John regarded his obligation to continue as just that, an obligation to his father. He'd much rather be on the golf course than operating the business.

I performed a turnaround analysis for John and concluded with the recommendation that he should either, (a) hire a people–oriented manager to run the business for him, or, (b) sell the business and do something he enjoyed. But in either case, do it before he ruined the company!

If you don't like sailing it makes no sense to buy a sail boat. If you can't stand dirt and bugs, stay out of the woods. It also doesn't make any sense to continue running a business you don't like. Why every business owner doesn't plan for a contingent getting out position in the event of his death or disability is a mystery. When an heir ends up with a company he either doesn't want or can't manage, and then tries to dispose of it, a distress sale, or even liquidation, is very often the end result.

One of the greatest services a lawyer can perform for a small business client is to push for a definitive contractual plan for disposing of the business upon his death or disability. Your heirs will have enough details to worry about without trying to manage a business they know nothing about. It doesn't need to be a complicated plan, but with enough teeth in it should there be a dispute between heirs. A court battle over the inheritance of a business can, and probably will, signal the end of the company.

No matter how the details are worked out, an unplanned for and unwanted inheritance is a very real reason for the heir to want to get out. In addition, these companies can be very attractive from the Buyer's side. Although the personnel will undoubtedly be shaken, and probably disillusioned about their future with the company, a distress sale can often result in a very favorable price for the Buyer, and at least with the right Buyer, the employees will be protected.

DECIDING WHEN TO SELL

Except for certain external forces such as death or a divorce settlement, most business owners have control over when to sell their company and how to structure the sale. Chapter 4 discusses timing factors in greater detail and how they affect the price you can get for your business. Right now, however, when you are first considering selling, it wouldn't hurt to determine the major factors influencing whether you should put the company on the market now or wait for a more opportune time. I have found the following evaluation form useful in bringing the key elements into focus:

Evaluation Questionnaire to Determine When to Sell

Economic Considerations

    A. Are interest rates rising, falling, or stable?

    B. Are Dow-Jones stock averages on an increasing or decreasing trend?

    C. Are P/E ratios for your industry averaging above 10?

    D. Are unemployment rates rising or falling in your region? Nationally?

    E. What is the attitude of the business community? Optimistic? Pessimistic? Worried? Uncertain?

    F. Are the economic indicators affecting your industry improving or deteriorating?

Company Considerations

    A. During the past three years have you seen an increasing or decreasing sales trend?

    B. During the past three years have your profits steadily increased, decreased, or remained unchanged?

    C. Are your management and supervisory personnel in place and functioning properly?

    D. Has direct competition increased, decreased, or remained unchanged during the past two years?

    E. Have there been any favorable or unfavorable demographic or community changes or government restrictions directly affecting your business?

    F. Have all of your business taxes been paid?

    G. Are there any outstanding lawsuits against the company?

    H. What is the economic outlook for the next two years in your industry and your region?

Obviously, the weight given to each answer varies with the type of business. Some will be more sensitive to national economic indicators, some more susceptible to local conditions. If external indicators are favorable, and if the business can demonstrate recent growth in volume and profitability, it won't be too difficult to sell the company in the open market. On the other hand, if there are problems either with the company or in the national economy, other selling techniques such as a partnership, merger, or an employee buyout might be more appropriate. Chapters 7 and 8 examine which options might be applicable for your particular business.

Whatever structure you choose, when you put your company up for sale will, to a large extent, determine the ease with which the business can be sold as well as the eventual selling price. Valuing a privately held business is, at best, difficult, and, you will see in Chapter 4, how timing has a major influence on setting the selling price.

ARE YOU MENTALLY PREPARED?

Whatever your reason for selling, when it actually occurs, it will be a rare entrepreneur indeed who does not suffer some pangs of remorse and misgiving. Sometimes, the emotions accompanying this change can be minor and easily overcome by a stiff martini or a prayer for help. Most times, however, leaving your own business can be extremely traumatic, and can have a devastating effect both on yourself and your family. It took a very specific mentality to get into your own business regardless of whether you started it or acquired it.

The two personal characteristics you needed then—the desire to overcome challenges and the ability to take risks—are what you will need when you are ready to get out. You will need to rely on those same two personal strengths to overcome the challenges of a new life after you get out, and the ability and willingness to take on the risks of finding a new vocation or activity.

If you are getting out because your company is in financial difficulty or because the economics of the market or industry make continuing impossible, then you'll probably be faced with a different kind of emotional upheaval. Under these circumstances, you might feel as if you've failed. Others might feel you have failed also, employees, clients, and vendors. There is nothing wrong with failure. It happens to all of us at one time or another. Today's society, however, has no room for failures and, therefore, the hushed whispers, snide remarks, and subtle social rejection might be quite different than if you had merely sold a solid, profitable company and made a million dollars on the deal. The emotional trauma of failure can be severe, long lasting, and debilitating and you need to begin preparing to put it behind you now. Chapters 14 and 15 can help.

Anne was bored. The travel agency she started from scratch 10 years earlier was booming. Five employees effectively managed the business and two were even more talented than Anne when it came to arranging creative group packages. The challenge of accomplishment was gone, and Anne decided to sell the business to her agency manager. Her profit from the sale, plus additional savings over the years, provided Anne with a more than adequate retirement nest egg.

Two months after the deal closed, however, Anne realized that friends had grown distant and virtually shunned her at social gatherings. Even her adult children treated her differently. Friendly telephone chats became fewer and Anne soon realized that everyone believed she had sold the business because it was in financial trouble. They regarded her as a failure and she soon believed them.

Her feelings of inadequacy and lack of characteristic enthusiasm were evident when we met for lunch. Her perception of failure had drained her and she seemed to have aged 10 years since the sale. Though I suggested a three month cruise as a way to rejuvenate herself, Anne declined. She could not shake the myth of failure, and today, six years later, she is still trying to put her life back together again.

The Psychology of Change

The least understood result of getting out of a business is the psychological impact of a changed life. Everyone feels slightly different about getting out, but one characteristic common to all business owners is a feeling of sadness and regret at leaving their "baby," much the same way a parent feels remorse when his child finally leaves the family nest. You are probably very proud of your company and your achievements in bringing it along the often treacherous survival trail. Whether the company was acquired or started from scratch, or even if you inherited it, you're probably convinced that your efforts and abilities have been the driving forces behind the growth of the business. Whether you've owned it for one year or 20 years, no doubt you have developed relationships with employees, customers, and vendors who have helped the company prosper. It doesn't matter if its a one–man barber shop, accounting practice, consulting practice, or a manufacturing company with 500 employees, it's your baby. Nurturing customers and employees through good times and bad, you have done your best to be honest and caring and have come to regard the company, not as a business, but as a way of life. It's as much a part of your family as your spouse and children, and managing the company remains the primary driving force in your life.

In addition to a feeling of loss, many business owners suffer what can be a debilitating fear of their unknown future. The same characteristics of ambition, drive, and the need for power that make successful entrepreneur now can create anxiety about an inactive future after the sale. The human impact of such a drastic action on the psyche can be devastating. More than any other phenomena, the fear of human emptiness causes the business owner to ignore planning for a getting out position. Even though he knows he should do it, he's afraid to face up to such a major change in his life and, therefore, refuses to recognize the need to plan. This is precisely why so many entrepreneurs without any logical plan, either start another company or buy one after they have sold their company.

What if you're in bad health, or you feel you are too old or too tired to start over again? What if your cash position or family conditions prohibit going back into your own business a second time? There are actions you can take to help alleviate this psychological void, but they take planning and should be started well before you finally decide to get out, as Olaf A. did.

The Successful Politician

Olaf started a small advertising agency in a major eastern city and, for the past 17 years, managed the business all by himself. He was close to 60 and, on the advise of his close friend, Olaf began planning for his retirement. The plan called for an as–yet, unnamed partner to buy him out over a three–year period. While his consultant began the Buyer search, Olaf started thinking about his future and what he would do with his excess time.

He recognized that he didn't have any real hobbies to spend full–time on. Golf was fine, but not every day. The same with fishing and sailing. He didn't like working with his hands, so tinkering around the house or with his car held no interest. The idea of starting a new business held a lot of appeal, but he was getting tired and would probably not have the same motivations as in the past. None of the ordinary hobby–type occupations seemed to hold any interest for him, then he found a creative solution to the problem of what to do after the sale of his business. He decided to leave the business world behind and create a completely new life–style.

Politics fascinated Olaf. Over the years, he was always too busy to run for office in his small community, but now he would have plenty of time. Why not begin laying some groundwork for a modest political campaign in the next town election three years from now? Now that was appealing! Maybe he could get elected to the Board of Education and implement some of the changes to the school system he had felt strongly about for so many years.

His consultant found a suitable partner and, after three years, Olaf completed the sale and retired, or rather stopped working in the business world. He never did stop working in the community. Elected to the Board of Education, Olaf eventually helped initiate major changes in school curriculum. He also ran for other township and county offices and, at one time, held five separate posts. Olaf found a new career, and even though he missed the excitement of the business world, never regretted his decision to get out when he did.

Neither the psychological emptiness of selling or the cataclysmic emotional upheaval of real or imagined financial failure need be too unpalatable if you make the effort to plan for your post-business career. There are many ways of alleviating the pain of loss if you begin early enough and plan your moves. If you know what you will do after you get out, then the shock of the process itself will be much less. This subject is discussed further in Chapter 2.

Other Alternatives

Politics might not be for everyone, but there are a number of other avenues an ex-entrepreneur can follow after he gets out. Some require planning, some don't. A few of these ideas can actually create income, but many require the donation of your time and expertise. This list is not meant to be inclusive, but merely to give you a few ideas of how to cope with the fear of an empty future.

1. Hold a political office in your community.
2. Get involved with activities in social organizations such as the Rotary, Kiwanis, Shrine, etc.
3. Volunteer to work on the community planning commission, hospital, your church, or the Boy Scouts/Girl Scouts.
4. Try fund–raising for your college or publicly supported organizations.
5. Try consulting. After all of your years of experience in the business world you certainly have some expertise that could be a salable commodity.
6. Volunteer for public speaking engagements.
7. Try your hand at writing. Many fine writers have turned up from previous entrepreneurs.
8. Teach. Many small colleges welcome ex-businessmen to their faculty for teaching part–time courses. Your real–life experiences in a particular field are an invaluable vocational tool.
9. Go back to school to study for a new career in law, accounting, criminal justice, foreign languages, or whatever interests you.
10. Volunteer work for political parties or international social organizations such as Amnesty International.
11. Establish a drug addiction education program to be presented to local schools.

The list could go on. There are many contributions you can make to society and give back some of the benefits you have derived from others over the years. It's never too late to stand up and be counted for something important, and once you get out, there's no longer any excuse that you just don't have the time! Instead of feeling sorry for yourself about losing your baby, look around and see the myriad of things you can do for others. Helping others can make you feel great. Why not try it?

2

The Promise of Tomorrow

Preparing to Get Out

I MET DR. O. THOR AT A COCKTAIL PARTY. THE PHYSICIAN WAS FANTASIZING ABOUT his retirement years: how he would cash in his chips and move to the Colorado Rockies. Finally, after all these years, he'd have time to tie flies and cast for Brook Trout in the cool mountain streams. Already in his sixties, I suggested to the good doctor that it was not too early to begin planning for the sale of his successful practice, but he would have none of it.

"To hell with planning. That's for the big boys. My practice is too small. I know I'm sixty-two, but I have no intention of getting out of medicine now and even if I did, I can always find someone to take over. To hell with planning!"

Three months later, this reticent doctor was flat on his back with a brain tumor, unable to communicate and close to death. His wife asked for my assistance in selling his medical practice, and after eight months, I finally located a young physician to take over on a 10–year contingency buy out arrangement. Had Dr. Thor made the effort to plan a getting out position, the transition would have been faster, the price and terms substantially more favorable, and his wife would have been saved the anguish of dealing with business matters while her husband lay on his death bed. With Dr. Thor incapacitated, the practice deteriorated. There was nobody to care for his patients, and by the time I located a Buyer, the value of the practice was less than half of what it should have been.

Whatever your reason for leaving, it's never too early to begin preparing a getting–out plan. A detailed plan for selling your business has several beneficial results:

1. It will minimize the psychological impact on yourself and your family.
2. It will minimize the hurt to employees and customers.
3. It will allow you to choose the best way to structure the sale from several options.
4. It will ease the transition to a new career and/or life–style.
5. It will reduce the possibility of a forced liquidation in the event of a catastrophe.
6. It will ease the burden on your spouse or estate executor in the event of your death.
7. It will maximize the gain to your heirs.
8. It will ensure the inclusion of all requisite steps in the selling process and make the transition to new ownership smooth and of the greatest benefit to you.

Whenever the occasion arises, I encourage young entrepreneurs just starting out on their own to begin planning immediately for a getting out position. You never know when catastrophe might strike. You never know what economic conditions are going to be in the future. You never know what misfortune might hit your family that requires ready cash. And you never really know how prosperous the business will be. For these and many others, you need to begin planning a getting–out position now.

Selling a business is never simple, and without adequate planning, it can be a nightmare. The minimum planning period should be three to five years in advance of a sale. Obviously, an unexpected death, or a rapid demise of the business calls for a much shorter interval. If you have a choice, however, allow yourself five years to begin planning and organizing.

PREPARING TO SELL

To reduce the psychological trauma on yourself, your family, and your employees, as well as to ensure the optimum combination of the right time, the right Buyer, and the right price, you should begin to prepare:

1. Yourself and your family for a new life–style.
2. Your employees, customers, clients, and other business associates for a new owner.
3. Your company for the right Buyer.

Preparing your company for a sale is obvious. Even more important, however, is preparing yourself and others that your business affects. Just as there are a series of steps to clean up the loose ends in your business, there are ways to prepare your employees and customers. There are also steps you can take to mitigate your own mental and emotional anguish when the realization finally hits that you are no longer an entrepreneur.

Preparing Yourself

As easy as it sounds, preparing yourself is often the most difficult phase of any business sale. Why? Because you probably have so much self-confidence and optimism that you believe you are invincible. Nothing can hurt you. In fact, you're looking forward to getting out, so why bother with what might become problems when you know there won't be? After all, haven't you run your business successfully for all these years? You certainly should be able to handle a simple thing like selling it.

Selling a business is different from running it, however. Suddenly, not only does your career come to a screeching halt, but your entire life–style changes. No longer faced with the daily challenges and excitement of managing a business or a practice, you must seek new horizons and new activities to fill the void. Also, the older a person is, the more difficult it is to change.

It's also very natural for an entrepreneur to worry about his financial future. We might not openly admit it, but many of us are deeply concerned about having enough cash to maintain our standard of living during our retirement years. As long as you can continue to take home cash from the business, this fear never surfaces. Without the business, however, where will your retirement cash come from? This is why it's so crucial to prepare yourself mentally, emotionally, and financially *before* putting the business up for sale.

I have been involved in over 65 cases of entrepreneurs and professionals disposing of their business, and I have never seen or heard of anyone preparing himself adequately for the psychological trauma that follows. With the hope that you are different, the following 10 Steps can help you prepare:

1. **Broadcast your intentions.** Well in advance of selling your business, tell your family and friends of your intentions to sell and why. The better informed everyone is about your plans, the less the shock will be when you finally get out, and the less implicit criticism of your actions in "quitting."

2. **Build a nest egg.** Financial security is crucial to mitigate the fear of the unknown future. If you know you can survive financially, no matter what happens, you'll be able to concentrate on developing a new life–style rather than worrying about paying the rent and buying the groceries.

3. **Broaden your interests beyond your business.** Try new hobbies, new vacations, or new clubs or organizations. Experiment with new

ideas and concepts. Most entrepreneurs who have spent years developing and running their own business (and I know I might get myself in
hot water with some of you) become narrow–minded and stagnant. The
more interests you have when you get out, the more options will be
open to you.

4. **Meet new people.** Actively seek to meet new people—the more the
better. Join church groups, civic groups, bridge clubs, or golf or bowling
leagues. The more friends you have, the greater the likelihood of having people to talk to when the pressure of the sale starts building.

5. **Protect your assets.** With personal lawsuits escalating at alarming
proportions, never leave your personal assets unprotected. Consult
qualified legal counsel to develop a strategy to protect your business
assets, as well as your home, car, investments, and bank accounts.

6. **Research different occupations and life–styles.** As part of the
planning process, investigate what options you could become involved
in after the sale that meet your personal criteria. If possible, begin the
education or preparation to enter your new life–style or career before
you put the business up for sale.

7. **Develop your knowledge.** Expand your knowledge in as many areas
as possible. Nothing reduces fear of the unknown faster than knowledge. Once the unknown becomes the known, there is nothing more
to fear. Read, study, take some courses, attend seminars.

8. **Seek qualified counsel.** I can't emphasize this step enough. Usually
because of pride, most entrepreneurs think they can handle everything
themselves. But qualified counselors, psychologists, religious leaders,
social services leaders, lawyers, even medical doctors can help you
through the rough spots. Most of the time, their advice is well worth
the cost.

9. **Talk to other entrepreneurs who have sold their business.**
Find out what problems others have faced. No business situation is
totally unique. If someone has found the solution already, there's no
need to reinvent the wheel.

10. **Analyze your own emotions.** This is the most important step of all.
If you know yourself—your strengths, weaknesses, likes, dislikes,
prejudices, and fears—nothing will seem insurmountable. Know yourself and you will love yourself, no matter what new challenges you face.
Once you take the first step, the realization that you are actually going
to sell your business will hit home, and fears and doubts will follow close
behind. About this time, many business owners get cold feet and

change their minds about selling. There's something about making public what should be a very personal decision, suddenly real. Eventually, however, talking openly about your plans will be like a catharsis, cleaning away misgivings and uncertainties. The more you talk about it, the more you'll find yourself adapting to the realism of your decision, and the easier it will be to mitigate emotional turmoil for yourself and your family, which is why broadcasting your intentions should always be the first step.

Planning for Financial Requirements

The next biggest headache to overcome is the fear of not having enough money for financial security, which is why building that nest egg as early in the game as possible becomes so important. Once the sale is completed, it's too late to begin financial planning. This should be done early in the planning cycle to put at least one fear to rest. The following personal financial plan should help you determine how much of a nest egg you really need and how much you must get for your business to meet your new life style:

Personal Financial Plan

1. What assets of yours can be converted into cash should you need it?
2. What income is available other than from your business—interest, dividends, spouse's job, pension, social security?
3. What are your monthly expenses—mortgage payments, utilities, taxes, insurance, college bills?
4. Deduct the total of item (3) from the combined total of (1) and (2). The difference is discretionary cash available to live on right now.
5. What changes in expenses or income will result from your changed lifestyle?
6. Add or subtract item (5) from item (4). The difference is the amount available to live on while preparing for your new career.
7. Estimate discretionary expenses after the sale—i.e. travel plans, relocation, gifts, new home, or car. The difference between (7) and (6) is the amount of cash you will need to realize the first year from the sale of your business. This amount should be added to the total of item (6).
8. From all of the above, calculate the amount of net cash after fixed expenses available to live on each year.
9. The difference between item (8) and what you really want to have available is what you will need to build into the terms of sale to provide the incremental income stream you want.

By following this plan, any stream of income you can generate from a new career after the sale will be incremental to your needs, and by not relying on such income to survive, selecting an appropriate life–style becomes that much easier.

Personal Credibility

One final comment about personal preparation. As part of the personal planning process, try to develop a public image of yourself. Write letters to the editor of your local newspaper, volunteer for speaking assignments with civic or trade organizations, take a part-time teaching assignment at a local college, become active in your local political scene, write magazine articles, or conduct a seminar. Anything you can do to bring your abilities and talents to the attention of the public will be of immeasurable help in establishing a new career after the sale. It can even help you sell your business. Even if you choose to retire, public credibility will enable you to smooth out the transition stage to your new life–style.

The Disenchanted Entrepreneur

Although few will readily admit it, there are a number of business owners who, for one reason or another, have become unhappy with their own business. Perhaps the rewards are not what was expected, the stress became too great, there is no time to spend with the family, or conditions have changed and the fun has gone out of running the company. Because change is continuous, any number of reasons could cause someone to become disillusioned with their present life–style. When this happens, a different type of personal preparation is necessary. Before selling, you need to reassess your personal motivations and attitudes, not only about the business but also concerning your personal goals and objectives, your desire for spiritual growth, and how you want to live the rest of your life.

Personal goals and beliefs dictate what type of life–style to go after. Perhaps you are disenchanted with the business scene per se, in which case a career outside the business world—teaching, politics, social work, and so on might be appropriate. Perhaps the profit motive and accumulation of wealth no longer holds any interest, but dedication to helping others has become important in your life. Or, if you strongly disagree with those organizations setting the rules for your trade or profession, perhaps a dedicated effort toward reforming professional standards might be the answer. Such was the case with Jay K.

Jay had been a practicing CPA for more than 20 years. Specializing in small businesses, Jay became disillusioned with new audit standards imposed by the AICPA. He felt this professional body was controlled by members from the Big 8 accounting firms who structured accounting rules to satisfy their own large, corporate clients. When applied to small businesses, Jay felt many of these rules were redundant, superfluous, costly, and actually harmful to his clients. Attempts to gain relief failed, and Jay turned bitter toward the profession. He recognized that not only had the profession changed since he began practicing, but his own values and personal objectives had also matured. He was no longer satisfied to follow rules and standards detrimental to his clients, he wanted to help people rather than hurt them. His own spiritual growth caused him to recognize the value of a caring and compassionate attitude.

Asking for my assistance in disposing of his practice, we structured a selling plan, and three years later, Jay was out. Earning his Master's degree in sociology, Jay founded a non-profit foundation to lobby for new auditing standards for small businesses. Unfortunately, he has not been successful in effecting changes yet, but he keeps trying, and the effort alone has brought him a level of satisfaction unknown before.

DO YOU REALLY CARE?

Leaving is never easy. Acknowledging that some day you will have to step down and turn the business over to someone else can be disconcerting. By beginning the planning process, you are, in effect, recognizing the inevitability of such a move. But you, as a business owner, also have a responsibility to other people: your spouse, your family, and certainly your employees and customers, patients, or clients. The best way to reduce the emotional hurt and mental anguish to others is to plan for their continued welfare after you leave.

A straightforward approach is the only honest way to deal with the problem. Honesty with yourself and others can do more to mitigate hurt and disappointment than anything else. Yet, for some reason, many people find that being open and truthful about getting out is a most difficult task. As mentioned in Chapter 1, the free enterprise system looks upon getting out as quitting, and regardless of the reason, somehow un-American. A captain abandoning his ship in a storm, a general deserting his troops in the heat of battle. Nevertheless, trying to hide your intentions from your employees can only lead to trouble in the end.

Not that you're responsible for the personal welfare of every person on the payroll! That would be an impossibility. You are responsible, however, to try to plan your getting out position so that it causes the minimum amount of hurt and confusion to others. Your employees have been loyal to you over the years and worked hard to make your company a success. Although you can't guarantee anything, the least you owe them in return is your best effort to provide for their continued employment and the continuity of their benefits after you leave. You might even find that by being honest and open, your employees will actually help you structure a sale.

One day, a client asked me to help him sell his company. He was ready to retire to the Caribbean to try to control his ulcer, but first he had to dispose of his $5 million manufacturing company. He wanted me to find a Buyer without advertising and without revealing publicly that his company was for sale. He reasoned that if his management team knew of his plans to get out, at least two key people would resign, and this would make the company harder to sell. He was also afraid that the union would delay negotiations on the expiring contract until a new owner appeared, making it more difficult to find a Buyer.

I advised him that I thought this was the wrong approach. He would be much better off revealing his plans to his employees and clearing the air before finding a Buyer. I explained that, without advertising or specific networking, it could take a very long time to find the right Buyer; and he would still need to reveal his intentions some time before the due diligence process began.

"No," he was adamant. "If everyone knows I'm selling, all hell will break loose in the plant, and I know I'll lose some key customers and employees. Also, the union will have me over a barrel. No, do it my way or I'll find someone else to handle the job!"

I took the assignment against my better judgment and proceeded to pass the word through my consulting network that a mystery company was for sale. Because I could only use generic terms to describe the business, a year went by before we had a viable candidate. Even with the identification of a Buyer, my client still would not announce his intention to sell.

I finally recognized that his reluctance had nothing to do with a fear of hurting the company. Instead, he was afraid of being called a "quitter" by his friends. After all, nobody quits unless they have failed! I tried to convince him this was nonsense, but even if it was true, so what! He had his own health to consider and that should come first.

During the Buyer search, two key employees left anyway, and the union contract was almost a giveaway. Although continuing to deny his intentions right up to the end, word leaked out and employee morale was terrible. The Buyer observed this disillusionment and discounted the price he was willing to pay for the very reasons my client hoped to avoid by not being honest up front.

Just the opposite situation occurred with another client who was honest with his employees. Robert spoke with the management team first to explain his situation and the reasons leading to his decision. He didn't have a specific deadline but did let the employees know that one more year would be more than enough for him, and if he could manage a way out earlier than that, he would take it.

Obviously, the news was greeted with shock. John E., the vice president of marketing, however, approached the problem from a positive viewpoint. John felt this might be a terrific opportunity for some, or all, of the employees to have their own business and control their own destiny. After several weeks of conversations and planning with other key employees, the group decided that they would go for it.

John approached Robert with a viable plan. "We would like to establish an Employee Stock Ownership Plan—an ESOP—to buy your company." Robert was delighted. A management buyout would save weeks, maybe months, of trying to find a viable outside Buyer. "Sounds good to me, John. Let's sit down and do some negotiating!"

Under the then–current tax laws, contributions made by the company to the ESOP were tax deductible, so Robert could see he could win on two fronts, a satisfactory way to get out, and a tax savings at the same time. Within a matter of weeks, the parties agreed to a price, terms, and ESOP funding requirements. The whole procedure took less than six months, the client received a fair price and the employees were exuberant that they were now the proud new owners.

I have always believed in treating employees fairly. The term merciful management defines the state of mind of the entrepreneur who cares enough to treat his employees as if they were family. Just as you would inform your spouse and children of your intentions, you should keep employees abreast of your plans. Merciful management can be carried too far, however and actually do more harm than good when it comes to selling, as in the case of Simon P.

When it came time to sell his auto accessories business, Simon was faced with a very difficult decision. He had built the company over a 35–year period and now, approaching his 70th birthday, was ready to get out. Simon's 65–year–old brother and his son, along with several other relatives, were employed at the company. No one had any interest in taking over responsibility for the entire business, so Simon announced his intention to sell.

I arrived on the scene representing a Buyer client, and quickly negotiated a deal with Simon, but could see something was troubling him. "What seems to be the problem?," I asked one day after a quiet lunch.

"I don't know, Larry. I'm satisfied with our negotiations and I think the world of your client. I guess I'm just upset about my employees. I really do care about them and no matter how reputable your client is, I know that he'll find some of my people unsatisfactory or perhaps bring in some of his own people. Also, I'm concerned that some day he might want to relocate the facility to another town or part of the country. Then what will happen to my people?" I tried to soothe his worries, but to no avail. The next day, I returned to my office to inform my client that a closing date had been set, but that Simon's concern for his employees might kill the deal yet. As it turned out, that's exactly what happened. Two weeks before closing, I received a call from Simon. "I just can't do it, Larry. I apologize for taking so long, but I've finally decided to keep the company, at least for another three years. I'll keep sending you quarterly financials and maybe we can get together in three years."

Merciful management, carried too far, actually harmed his employees. Simon is still running the company and still in good health, but he knows he can go at any time and, if he does, his employees will suffer a great deal more than if he had sold the company as planned. Although he cared for his employees, he let his pride get in the way. He really thought that he was the only person who cared about people. Clearly, this is not what I mean by caring and compassionate management.

Being Honest with Customers/Vendors

Your customer and vendor contacts are also entitled to personal consideration. You can be sure that once your plans are announced to employees, word will spread to customers and vendors anyway, so you might as well take the initiative. Breaking the news to these people, however, is a bit trickier. Whereas up–front honesty with employees can only be helpful, announcing intentions to sell to the outside world might get you in trouble. Vendors will worry about getting paid for their deliveries and customers will be concerned about deteriorating delivery schedules and quality. Nevertheless, it's better to take the risks than ignore the problem. It's better in the long–run that customers and vendors receive the true story directly from you rather than a distorted versions through the grapevine.

The checklist in Fig. 2–1 can help remind you of all the parties you should contact about your intentions to get out. Openness won't eliminate the disillusionment, but it will reduce the hurt.

CHOOSING A SELLING METHOD

There are a number of ways to sell a business. The reason for selling, as well as the size of the company, type of business it conducts, and its profitability, dictates which form to choose. Some of the more common ways include:

- On the open market
- Merger
- A public stock offering (IPO)
- An employee profit sharing plan (ESOP)
- To a successor, either family or outsider
- A partnership
- Bankruptcy
- Liquidation of assets

If a business is profitable, it can generally be sold on the open market, although this might not be the most advantageous way. For example, if the busi-

Fig. 2-1. Use this checklist as a reminder of who you should inform about your plans to get out.

CHECKLIST
Who to Notify of Intention to Sell

Personal

Family and Friends (Use separate sheet if necessary)   _____

1. _____   _____

2. _____   _____

3. _____   _____

4. _____   _____

5. _____   _____

6. _____   _____

My Attorney   _____

My Accountant   _____

Others

1. _____   _____

2. _____   _____

3. _____   _____

4. _____   _____

Business

Employees:

   Management Team   _____

   Salaried employees   _____

   Union committee   _____

   Hourly employees   _____

Customers (Use separate sheet if necessary)

1. _____   _____

2. _____   _____

(Fig. 2-1 continues)

Fig. 2-1 continued

3. _____ _____

4. _____ _____
(Note: If there are too many customers/clients to notify each personally, use a mailing to make the announcement.)

Vendors (Use separate sheet if necessary)

1. _____ _____

2. _____ _____

3. _____ _____

4. _____ _____
(Note: If there are no major vendors use a mailing to make the announcement.)

Banks (Use separate sheet if necessary)

1. _____ _____

2. _____ _____

3. _____ _____

4. _____ _____

Legal counsel _____

Accounting firm _____

Insurance broker _____

Pension trustee _____

ness assets consist mainly of goodwill, such as in a law practice or other highly personalized business, you, the owner, are the business. Without you, the business will have little value on the open market. Assuming you can even find a Buyer, he will demand a significantly discounted price. A partner or a planned successor who gets to know the client base before taking over will value the business much higher.

If you own a larger business or one with a particularly glamorous product, selling stock to the public might be the best way. To do this, you'll need at least three years of continually increasing sales and profits as well as a promising future. It's also a very expensive undertaking to put together. If market conditions are favorable, however, and you plan for the offering far enough in advance, an IPO can very easily be the most profitable way to get out.

A merger with another company achieves much the same results as an IPO but it is much less expensive and can be utilized by small, personal service businesses as well as larger companies. Merging a medical practice into a larger clinic or a one–man accounting practice into a multi-partner CPA firm can be extremely lucrative for the Seller. The downside is that a merger generally requires continued participation in the merged business, at least for a transition period. The biggest difficulty, however, is to find the right company to merge into. A public company with stock traded on the open market can yield results identical to an IPO. A merger with a private company requires a more elaborate contractual agreement to permit you to sell your share of the merged company at an appropriate time in the future.

Selling a business under the protection of the federal Bankruptcy Code is a very special case and applies only under unusual circumstances. Though costly, time consuming, and fraught with psychological trauma, bankruptcy is fast becoming an accepted means of disposing of a financially troubled company. There is a catch, however. If there is little or no chance of recovery, and getting the company out of bankruptcy through a reorganization, you'll never find a Buyer. The what, when, and how of this method is explored in Chapter 12.

A liquidation sale or auction is also a very drastic means of getting out. When a Buyer cannot be found or when the market price of the business is substantially less than the auction value of its assets, however, liquidation might be the only way. Planning for a liquidation sale is also dealt with in Chapter 12.

PREPARING THE COMPANY

The steps in preparing for a sale are done in parallel, not in a series. Consequently, at the same time you are taking the requisite human relations actions for your family, friends, employees and customers, and redefining your own goals, attitudes and objectives, you should begin getting your company ready. There is no need to decide on the proper structure first. This can be done later, because the same procedures apply regardless of how you sell it.

A thoughtfully prepared selling plan will provide guidelines to lead you through the labyrinth of decisions and activities involved in the selling process. As with any complex activity that stretches over a period of time, without a road map, it is very easy to get lost. To illustrate the various steps along the way, I have used a hypothetical company, complete with financial statements, market assumptions, and economic premises, as the primary example. As a starting point, we'll prepare a Selling Plan for this hypothetical company, but first some background data.

Background for MAKE MONEY FILTER CORP.

A fictitious company is used to illustrate the selling process. MAKE MONEY is probably a bigger company than many of you will need to deal with, and some of you will have trouble relating to such large numbers, but don't be scared off if your business is smaller. Most of the same selling techniques are applicable to small retail or service businesses and even professional practices. Differences in emphasis and techniques for smaller businesses will be pointed out as we move along through the selling process.

MAKE MONEY FILTER CORP., a manufacturer of metal filters for the water industry, had a sales volume of approximately $20 million five years ago when it was acquired by John E. Joe and yielded an after–tax profit of slightly over 5 percent of sales. Net worth was nearly $10 million.

Over the next three years, profits increased to over 9 percent of sales, but then the market turned. The residential water industry reverted to its normal 3 percent per year growth curve and sales for MAKE MONEY FILTER CORP leveled out at about $30 million. Profits began to slip a bit, but by cutting costs and adding some state-of-the-art equipment, the company held profits to almost 9 percent of sales. The economy headed into a downturn, but not a bad recession—only an adjustment, as the economists like to call it. The forecast is for a return to stronger markets next year, however, and a tapering off again over the ensuing four years. In the long–run it now appears that, although the residential water industry will continue healthy for an indefinite period, some downturn can be expected next year. Competition is becoming stronger, but pricing should hold and probably continue to yield satisfactory margins. With that background to go on, let's move ahead and put together a selling plan for MAKE MONEY.

The Selling Plan

Regardless of the structure of the sale, using a well–thought out selling plan will keep expenses to a minimum while maximizing your return from the transaction. The selling plan consists of nine steps:

1. Determining the proper timing.
2. Examining tax implications.
3. Calculating the selling price.
4. Cleaning up the company.
5. Preparing an offering prospectus.
6. Locating a Buyer.
7. Negotiating price and terms.
8. Assisting the Buyer in arranging financing.
9. Negotiating and writing a Buy/Sell Agreement.

There is also a possibility that the new owner will want some assistance in managing the transition period.

MAKE MONEY FILTER CORP.
Selling Plan

	Start	Stop	Cost
Timing	Not Applicable		−0−
1. Stock market trends			
2. Water filter market business cycles			
3. Growth trends for three years			
Examine Tax Implications	3/10	3/20	$2,000
1. Meet with CPA			
2. Asset sale or stock sale			
3. Deferred payments			
4. Allocation of sell price			
5. Construct personal tax plan			
6. Estate planning			
Calculate Valuation and Sell Price	3/1	3/15	$5,000
1. Prepare pro forma forecasts			
2. Determine personal financial needs			
3. Arrive at asking price and terms			
Preparing the Company for Sale	1/1	11/1	Unknown
1. Notification of employees, etc.			
2. Get key employees in place			
3. Clean up the company			
4. Develop public relations image			
The Offering Prospectus	1/1	4/1	$15,000
1. Write five–year strategic plan			
2. Gather data			
3. Hire photographer			
4. Write prospectus			
5. Package prospectus			
Hire M & A Consultant to Locate Buyer	3/1	6/1	Contingent
Negotiate Deal with Buyer	6/1	6/15	−0−
Assist Buyer with Financing	6/15	9/1	−0−
1. Contact current bank			
2. Determine need for buyer paper			
3. Negotiate other deferred payments			
The Buy/Sell Agreement	9/1	11/1	$15,000
1. Hire competent lawyer			
2. Help draft warranties and representations			
3. Establish satisfactory collateral to buyer paper			
The Closing and Formal Announcements	11/1		$1,000

Fig. 2-2. Keeping track of all of the details of selling your business can be overwhelming. Use this selling plan to organize your thoughts. Even if you never use it, you will have at least thought through the process.

While it's very difficult to anticipate how long the selling process will take, you should go through the exercise of writing out a detailed plan with dates and budgeted expenditures if for no other reason than to force the discipline of thinking through the sequence. It might take one month to find a Buyer, it might take a year. You might have to wait several years for the right timing. Lawsuits could take years to resolve. Nevertheless, once the timing problem is overcome, you can lay out at least a tentative plan. A selling plan for MAKE MONEY would look as shown in Fig. 2–2.

Figure 2–2 tells us it will take 10 months to sell the company (probably reasonable) and will require a cash outlay of about $38,000 (probably excessive). It should certainly cost less than $38,000 to sell MAKE MONEY, but it's better to be conservative.

Obviously, the smaller your business, the less it will cost to sell it. Yet, there are certain expenditures that must be planned for. The Offering Prospectus will cost something, and you shouldn't skimp. A professional looking package will sell faster than one quickly thrown together. You'll always need a lawyer. Maybe $15,000 is a bit steep, but they don't come cheap. Don't make the mistake Roy S. made in trying to save costs by doing the legal work himself.

Roy owned a thriving one–man dental practice. Approaching retirement age, he located a young dentist to join him in a partnership with an agreement to buy Roy out in two years on a deferred payment plan. Roy thought he could draft the simple contractual agreements himself and never consulted a lawyer. Now, four years since Roy left the practice, he has yet to receive his first payment. His partner found a loophole in the Buy/Sell Agreement and there is nothing Roy can do about it now. So plan conservatively and you won't be sorry. There are additional steps in preparing your company such as resolving contingent liabilities and outstanding disputes, cleaning up accounting records, and getting the facilities in shape, which are discussed later in Chapter 5.

With adequate preparation and the right structure, there is every reason to believe that you can efficiently and profitably sell your company in a reasonable period of time. With care and consideration, and the willingness to take appropriate action with employees and customers, you can relieve others of much of the anxiety accompanying the sale. Also, thoughtfully structuring your personal goals and sufficiently planning for your post-closing life–style, you can mitigate much of the psychological trauma normally accompanying a sale.

Having taken these preparatory steps for yourself, your family, your employees and customers, and your company, you should consider the tax implications of selling and how to minimize both your personal and company tax liabilities.

3

The IRS is Waiting

Preparing to Minimize Taxes

BEFORE GETTING TOO FAR ALONG IN THE PLANNING STAGES, IT IS A GOOD IDEA TO check with your tax advisor about the current status of income tax regulations that could affect the sale of your business. Federal and state income taxes have always been a major expense both for individuals and corporations, yet it's interesting to note the change in the current attitude toward paying taxes as reflected in the H & R Block television commercials. No longer does the tax return preparer advertise how much they can reduce your taxes; now it's how big a refund they can get you. Of course, they neglect to mention that any refund assumes the government has used a taxpayer's money—interest free—all year. Fortunately, most entrepreneurs are smart enough to realize this fallacy and do their utmost to reduce the tax liability so they won't have to pay the IRS any more than absolutely necessary in the first place.

DEFINE WHAT IS TO BE SOLD

What are you really selling? On the surface this sounds like a dumb question. "I'm selling my business, what else?" But what is your business? A collection of assets, some recorded in the books, some not, but all with value. Perhaps you want to keep some of those recorded assets, such as a personal car, computer equipment, and office furniture. If you own the building the business is in, maybe it would be beneficial to hold onto it and lease it back to the new owner. Some Seller's prefer to collect their own receivables and exclude them from the sale. You will probably want to retain the life insurance policy carried by the company. If the deal is structured as an asset sale, designating assets to be sold becomes fairly obvious. But in a stock sale, typically everything on the books of the company goes with the business. If there are any assets you want to keep, you need to transfer the title before putting the company on the market, or write exclusions into the Buy/Sell Agreement. No matter how you accomplish it, planning what will be sold is a crucial, first step to selling your business.

Jack owned a delicatessen that operated as a corporation. Several years earlier, on the advice of his CPA, the corporation purchased the building that housed the store. He didn't pay much attention to taxes. His CPA took care of all that for him, including the preparation of his returns. For years, Jack included everything he could think of as business expenses, including his two cars, personal computer, some furniture in his home he used as an office, and a sailboat—all of which were carried on the company's books, even though they were fully depreciated. The sale was negotiated as a stock deal and the Buyer wanted to pay Jack 40 percent down, with the balance due over a three–year period. Jack would have none of that and insisted on a full cash deal with no deferred terms. He wanted the cash now to make new investments. When the Buyer took over, Jack attempted to claim the assets he considered personal and not part of the business. "Sorry, Jack," was the reply. "I bought the stock of the company and that included everything on the books—including the building, cars, computer, furniture, and boat."

Jack received cash all right, but now he had to turn around and buy new cars, a new computer, and new furniture for his office at home. He also lost the real estate that could have been an excellent long–term investment, reducing personal taxes for years to come. Not only did he sell assets he should have kept, but by taking the entire payment in cash, he paid about three times as much in taxes on the deal as he might have with deferred payments.

Jack missed out on one of the best tax shelter investments around. In many parts of the country, commercial real estate has been an excellent investment as well as a viable tax shelter for years. As the commercial real estate market continues to escalate, a property increases in value every year. As rents continue on an upward spiral, ever higher cash income accrues to the property holder. And with a tax deduction for depreciation, much of this income can be sheltered for many years. Consequently, a popular maneuver by the entrepreneur owning business real estate is to exclude such property from the sale of the business. By leasing it back to the Buyer, he benefits from a long–term, steady source of income and a tax shelter. There can be no doubt that tax planning is important—right from the beginning. Define what you are selling, and let your tax advisor help in determining how to structure the deal.

This book does not purport to be a definitive work on income taxes. To minimize taxes on a specific sale, consult your tax lawyer or CPA. It is also not possible to predict what changes in tax laws congress might contrive in the future. Sweeping changes in the recent tax reform acts radically changed the rules from prior versions and there is every reason to believe that congress will continue to muddy the waters. There are, however, some broad provisions that applied in nearly all revisions. Consequently, as a Seller, you should be cognizant of these common denominators so that you will know what questions to ask your tax advisor.

In addition to defining the specific assets included in the sale, there are three key tax questions to resolve during the planning stage:

1. How can I structure the sale to avoid double taxation—first to the company and then to myself?

2. How much of the gain will be treated as long–term capital gain and which part as ordinary income?

3. Is there any benefit in taking part of the purchase price in deferred payments?

DOUBLE TAXATION

Double taxation arises only when business is conducted through a corporation. Unless an S corporation election is made, the IRS treats the corporation as a taxpayer itself, without regard to who owns its shares. Therefore, any income to the corporation is taxable to the corporation. When the corporation makes distributions of property or pays non-deductible dividends, taxes are paid twice on the same income. Once by the corporation, because such distributions are not deductible, and again by the individual as income on his personal return. That's double taxation.

Prior to 1986, if a corporation sold all of its assets, it could then distribute the proceeds to shareholders under Code Section 337, called a tax–free liquidation. Current laws, however, repealed this provision. Tax experts call this the repeal of the General Utilities Doctrine. Even though our system of taxation remains dynamic and continuously changing—and this whole subject will probably change again next year—if you sell under the current laws, you'll have to contend with the possibility of paying double taxes.

Obviously, if the business is operating as a partnership or a sole proprietorship, double taxation problems don't exist. If the business is incorporated, however, how can you avoid this completely inequitable and excessive taxing of income? There are a couple of ways to structure the sale to accomplish this:

1. Sell the stock of the corporation rather than its assets.

2. Elect to be taxed as an "S" (small business) corporation.

Unfortunately, thanks to the repeal of the General Utilities Doctrine, conversion to an S corporation, which has been a viable tax planning alternative for years, is no longer straightforward. Congress has now nullified some of the advantages by imposing built-in gains provisions, which is examined later.

Stock Sale or Asset Sale

In virtually every instance, a Seller operating in a corporate form is better off selling his common stock in the company than having the corporation sell assets. There are three reasons for this:

1. The sale of stock qualifies as a sale of a capital asset by the individual and thus, subject to capital gains provisions in the Code.

2. The transfer of stock ownership automatically relieves the Seller of any potential future claims or lawsuits against the company. He gets out free and clear and never needs to worry about contingent liabilities from prior actions.

3. He can avoid the problem of double taxation.

Of course, the Buyer will probably want just the opposite (an asset sale) for the reverse reasons. This subject usually deserves a fair amount of negotiating time and, if there is radical disagreement, it can be a deal breaker. One possible compromise allocates part of the purchase price to the common stock and part to a non-compete covenant.

A non-compete covenant states that for a specified number of years the Seller will not enter into any activity that would hinder or detract from the business being sold. Although any length of time can be used, generally, if tested in court, five years is about the longest enforceable period. More common, three years offers sufficient restriction to allow the new owner to develop his own expertise and goodwill in the marketplace. A Buyer usually tries to get as much of the purchase price as possible allocated to a non-compete covenant. Aside from keeping you out of the picture, he can write off the cost of the covenant over its life span and take these write-offs as deductions for tax purposes, much the same way as depreciation of hard assets. On the other hand, he cannot take deductions for any amounts allocated to goodwill. Regardless of revisions to the tax code over the years, neither a deduction for purchased goodwill nor a deduction for its amortization has been permitted.

Assuming you, as an individual, own the stock in the corporation to be sold, and there is no intermediate holding company, proceeds from the sale go directly to you without passing through the corporation, thus avoiding any double taxation.

Tax Rates

For years, there have been different tax rates applied to ordinary income and net, long–term capital gains. Prior to 1986, the Alternate Minimum Tax imposed a minimum tax rate of 28 percent on capital gains for corporations compared to a maximum rate of 46 percent on ordinary income. Individuals were also allowed to limit their effective tax rate to 20 percent of capital gains, substantially less than the maximum 50 percent on ordinary income. The avowed purpose in such discrepancies between types of income was to encourage long–term investments of capital by both types of taxpayers in the belief that these investments would stimulate the economy. In fact, many companies and individuals did take the bait and productivity throughout the country increased. Now, however, in its infinite wisdom, congress has seen fit to eliminate this incentive. No longer do either corporations or individuals get any tax break in rates between ordinary income and capital gains. Instead, under the 1986 Code revision, corporations pay a maximum tax rate of 34 percent on all income over $75,000 (15 percent on the first $50,000 and 25 percent on the next $25,000), and individuals are taxed at a maximum of 15 percent on income up to $29,750, 28 percent on the next $42,150, and 33 percent for all income over $71,900.

There are still two quirks in the tax law that encourage capital gains, however. If a taxpayer realizes capital losses in a given year, these losses can be absorbed against capital gains and only the net gain taxed. Without capital gains to offset, capital losses in excess of $3,000, cannot be deducted against ordinary income in any one year, although the deduction can be deferred to future years. Therefore, assuming he does have capital losses, there is still some tax advantage for the Seller to allocate the purchase price to his stock (a capital asset) rather than a non-compete covenant, which is taxed as ordinary income. How advantageous this is will be determined by his other investment transactions during the year. In addition, new provisions restrict the use of installment sales to report gains realized from the sale of capital assets. Before beginning negotiations, be sure to get competent tax advice about the benefits of allocating part, or all, of the selling price to capital assets.

Using Deferred Payments to Reduce Taxes

Other than the questions of double taxation and offsetting capital gains against capital losses, the third major tax question in planning your sale is: What are the benefits of taking deferred payments rather than all cash at closing?

The basic ingredients of installment sales are fairly straightforward. For a taxpayer, using the cash basis to report both income and expenses, and most individuals are on the cash basis, an installment sale is one in which you receive payments over a period of years, not all at one time. Income is reported in the year the cash is received and calculated on the same proportionate gain—that is, total gross sales price less your cost basis, multiplied by the fractional cash received each year.

But, once again, congress has put it to the small business owner. In the case of an asset sale, all forms of gain normally taxable as ordinary income, such as the sale of receivables, inventory, or a non-competing covenant, are taxed in the year the asset is sold, not when cash is received for it. Consequently, although installment sales can benefit a Seller for the sale of capital assets, or in total for a stock sale, deferring payment isn't as beneficial as it once was.

Deferring payments when selling capital assets or stock, however, can help. By spreading income over a period of years, the taxpayer's total income in any one year might qualify him for a lower tax rate than if all of the cash were received at one time. For example, if you sold stock for $350,000 and had a cost basis of $200,000, the gain would be $150,000 (assuming no outside capital losses to offset it). If this was all received in the first year, it would be taxed at the maximum individual rate of 15 percent for the first $29,750, 28 percent on the next $42,150, and approximately 33 percent on the balance of $78,100 (assuming a married taxpayer filing a joint return) for a tax of $42,000. On the other hand, if the gain was realized in equal installments over a five–year period at $30,000 a year, the minimum rate of 15 percent would apply and the tax would be about $22,000. A cash savings of $20,000 could pay for a long vacation, a new car, or perhaps a sailboat.

The definition of type of income—ordinary income or capital gain—is the same for deferred payments, just as if it were an all cash deal, except for one very big difference. If part of the sale price is to be paid on an earn–out contract or other form of contingency payment made out of profits of the company, it will always be treated as ordinary income, not a capital gain. In addition, contingent payments without fixed, minimum amounts will not be treated as part of the sale price of the business for tax purposes and, therefore, will not be used to calculate installment sale income.

If deferred payments are made using Buyer paper with designated payment terms, that's a different story. They are fixed payments regarded as part of the sale price and included in installment sale calculations. Of course, the interest income earned on these promissory notes will be just that, interest income, and not part of the installment sale. By the way, if you take a Buyer's promissory note, be sure to include an interest rate not less than the prevailing federal rate at the time of closing. If you don't do this, the IRS will calculate an implied interest rate on each of the payments, and the benefits of the installment sale are diminished by the amount of cash received that is attributable to this interest income.

You can see how complicated tax planning can become, and that's why it is imperative to work closely with a tax advisor during the planning stages of the sale, during negotiations, and finally, before the closing documents are finalized.

THE "S" CORPORATION

Over the years, the advantages of electing to be taxed as an S corporation (small business corporation) have come and gone. Under some revisions to the code, it has been extremely advantageous. Others make it a burden. It's hard to know what congress will come up with next. At the current time, however, there is a distinct advantage to the business owner in using this election. All income or losses as an S corporation are passed through directly to shareholders and included in their personal returns. An S corporation is treated by the IRS as if it were a partnership, not a corporation at all. Each type of income or loss incurred by the company passes through in the same form to its shareholders in the proportion that their stock holdings bear to the total shares outstanding. Because the corporation pays no tax at all, there can be no double taxation.

All shareholders of a corporation must agree to the S election. It is a simple procedure requiring only that Form 2553 be filed with the IRS. Except for very unusual circumstances, permission is always granted. There are three problems to be aware of in making the election, however:

1. The form must be filed within 75 days of the beginning of the tax year to which the election applies.

2. If the corporation reverts back to be taxed as a standard, or C corporation at a later time, it must wait a full five years to once again make the S election.

3. If a C corporation converts to a S corporation, and the S corporation sells its business assets within 10 years of the election, built-in gains provisions apply.

This is certainly not something to do without a well, thought–out tax plan that anticipates (1) the amount and type of income the company might generate in the future; (2) the other income or losses you, as an individual, might have independent of the company; and (3) whether the company will be sold this year or sometime in the near future. You can't vacillate. Once the election is made, it will be more costly and less beneficial to cancel the election than not to make it in the first place.

Congress has devised insidious built-in gains provisions in its current revisions to the code that often penalize the small business owner. To discourage business owners from using the S election to avoid double taxation, these provisions specify that if assets are sold within 10 years from the date of conversion from a C corporation to a S corporation, the corporation itself, not its shareholders, is taxed on any gain realized between the tax basis of the asset and its fair market value at the time of the election. This means two things: (1) The gain is taxed at potentially higher corporate rates, and (2) when the cash realized from the sale is distributed, it is taxed again to the shareholders as a dividend. For cash basis corporations it is even worse. An S election conversion creates built-in gains to the corporation, and hence is taxed at corporate rates, even if the company is not sold. For example, if any asset owned by the corporation is sold within the 10–year period, the corporation pays a tax on the difference between the tax basis and its fair market value at the date of the election. This tax is in addition to that levied on shareholders for the gain on selling the asset.

It should be noted that the built-in gains provisions apply only to the sale of assets, not the sale of the corporation's stock by its shareholders.

In spite of the insidious built-in gains provisions, an S election can still be a viable tax savings device, and hopefully, within the near future, enough pressure will be placed on congress to modify this inequitable provision.

Getting back to the problem of double taxation, because in an S corporation all income, including gains on selling its assets, are passed to its shareholders, you'll never need to worry about paying double taxes (except for potential built-in gains). This is especially useful to small retail or personal service businesses when negotiations will probably result in an asset sale. In addition, the Seller retains the corporate shell for any new business in the future. The election must be made in a timely fashion, however, or it won't count. Consider what happened to Mike, who owned a small chain of auto repair shops and forgot to make the election.

Mike operated his four repair shops under four different corporations. Developing a malignant tumor, he decided to sell his businesses to provide cash income to his spouse and family in the event of this death. Neglecting to seek tax advice early enough, there was no time to make the S election. Selling each company separately—and all four were asset sales—Mike realized gains of $100,000, $35,000, and $42,000 respectively on the first three, and a loss of $82,000 on the fourth because of its location in a deteriorating neighborhood. If he had elected to be taxed as an S corporation for all four, his net gain would have been $95,000, and his tax bill would have totaled $31,350. By forgetting to make the S corporation election, he was unable to offset the loss on the fourth company against the gains of the others and the corporations paid total taxes of over $60,000. When he distributed the proceeds to himself, Mike paid personal income taxes again of over $60,000. He netted only $57,000 on the sale as opposed to nearly $150,000 had he made the S election.

The S corporation has definitely come back into vogue and should be carefully considered as a viable tax saving mechanism. Just remember, the election must be made early in the tax year, and you can't go back and forth between an S and a C corporation. Also, be aware that using a holding corporation to own more than 80 percent of the stock of the operating company negates an S election.

AN UNINCORPORATED BUSINESS

All this talk about tax strategy for corporations is fine, but what if you operate as a sole proprietorship, not a corporation? Until recently, the standards of many professions prohibited using the corporate form. Many physicians, lawyers, CPAs, consultants, and security advisors continue to operate without the corporate shield. Even corporations in small retail businesses are still a rarity. What can the unincorporated small business owner do to reduce his tax burden on the gain from a sale, or can he do anything other than pay the taxes?

There are ways to minimize taxes, and the available options are no different than operating under the corporate form with the S election. The same rules apply to types of income and installment sales. Just be sure to get qualified tax advice far enough in advance of the sale to ensure timely personal tax planning. If capital losses are anticipated on outside investments, see if you can take them in the same year as the sale of the business and offset capital gains against losses. Also, be sure any retirement plans are fully funded before the sale. If you own the real estate housing the business, consider excluding it from the sale and lease it back to the new owner. If your automobile is used for company business, you might want to keep it or other vehicles or equipment out of the sale. If so, get the titles transferred before the sale. Take a look at potential deductions against Schedule C business income this year instead of taking them as personal deductions (or no deductions at all) such as expenses of keeping an office in your home. There are a myriad of tax–saving possibilities on your personal return.

PERSONAL TAX PLANNING

What are some of the steps to minimize taxes on ordinary business income in the year of sale and to take advantage of possible tax savings in your personal finances? Some of the questions you should ask a tax advisor include:

1. Is there a possibility of shifting non-business personal income to next year?
2. What about taking deductible expenses this year instead of next?
3. Should I increase my salary this year or take more dividends?
4. How about dumping obsolete inventory a Buyer wouldn't want?

5. Should I try to increase collections from receivables?

6. Should a company pension plan be set up or funding increased for one already in existence?

7. Are there any fully depreciated hard assets such as automobiles that should be transferred out of the business before the sale?

8. As the only employee in the company, are there any advantages or disadvantages to setting up a personal holding company?

This list of questions certainly doesn't cover everything, but it should get you started. The following checklist broadens the coverage of tax planning ideas and includes potential tax savings items for both the company and yourself. The main thing to remember is that taxes are one of the biggest expenses either you or the company will ever have, and cash payed to the IRS means less cash available for your personal use. Therefore, the idea is to keep cash at home. Don't give it to Uncle Sam.

A Tax Checklist

The following list of questions points out possible deductions or other ways of saving taxes you might have forgotten about. At a minimum, use it to review with your tax advisor.

1. Should I incorporate the business?

2. If incorporated, should I elect to be taxed as an S corporation?

3. Should I consider a Personal Holding Company?

4. Have I looked at the new preference items?

5. Do the retirement programs currently in place still qualify?

6. Should I consider a fiscal year end for my company?

7. Should my company put my spouse on the payroll to take advantage of additional IRA deductions and the child care credit?

8. If my corporation is earning more than $75,000, what can I do to transfer some income to myself to keep the current rate at 28 percent rather than 34 percent?

9. Should I implement a medical reimbursement plan?

10. With two or more corporations, should I use a common paymaster to minimize payroll taxes on myself or my spouse?

11. Should I set up a 401(k) or a SEP retirement plan?

12. Should the company have a group, term–life insurance plan?

13. Are there changes I can make in my group health plan to increase benefits to myself and my family?

14. How about director's fees, should I pay myself and my wife to qualify for Keogh retirement plans?

15. Does my recordkeeping for travel and entertainment expense meet IRS requirements?

16. Should I have a review made of all retirement, profit-sharing, and other compensation programs in light of new tax laws?

17. Is there any benefit in setting up new IRA plans?

18. Would setting up an ESOP be beneficial?

19. Can I make additional contributions to charities to save on taxes?

20. Do I have the appropriate depreciation schedules in effect for all hard assets?

21. Am I handling my company cars correctly to maximize benefits?

22. Do I need to worry about changes in the tax laws affecting foreign tax credits?

23. Should I sell or scrap unused equipment?

24. Can I gain anything by writing off old inventory?

25. Can I file an amended return for last year to take my casualty loss in that year instead of now?

26. Should I change from single dollar value LIFO to simplified dollar value LIFO for my inventory?

27. Should I sell or give some of my stock in the company to my spouse? My children? A Trust?

28. Can I use a Foreign Sales Corporation (FSC) for export sales?

29. If I can, how do I set it up?

30. Can I use a stock redemption agreement?

31. Do I have a contractual agreement in place to dispose of the company if I should become disabled or die?

32. Should I have key–man life insurance?

33. Is there any way to shift either income or expenses from one year to the next?

34. Is there any way to shift income or expenses between myself and my company?

35. Is my salary and my spouse's salary reasonable for my size business? Can I increase it? Should I decrease it?

SHOULD YOU INCORPORATE?

The preceding sections have described a variety of tax consequences that affect the sale of a business. Double taxation is an ever–present problem if you own a corporation and do not elect to be taxed as a S corporation. Then why bother with the expense and recordkeeping of a corporation when it can only cause problems? Why not stay as a sole proprietor or partnership and forget about incorporating?

There are several reasons why the corporate form of doing business is preferable, some of which have nothing to do with the tax laws. This is probably as good a place as any to look at the advantages and disadvantages.

A corporation is regarded as a legal entity, with a separate life, actions, and abilities to perform acts distinct from its shareholders. It can sue and be sued, pay taxes, declare bankruptcy, and live forever, with or without the owner(s). To some extent the size of the business influences whether the corporate form could be beneficial. Although incorporating might not save much in costs, many times it's easier to do something through a corporation than as a sole proprietor or partnership. For example, for a company with many employees, such as most manufacturing companies, the corporate form makes it much easier to set up benefit programs, including retirement and profit-sharing plans, group health and life insurance programs, liability and casualty insurance coverage, and so on. On the other hand, for a one–man business, benefits can just as easily be arranged for himself without a corporation.

The type of business also determines whether limited liability advantages apply. For example, a company that produces a product or a generic service such as an insurance agency or a real estate agency receiving limited liability from the corporate form is more likely to hold up in court in the event of a lawsuit. If a suit is brought against a one–man, personal services business such as an artist, athlete, actor, marriage counselor, or psychologist, where the service performed can only be done by him, not a corporate entity, a court would probably rule that the corporation is merely a sham and pierce the corporate shield.

Each business owner must assess his own benefits of incorporating. Generally, all retail, distribution, and service businesses, except for specialized personal service activities, can benefit from the corporate form. The following is a list of the principal benefits and risks of using a corporation.

Advantages to Using a Corporation
When it comes time to get out:

1. selling stock in a corporation, eliminates liabilities from the business after closing;
2. cumbersome Bulk Sales laws can be avoided by selling stock;

3. corporate title to assets clearly identifies which assets belong to the business and which are personal;

4. more options are available to negotiate allocations of purchase price (stock versus asset sale);

5. audited financial statements are cleaner; and

6. Buyers would rather deal with a corporate entity because:
   a. recordkeeping is generally more complete;
   b. tax returns more accurately reflect business income;
   c. business and personal assets can be easily segregated; and
   d. by acquiring stock, the business name remains intact.

When you need more flexibility:

1. it is easier to move money back and forth in the form of loans to and from the company;

2. accounting for transactions on the accrual basis is easier;

3. liability is limited in case of a lawsuit;

4. you can use an intermediary corporate holding company to hold stock to provide further protection from liability; and

5. banks prefer lending money to a corporation rather than an individual.

For planning your estate:

1. give shares of stock to your spouse, children, or trusts before death to reduce estate taxes. (You might have to relinquish total control of your company, however, three years before your death. Your tax advisor should advise on the details);

2. spread your ownership to reduce income taxes if using an S corporation,

3. benefit and retirement programs are easier to establish and administer.

Disadvantages

There are also some glaring disadvantages in the corporate form:

1. It can be costly to set up a corporation.

2. Additional state income taxes might be required even though the corporation reports a loss.

3. There are annual agent fees and registration fees.

4. More bookkeeping and corporate records are required, such as stock transfer records, board of directors minutes, and stock certificates.

5. Limited liability might not apply if the court breaks the corporate shield.

6. Potential for double taxation.

7. Corporate tax rates could be higher than individual tax rates if an S corporation is not used.

Using the corporate form isn't for everybody, but if it appears to be beneficial, the next questions to answer are how to do it and in what state. Nearly any law firm will be happy to do the incorporating and filing work. You can expect to pay legal fees ranging from $400 to $2,000, which is outrageous for the time and effort expended, but the going rate nevertheless. Normally, a secretary does all of the work, not the lawyer. To pay such prices for a few hours of clerical work seems a bit much. Registration fees to the state and annual agent fees to be represented in that state are additional.

Over the years, I have formed 11 corporations of my own, and many more for clients, and have never used a lawyer. There are many service companies around whose only business is to form corporations for others and then act as registered agents. You can find them listed in the *Wall Street Journal* ads every week. Many are reputable, but I have used one company almost exclusively: The Company Corporation, 725 Market Street, Wilmington, DE 19801, (302) 575-0440.

A phone call will get you their brochure and complete incorporation forms in the mail within a day. When calling, give them the name of the corporation and, assuming you want to incorporate in Delaware, they will do a computer name verification search while you wait. For other states, it takes about 24 hours. The total cost to form a corporation is about $150. Sixty-six dollars to the state and county for registration fees, $25 to The Company Corporation for the first year's registered agent fee, and about $60 for a gold–embossed corporate minute book, imprinted stock certificates, stock transfer records, and a corporate seal. Thereafter, the annual agent fees run about $50 to $60 for a Delaware corporation. Quite a difference compared to standard attorney's fees for the same service, and at least twice as fast. Also, if you decide to incorporate in a state other than Delaware, they can do that too. The only difference in cost is the state registration fee.

Which state to incorporate in is completely up to you. It has no bearing on where the facilities or accounting records are maintained. It makes no difference where most of the business is conducted. You don't even need a legal address in the state of incorporation, the registered agent provides that. So how do you choose the right state? It really comes down to three questions:

1. Which state has the lowest fees, annual franchise taxes, and corporate income taxes?
2. Which state has the best business climate with the least harassment?
3. Which state laws offer the best protection for officers and directors against personal liability?

Although state laws change from year to year, Delaware has always been a favorite of many Fortune 500 companies, as well as small companies, principally because of the pro–business attitude of the state government. Incorporation costs are low and state taxes are minimal. Recent legislation has also been enacted to afford further legal protection to officers and directors. Nevada is another favorite state with minimal costs and taxes. Some states, seeing that Delaware and Nevada have been making good money from incorporating foreign businesses have tried to get into the act by reducing fees and making it easier to become registered. To my knowledge, however, none offer the liability protection or are as pro–business as Delaware and perhaps Nevada.

On the other hand, there are some states to avoid. Some of the worst include: New York and California, which have complex tax laws, Minnesota which has an anti-business philosophy, Massachusetts and Connecticut have high tax rates, and Wisconsin and Michigan have unpredictable legislation. Remember, if you do incorporate, it need not be in the state in which you are located or do business.

This chapter presented an overview of the tax implications of selling a business and some advantages to incorporating before putting your company on the market. The next step in the selling process is to calculate the value for the company and set a selling price, which is discussed in the next chapter.

4

Pay Me What It's Worth

Setting the Selling Price

YOU CAN'T SELL A BUSINESS WITHOUT FIRST SETTING A SELLING PRICE. THE PRICE must be supported by factual economic and financial data, not contrived from emotional opinions or haphazard conjecture. In today's sophisticated market, merely guessing at a selling price just won't work. You own a terrific company, but a smart Buyer will insist on documented financial statistics to substantiate this claim. My good friend Nigel Brooks tried it without the numbers and failed miserably.

Nigel owned a small engineering firm near London specializing in the design and manufacture of automobile transmissions with sales of about three million pounds sterling. He founded the business 30 years earlier and now wanted to retire. There were no heirs to take over so he decided to put the company on the market.

The British business community is not known for practicing open communications, and Nigel was probably worse than the average businessman. One day in March, he called his solicitor and his tax accountant and told them both, "Find a Buyer for my company. I want to get out. I don't want to pay any taxes, and I want to spend the summer in the South of Spain, without worrying about the business."

Fine, they both told him, but how much was he asking? His answer was a classic British no decision. "Well, we'll just see what the market will pay." What Nigel did not tell them was that he had already estimated he needed six million pounds to retire in comfort, therefore, that's what he would take for the business.

For more than 14 months, the solicitor tried to sell the business, receiving 11 inquiries from viable Buyers. Offering prices ranged from 500,000 to 1,500,000 pounds sterling. Nigel turned them all down, much to the consternation of the solicitor. His accountant tried to impress upon him the need for a rational valuation to support the asking price, but Nigel would have none of that. He knew what he wanted and would settle for nothing less. The company never did sell, and Nigel continues to worry about retirement.

A TIME TO MOVE AND A TIME TO STAY

External economic forces, together with internal financial performance will dictate when you should put your company on the market so as to achieve the maximum results. If the timing isn't right, it will take much longer to sell the business, and the price you negotiate will inevitably be less than you should get. Therefore, proper timing is crucial. In most cases, the best time to sell is:

- when the stock market is bullish;
- at the peak of the industry business cycle; and
- when recent sales and profit history demonstrates continued strong growth.

Stock Market Trends

Stock market averages and trends reflect not only the current health of the national economy, but the projected conditions for the near future. Major corporate decisions for capital appropriations, expansion or contraction moves, and new product and service introductions are strongly influenced by the perceived well being of the economy. In turn, the magnitude of these corporate decisions affect investor confidence in the stock market. It is this "round robin" investment game that causes the price/earnings ratios of listed companies to have a major, and in some cases overwhelming, influence on the valuation of a business, whether it is a public corporation or a private company. The price an entrepreneur can get for his company will be heavily influenced by public investor attitudes.

Industry Cycles

Industry business cycles can be even more important than price/earnings ratios. In many cases, a particular industry cycle might not coincide with stock market trends, but, to a large extent, it controls a company's sales and earnings performance. On a downward trend it's unlikely that a company will experience increasing sales and earnings, although it is possible. If your sales and earnings are on a downward trend, it will be much more difficult to find an appropriate Buyer and the offering price will be less than you would get if the cycle was moving upward. Take a look at what happened to Joe R. and Jerry K., who wanted to sell when both the stock market and their industry cycle were down.

Joe and Jerry owned a heavy equipment dealership in the Midwest. They sold off-road construction equipment (bulldozers, graters, etc.) as well as rolling–stock farm equipment (tractors, balers, and mowers). Sales had dropped nearly 20 percent in the past two years and, although still profitable, the company had seen better times. They had purchased the dealership eight years earlier in a highly leveraged buyout, and hard times from the beginning forced the partners to refinance the acquisition debt twice. Although not disastrous, the past three years were less than what they had expected, and they still owed the banks a substantial amount of the original loan.

Jerry called one day and asked if I would help sell the business. Both partners were in their early sixties and wanted to spend their remaining years in retirement. Recognizing the depressed conditions of the markets, I suggested that to offer the company for sale now would mean taking a severe beating on price. The stock market had declined for two years and was now fluctuating around what appeared to be the bottom. The construction and agriculture markets that the company sold to had been depressed for several years. Interest rates were still high and the inflation rate was just coming under control. This might be a perfect market for a Buyer, but it was just the opposite for a Seller. The chances of selling at a fair price were so low that I strongly recommended the partners wait another 12 to 18 months to see how the market and business cycles were doing. If conditions improved, they could put the company up for sale then.

Jerry was willing to wait, but Joe had already decided to get out as soon as possible. Jerry acquiesced, and over my strenuous objections, the search for a Buyer began. If the timing had been optimum a P/E ratio of approximately 15 times earnings yielding a price of $13 million might be reasonable. But now, at the bottom of the market, this multiple was much too high.

An interested Buyer finally emerged, but negotiations extended for 15 months. When we finally closed (at a price of $8 million), the cycles had already started up, sales were increasing rapidly, and profits were improving. A terrific position for the Buyer, but Joe and Jerry took a beating. They would not believe the timing of the sale could make that much difference until they saw the results.

Financial Performance

The third timing factor, financial performance, also influences selling price. Unless you have mismanaged the company or there are severe extenuating circumstances, you should be able to command top dollar with a three–year record of increasing sales and profits. A strong growth record implies the good health of the company and industry. It also points the way toward projecting future growth, thereby supporting a still higher price. A Buyer reasons that if past efforts resulted in such a positive performance, his own abilities and talents should engender even higher marks in the future. In addition to commanding a higher price, companies with strong historic growth records generally sell much faster.

So even though you might be ready to get out, take a look at the economic conditions first. The stock market, industry cycles, and recent company performance all have a strong influence in determining how much you can get for your business and even whether you can find a viable Buyer. Timing is crucial in any acquisition or divestiture, from anyone's viewpoint.

Fortunately, there is one way to mitigate the effect of unfavorable timing factors. If you must sell during an unfavorable cycle, or when the fortunes of your company have been less than spectacular, a fair price might still be possible by agreeing to deferred payment terms. Buyers are far more apt to take a chance if they can delay payment for several years. Various deferred payment options are examined in Chapters 9 and 10.

The checklist in Fig. 4–1 supplements the questions used to prepare the Selling Plan in Chapter 2 and ensures the inclusion of all relevant external and internal factors in determining the timing of a sale. It's helpful to use this checklist when you first decide you want to get out. Economics are dynamic, however, and just because conditions are right when you make your first survey doesn't mean they will stay that way, so you'll need to update this checklist right up to the time you negotiate a deal.

Timing the Sale of MAKE MONEY

Using our hypothetical company, MAKE MONEY FILTER CORP., let's review it's record for the past five years and see how timing factors influence its sale. Table 4–1 shows its five–year historical financial statistics.

When John E. Joe acquired MAKE MONEY five years ago, sales were at $20 million and profits running about 7 percent. Since taking over, he has been able to improve sales by 40 percent and profits by nearly 3 percentage points—that's not bad!. A cash flow of over $8.8 million is pretty good too, considering debt service took $6.5 million of it, including a payoff of the entire Seller earn–out balance. That left over $2 million for John's draw and reserve funds.

MAKE MONEY's financial performance for the past five years has been stunning, which will be a very strong point when negotiating price. Unfortunately, most of the growth came during the first three years under new ownership. The two most recent years were nearly flat, indicating to the Buyer that the peak has been reached and a downward trend can be expected in the near future. John E. must come to grips with this argument and convince the Buyer that this won't happen. On a scale of 10, historical growth trends rate a score of eight!

Checklist of Economic Factors

National

1. Current trends in the stock market.
2. Average price/earnings ratios for companies in my industry.
3. Current interest rates.
4. Forecast of interest rates next year.
5. Inflation rate—last year, this year, forecast for next year.
6. National unemployment rate last year, forecast for this year.
7. Unemployment rate in my area, last year and this year.
8. Foreign exchange rates against free world currencies.
9. Current oil price per barrel and projected for next year.
10. National indicators
    a. Capital appropriations
    b. Inventory/sales ratios
    c. Housing starts/building permits—last year, this year, next year
    d. Other indicators affecting my industry

Industry

1. Industry growth rate during last three years.
2. Industry growth rate forecast for next year.
3. Major changes in industry technology.
4. Business failures in my industry last year.
5. Major changes in market position of competitors in my industry.
6. Recent major acquisitions in my industry.

Company

1. Sales and profits for the last three years.
2. Sales forecast for the next three years.
3. Debt-to-equity ratio for the last three years and this year.
4. Major work force additions or reductions anticipated next year.
5. Inventory growth rate versus sales growth rate—last year.
6. Capital expenditures for last year, this year, and next year.
7. New product introductions last year, this year, and next year.
8. Changes in competitive position or market share last year and this year.

Fig. 4-1. An economic checklist can help you determine whether or not now is a good time to sell your business.

The business cycle for residential water markets will detract from this strong performance. It looks as if it might already have peaked and started downward to put even more pressure on sales and profits. Selling on the downside of the cycle hurts, although not as bad as four or five years hence when the

TABLE 4-1
MAKE MONEY FILTER CORP.
Five-Year Financial Statistics

Actual	Sales	Profit	Percent To Sales	Cash Before Debt Service
Year 1	$24,200	$1,870	7.7	$1,470
Year 2	$27,000	$2,133	7.9	$1,710
Year 3	$30,000	$2,700	9.0	$1,060
Year 4	$29,800	$2,625	8.8	$2,510
Year 5	$30,600	$2,725	8.9	$2,100

curve will be at its trough. In spite of John's optimistic forecast on a downward curve, further market deterioration can be expected and this will put additional pressure on him to reduce his price. The industry business cycle doesn't rate more than a six!

On the plus side, the stock market has been strong for some time now. Most of the prognostications from Wall Street indicate the bull market should last at least through the next year. Well thank goodness! At least one out of three is favorable, and this one rates a ten!

There is a fourth element to consider in assessing the timing of the sale. How does MAKE MONEY's market position compare to its competitors? MAKE MONEY has gained market share over the past three years and this gives John E. an advantage. An improving market share each year indicates that existing marketing strategy is working and that sales personnel are doing their job. This, in turn, means that the Buyer need not worry about this aspect of the business, and that's worth money to John. If market share was declining, expansive historical financial results would probably be discounted as being controlled by external forces rather than good management and the Buyer would see a need to implement new marketing plans as soon as he takes over. This costs money, and he would argue that John should pay for it through a decreased selling price. Fortunately for MAKE MONEY FILTER, this is not the case. The company has a qualified marketing team on board and they have done their job well. The company's market share in most product lines has increased, although not dramatically. A rating of eight for market share!

On a timing scale where 10 is the optimum, a summary for MAKE MONEY FILTER, coming into Year 6, would be as follows:

- Company financial performance   8
- Industry business cycle   6

· Status of stock market	10
· Company's market share	8
Total timing score average	8

This method of quantifying the important timing factors works well in practice as long as you remain objective. Generally, if the timing score is seven or higher, you can expect to realize maximum price for your company. Anything less than seven means you probably must reduce the price. When the timing score drops below five, hold onto the business until internal problems causing the low score can be corrected or until external conditions are more favorable, assuming, of course, you are not under duress to sell.

VALUING A PRIVATE COMPANY

Valuing a private company is, at best, difficult. An owner always believes his business is worth more than the market does and, without some guidelines to follow, pricing at an inflated amount will surely preclude attracting viable Buyers.

Numerous books and articles have been written about how to value a going business. Self-proclaimed authorities in financial circles, academia, consulting, government agencies, corporate America, and even statisticians get into the act. Everyone has his own theory about the most equitable and accurate method. But keep in mind that everyone has his own ax to grind too, and chooses the method that best suits his own self–interests. Finance companies value a business at what the assets will bring at liquidation auction. Investment bankers and venture capitalists, interested in rapid appreciation and high returns on their investment, value a business at discounted future cash flow. Statisticians have devised complex deviation curves based on historical performance to project future earnings. Corporate America looks to the prevailing P/E ratios, unless the market is depressed, in which case they use book value. And on, and on, and on it goes.

The temptation to overvalue a business to support the asking price can backfire. When owners use replacement costs to value hard assets, restated prior years' earnings and book value to reflect so-called true earnings, and then believe their own forecasts of future growth, they can really get into trouble.

Don't forget that a business is more than a collection of tangible assets. It's a dynamic collection of people, product, and customer loyalty—a going concern. A going concern produces profits, and from profits, cash. Generally, the net cash a business can generate over time reflects the practical value of a business. Whether it is sold on the open market, to a partner or a successor, to an ESOP, or even through a public stock issue, without an asking price based on calculable, verifiable financial statistics, no reasonable Buyer will spend the time investigating and negotiating the deal. Five of the most commonly used valuation techniques are:

1. Liquidation method
2. Net asset value method
3. Historical cash flow method
4. Future cash flow method
5. Profitability method

There is no universally acceptable method for all businesses. Very small retail and personal service businesses require special techniques, which are discussed near the end of this Chapter. Let's use the financial data from MAKE MONEY FILTER CORP. to examine an acceptable compromise for companies with substantial hard assets.

Liquidation Method

As the name implies, the liquidation method values the business at an estimated amount to be realized from a liquidation auction. There is no going concern concept to worry about because, if the business fails, the only remaining value is in the hard assets.

Various liquidation methods can be used if quick disposal through an auction is not required. Given enough time to dispose of the assets, say one year, individual Buyers can be located for the real estate and each piece of equipment, resulting in a higher price than if they were sold at an auction. Similarly, with no urgency to sell the inventory, Buyers might be found to purchase most of the in-process materials as well as supplies and materials not yet in the production cycle. With time to resolve disputed accounts receivable, chances are high that more collections will be forthcoming than if the accounts were settled quickly.

Most owners view the liquidation method with disdain, and rightly so. No consideration is given to customer or industry goodwill built up over the years. The benefits of unique product/service identification or specialized market niches are ignored. Abilities and talents of company personnel are completely overlooked and no credit is given to the company's propensity to generate cash. The business is not viewed as a going concern but as a group of tangible assets to be sold at distressed prices.

No wonder a Seller shuns this concept. Most business owners look at a business as a group of assets, people, and opportunity to create profits and cash—a living organism, not a collection of nuts and bolts. An owner is certainly not going to sell his profitable company at an auction. So why even discuss the liquidation method? Because this is how bankers and asset–based lenders view the loan value of the business. The liquidation value will determine the amount a lender might loan a qualified Buyer for a leveraged buyout. He considers the liquidation value of the tangible assets the only valuable collateral to the loan. In a default, the liquidation of assets provides the only plausible means for the bank to collect its outstanding loan balance.

To combat Buyer arguments for this method during your negotiations, and also because you must be concerned about how a potential Buyer will finance the acquisition, you need to be aware of how a bank will look at the available collateral and how to make the calculation. If there are no recent appraisals of real estate or machinery and equipment, and if you can afford the time and money to hire such appraisers before putting the company on the market, do so. It will pay off at the negotiating table. Look at Table 4–2 which shows the Liquidation Method calculation for MAKE MONEY FILTER CORP.

Liquidation factors are those reductions from book value used by a bank to

TABLE 4-2
MAKE MONEY FILTER CORP.
Liquidation Method Calculation

Asset Category	Book Value	Liquidation Factor	Liquidation Value
Cash	100	100%	100
Accounts Receivable	5,100	75%	3,825
Inventory	4,800	25%	1,200
Prepaids	75	–0–	–0–
Land & Bldgs.	1,200	60%	720
Mach. & Equip.	3,500	80%	2,800
Other Assets	150	–0–	–0–
Gross liquidation value			8,645
Less: Liabilities assumed:			
Accounts Payable			(1,000)
Accrued Expenses			(1,000)
Notes Payable			(1,000)
Net liquidation value			5,645

give it a cushion in the event of default and liquidation proceedings. Though they vary somewhat with the type of business and quality of assets, the percentages used here are fairly common. Rarely will a financial institution lend more than 75 to 80 percent of receivables, 20 to 30 percent of inventory or 70 to 80 percent of equipment and machinery, although land and buildings might deserve a higher factor if the location is superior and the building relatively new.

Of course, this method would never be used in a sale to a partner, a successor, an ESOP, or a public stock offering. These Buyers are concerned with the potential cash generation of a going business, not liquidation of the company.

Net Asset Value Method

Net asset value is similar to book value. The assets minus the liabilities of the business as shown in the accounting records. All amounts must be reflected on the company's Balance Sheet in accordance with generally accepted accounting principles set forth by the American Institute of Certified Public Accountants. Simply put, net asset value is the recorded book value of the business, with a few adjustments. It is also referred to as net worth or owner's equity.

The book value reflects neither the actual value of assets today, nor their original cost. Consequently, the true current value of the business is distorted. For example, hard assets such as buildings or machinery and equipment are stated on the Balance Sheet at original cost, less depreciation recorded to date. Conceivably, some hard assets might be fully depreciated and, therefore, not shown on the Balance Sheet at all yet still be in use. Or, the company auditors might insist on writing off old inventory and not include this asset on the Balance Sheet even though these materials might still be present and have a value. Slow paying or disputed accounts receivable might be written off and not appear on the Balance Sheet either but still be collectible.

A second difficulty is that this method does not take into account the company's profits or cash. The net asset value method looks at a business at a fixed point in time and ignores the benefits these assets generate over time. It is a static measurement, and therefore, confuses the accounting measurement of assets with the value of the company as a going business.

Nevertheless, accountants, analysts, and business executives continue to use the net asset value method as a viable valuation technique. With all its faults, this method at least gives some measure of a company's value and can easily be calculated from existing financial statements. It also provides a measure of consistency between companies for comparative purposes. Using the balance sheet accounts from MAKE MONEY FILTER CORP., the calculation shown in Table 4–2 would result. Only those balance sheet accounts that reflect assets with a true value to the Buyer are included in the calculation. Accounts such as prepaid expenses, other assets, purchased goodwill, or unamortized organization ex-

TABLE 4-3
MAKE MONEY FILTER CORP.
_____ *Net Asset Value* _____

Category	Amount
Cash	100
Accounts Receivable	5,100
Inventory	4,800
Net Fixed Assets	4,700
Total assets	14,700
Less: Accounts Payable	(1,000)
Accrued Expenses	(1,000)
Notes Payable	(1,000)
Net asset value	11,700

pense are excluded because they are not used to run the business and generate profits or cash. Because such intangible assets are excluded, the net asset value will obviously be somewhat different from the net worth or owner's equity shown on the balance sheet. For purposes of valuation, however, it does, theoretically, reflect the amount invested in the business.

Historical Cash Flow Method

For many prospective Buyers, historical cash flow is the only meaningful way to value a business. Most Buyer's value a business at how much cash it will throw off, and how much he can put in his own pocket. The value of assets might be interesting to know, but hardly anyone buys a business only for its balance sheet assets. The whole purpose is to make money, and most Buyers feel that they should be able to generate at least as much cash in the future as the business yielded in the past.

A knowledgeable Buyer will inevitably argue that the business is only worth what it can generate in cash, and the historic record of achievement measures this ability. Typically, the most recent three years are used as an appropriate measure. Anything prior to three years is ancient history and probably not reflective of the current condition of the company. Also, three years should be enough to eradicate any unusual swings in the business. The trend in cash flow over this period becomes far more important than one year's performance. A Seller faces two major obstacles in using this method:

1. Because management decisions and actions taken in the past will create a greater cash flow in the future, the trend in cash flow should be projected over several years to recognize the true value of the business as a cash generator. Because a Buyer is really purchasing future earning power, he should pay for the future potential, not the past.

2. A price based on historic cash flow does not compensate the Seller for his investment in the business and the risks he has taken to build it.

Again, using MAKE MONEY financial statements as a source of data, the calculation shown in Table 4-4 would be made.

It's easy to see the fallacy in this calculation from the Seller's viewpoint. Cash flow generated by the profits of the business averages $3,010 and multiplied by the factor 3, yields a valuation of $9,030, not $3,132. The difference,

TABLE 4-4
MAKE MONEY FILTER CORP.
Three-Year Cash Flow Comparison

Category	Year 1	Year 2	Year 3
Adjusted pre-tax profit	3,964	4,222	4,364
Add:			
Depreciation	700	700	800
Interest Expense	100	100	100
Re-adjust. pre-tax profit	4,764	5,022	5,264
Less: Taxes	1,905	2,008	2,105
Adjusted after tax cash profit	2,859	3,014	3,159
Less:			
Increase in working capital	(1,500)	(1,000)	(500)
Purchase of fixed assets	(500)	(1,000)	(1,400)
Net cash flow	859	1,014	1,259
Average cash flow three years	1,044		
Factor Applied	× 3		
Cash flow valuation (Historical)	3,132		

nearly $6,000, was plowed back into the business for working capital and new equipment. This amount is discretionary, and the Seller should not be penalized for using his cash to help the business grow. Not only did this reinvested cash help the business grow during the prior three years, but it laid the foundation for future growth and higher cash flows.

The Buyer, of course, will argue that the reinvested cash was necessary to achieve the profit and cash levels already recorded, and therefore should be properly deducted from the profit cash flow in arriving at a valuation.

It should be noted that the calculation begins with an "Adjusted Pre-Tax Profit," not the profit reported on the financial statements. A common practice in private company valuations, is that all compensation to the business owner gets added back to the reported profit. Items such as the owner's salary, bonus, dividends, and benefits are discretionary items and distort the true cash flow of the business. Presumably, a new owner will structure his own cash draws and benefits program, and therefore, the Seller's compensation should be excluded from the computation.

The factor 3 that is used to value cash flow is also discretionary, and certainly conservative. Current investment banking philosophy uses multiples of three to five depending on the desired payback period for an investment.

Future Cash Flow Method

Just as the Buyer wants to look at historic cash flow, the Seller wants to look to the future. Entrepreneurial optimism invariably assumes that the business will do better in the future than in the past. Unless the company experiences a financial disaster or happens to be in a clearly dying industry, the future will always look brighter than the past. Also, the Seller rationalizes that his prior efforts and decisions were made with the future in mind and should be compensated accordingly.

Realistically, this argument has merit. No Buyer should acquire a company unless he believes the company can do better in the future than in the past. Unless the Seller has been totally incompetent, and very few business owners are, steps taken by the Seller, and his reinvestment of cash in facilities, product development, personnel organization, and marketing promotions, should benefit the future more than the past. Therefore, he should be compensated for these actions.

Another way of looking at future cash flow recognizes that the goodwill engendered by the Seller during his ownership of the business has established customer loyalties, industry reputation, and personnel efficiency which are assets of the business as much as the real estate, equipment, receivables, and inventory recorded on the balance sheet. Only prohibitions by the accounting fraternities and government and banking regulations prohibit monetary recognition of these intangible assets. He should be compensated for this intangible goodwill the same as recorded assets.

The MAKE MONEY five year forecast yields the valuation shown in Table 4–5. Financial analysts usually like to apply a discount rate to arrive at the present value of such cash flow, and there is merit in such an approach. Cash earned five years from now is not worth as much to you today as cash earned today. Many business owners, however, unsophisticated in financial analyses, just do not understand the meaning of discounted cash flow. Therefore, the layman might find it easier to think in absolute terms.

A five-year period is purely arbitrary. It could just as well be three or seven years. The financial community generally accepts five years as being a reasonable time period to project a business, however. Three years is too short because most business investment in hard assets and personnel will be influential beyond this time frame. Seven to ten years is too long because too many un-

TABLE 4-5
MAKE MONEY FILTER CORP.
Valuation

Category	Year 1	Year 2	Year 3	Year 4	Year 5
Adjusted pre-tax profit	5,095	6,488	7,714	9,205	10,429
Add:					
Depreciation	800	900	1,000	1,100	1,200
Interest Expense	150	150	150	150	150
Re-adjust. pre-tax profit	6,045	7,538	8,864	10,455	11,779
Less: Taxes	2,418	3,015	3,545	4,182	4,711
Adjusted after tax cash profit	3,627	4,523	5,319	6,273	7,068
Less:					
Increase in working capital	(1,300)	(1,800)	(1,200)	(1,300)	(1,700)
Purchase of fixed assets	(600)	(1,000)	(800)	(1,000)	(1,500)
Net cash flow	1,727	1,723	3,319	3,973	3,868
Average cash flow five years			2,922		
Factor Applied			× 5		
Cash flow valuation (future)			14,610		

foreseen events might occur, making the forecast meaningless. Consequently, five years is the accepted length for forecasts, although some Buyers will argue that any forecast is meaningless. The entire subject of forecasting accuracy, however, is subjective and completely beyond the scope of this book.

It should be noted that the same arguments for using the future cash flow method are also used for the historic cash flow method regarding reinvestment of cash in working capital and equipment. Also, remember that the beginning point is "adjusted pre-tax profit," which equates to reported profit plus the owner's draws and benefits.

Profitability Method

The profitability method recognizes only the prior year's profits and current stock market price/earning ratios. This computation is too simplistic for most sophisticated financial analysts, although this very simplicity appeals to the corporate Seller. The emphasis placed on P/E ratios is ideally suited to publicly traded companies. Most corporate Sellers assume that because the stock of the parent company sells at a given P/E ratio, each of its subsidiaries and divisions should also sell for the same multiple. The only merit in this approach, however, is it's ease of calculation and because it can be used as a starting point in negotiations. The profit of MAKE MONEY for the prior year yields the following calculation, assuming a published average P/E ratio of 12 times:

	Amount
Prior year's profit, as restated	2,619
Current NYSE average P/E ratio of 12 times	× 12
Valuation	31,428

Although not used by itself, if your company is publicly traded, you can point to this method in arguing for a higher price in negotiations. In most cases, however, the many extenuating circumstances in private companies, or even in owner–controlled traded companies, prohibit meaningful measurement by such an external standard. This method is presented here for illustrative purposes only to alert the Seller to the impact of P/E ratios on his own business valuation. If the stock market runs bullish when he puts his company up for sale, this is a good arguing point for a price in excess of either cash flow or book value. When the market is down, you should probably try some other way.

CHOOSING A VALUATION METHOD

The next step gets rather sticky. With so many methods available, how can you determine which one fits your specific situation best? Or, alternately, how do you weigh the calculations to arrive at an average? Let's summarize the valuations we have so far for MAKE MONEY:

Method	Amount
Liquidation method	5,645
Net assets value method	11,700
Historic Cash flow method	3,132
Future cash flow method	14,610
Profitability method	31,428

What a spread! How can the negotiating parties ever get together on a price with this much variation? Well, it's not easy, but for starters throw out the high and the low. With a book value of about $10 million, in an industry growing at 3 percent per year, a Buyer will probably not be willing to consider a price even approaching $30 million. A 12–year payout is just too long in a stable industry. So John should throw out the profitability method. He can also eliminate the historic cash flow method. He's selling a going business based on the opportunity for a Buyer to earn cash in the future. The fact that a given cash flow resulted in the past should only indirectly influence what a new Buyer could do in the future. So from John's perspective, $3,132 is much too low. Throw it out. That leaves three possibilities to deal with:

	($000)
Liquidation method	$5,645
Cash flow method (Future)	$14,610
Net assets value method	$11,700

To base an offering price on liquidation value is tantamount to conceding the company will soon go out of business. Liquidation value might be fine for conservative bankers, but it certainly doesn't recognize the value of earnings and cash flow generated by a going business. Therefore, throw out the liquidation value also.

Now we're down to what it's all about. How much investment John has in the business (net asset value) and what cash it will generate in the future. If your business is profitable, such as MAKE MONEY is, then you should get back your investment, or book value, plus a premium for customer and employee goodwill built up over the years. Whether or not a multiple of five times future cash flow accurately reflects a company's value, depends on the economics of the moment.

Maybe it should be seven, or ten, or maybe four. But having chosen a factor of five, let's stick with it. With this multiple, an asking price of $15 million for MAKE MONEY looks like a good going-in number. The minimum John E. should take is the net asset value of $11.7 million. That leaves approximately $3 million to negotiate.

DOCUMENTING GROWTH AND SALES TRENDS

In addition to valuation calculations, trends play a major role in setting the selling price for a business. Current financial history will be the first thing a prospective Buyer looks at, and his first questions should be:

1. Is the sales curve increasing or decreasing?
2. Has the profitability and return on sales percentage improved along with the sales?
3. Has inventory increased or decreased?

To be able to answer these questions, you'll need at least three annual financial statements available for the Buyer's inspection. Don't try to cut costs by using unaudited statements. Nothing scares a Buyer more than internally prepared financial statements or statements prepared by a non-certified outside accountant. A certified audit by a reputable CPA firm doesn't cost that much more, and it is well worth the extra cost to prove to the outside world that your financial statements are reasonably presented. Even if your bank doesn't require certified audits, you should have them for your own peace of mind. Additionally, certified financial statements are required by the Securities and Exchange Commission should you ever decide to issue stock to the public.

If the previous three years have not seen a growth in sales and improved profitability, the logical question from a Buyer is, why not? Is the industry in a downward cycle? Is the economy taking its lumps? Have you lost key marketing people? Have you just mismanaged the business? You'll need some plausible answers to these questions to continue to interest the Buyer. There might be perfectly reasonable explanations, but to reduce the possibility of prolonged negotiations or of possibly losing the Buyer, you'd better be prepared. On the other hand, without solid explanations, you probably better look to internal Buyers rather than in the open market.

VALUING A SMALL RETAIL BUSINESS

Like most small business owners, you most likely haven't kept very extensive, or even accurate, financial records over the years, probably just enough to file income tax returns. Also, if your company is not incorporated, there are no legal requirements for recordkeeping other than for tax purposes. It's futile to try to use the above valuation techniques under these conditions. Much better that you work with what you have—Schedule C from your personal tax return and bank statements.

The three most important valuation criteria for this type of business are: (1) how much cash did you withdraw last year; (2) what are the equipment, fixtures, inventory, and receivables worth; and (3) has the markup on purchases been consistent for the past three years? If the answer to the third question is yes, and in most retail businesses it will be, then you only need to deal with your cash draws and the value of the assets.

The Buyer of a small retail business will normally assume fairly constant sales in the future and, therefore, should be confident that he can draw at least as much as you did. This cash will have to cover both his draw and principal and interest payments on acquisition debt. Whether a bank finances the deal, you hold Buyer paper, or the Buyer invests his own cash, the selling price should be predicated on cash flow plus the value of balance sheet assets. Of course, you might be able to convince the Buyer that he can make the business grow more than you have, in which case he'll have more cash than in the past. Although many retail owners are tempted to value their business on gross sales, an intelligent Buyer will insist on using cash flow.

Using some hypothetical numbers, let's take a look at how this works. Although always subject to negotiation, the valuation factors shown in Table 4-6

TABLE 4-6
MAKE MONEY FILTER CORP.
Valuation Factors

Asset	Asset Value	Valuation Factor	Valuation
Receivables	$ 50,000	80%	$ 40,000
Inventory	15,000	75%	11,250
Store Fixtures	50,000	25%	12,500
Office Equipment	10,000	80%	8,000
Vehicles	7,500	25%	1,875
Total assets	$132,500		$73,625
Owner's draw	$ 40,000	3 times	$120,000
Total valuation			$193,625

are generally acceptable to financial institutions and most Buyers. A factor of three applied to owner's draw assumes that a reasonable payback period for the Buyer of a small retail business is three years and that he should be willing to pay you that amount for goodwill. Of course, you might have to negotiate away some to make the sale, but in this example, $193,000 would be a good starting point. Obviously, the asset values must be substantiated from tax returns or other documentation.

One thing to be aware of when trying to value a small business without a complete bookkeeping system is that a Buyer will always assume that one of the perks of having such a business is to charge off as many personal expenses as possible to the business, regardless of IRS regulations, and usually he'll be right. Few small business owners play strictly by the rules and keep all personal expenses out of the business. At a minimum, the owner's car and its operating expenses are usually charged as a business expense. Health and life insurance premiums are also handled as business expenses. Depending on the type of business, personal food purchases, vacation trips, home remodeling, or home appliances might be paid for by the business. Some owners are even clever enough to get some clothing and children's college costs paid out of business funds, even though these are usually not deducted for tax purposes.

The main point to remember is that a Buyer is not dumb, and most will realize you do these things. So be sure to accumulate whatever personal expenses were charged to the business during the past year and add these back to cash draws actually taken. It's really for your own benefit. If the Buyer works from Schedule C of your tax return and it includes inflated expenses, his calculation of owner's draw will be less than it should be and you'll be shortchanged in the valuation.

VALUING A PERSONAL SERVICE BUSINESS

Because a personal service business typically has few, if any, hard assets, inventory, or receivables, a slightly different approach is needed. Normally, a professional practice, as well as other personal service businesses, is valued on gross billings plus any equipment, supplies, tools, reference libraries, or real estate included in the business. The reason is simple. Expenses such as office costs, payroll, reference libraries, transportation, and so on are totally under the control of the owner. A Buyer will probably have an entirely different cost structure, maybe even a different location. Therefore, historical expenses are not really very important to him. He might like to know how much rent, utilities, and taxes apply to the current location, but for information purposes only. He'll never use these statistics in valuing the business.

The important consideration in valuing any personal service business is how much gross billings can be generated from the customer/client base, not what profits have been recorded or how much cash you have taken out. Let the Buyer calculate whatever expenses or cash flow he wants. The price should be set on two factors: annual gross billings and the value of hard assets included in the sale, whether they are recorded on the books or not.

Factors of one or two times gross billings are applicable for most professional practices. The rationale a Buyer will use is that, by the end of a year, any goodwill built up by the Seller will be dissipated. Out of sight, out of mind. From then on, he believes any goodwill will be generated by himself, not the ex-owner. In a tax practice, for example, once the Buyer goes through one tax season, the clients will come back the second year because of his expertise, not the Seller's. Depending on the type of business, a Seller might have cause to argue that his goodwill extends beyond a year, or even two. An insurance agency, for example, generally sells policies on an annual basis. The policyholder keeps coming back, not because of a new agency owner, but because he has been doing business with the agency for years and doesn't pay too much attention to who the agent happens to be. As an owner, you have built up this business over a period of years and goodwill attached to customer policy lists should continue for several years to come.

Obviously, negotiations are necessary to resolve the question of what multiple to use. Nevertheless, gross billings remains the measurement of goodwill. For example, using a factor of two, a dental practice grossing $200,000 annually would have a goodwill value of $400,000. The value of the equipment and supply inventory should be added to this to arrive at the final asking price.

A key consideration to keep in mind if you are selling a professional practice is that the goodwill you have built up over the years is really what you are selling. Sometimes, it is called customer or client lists, or client files, but it is really just goodwill. Because a Buyer's main concern will be his ability to retain your customer or client base, the most logical way to maximize your return would be to bring the Buyer in as a partner for a training period. This way, your customers will get to know him and develop confidence in his abilities to carry on before you leave. Many lawyers, physicians, dentists, and consultants use this technique to sell their practices. Even though bringing in a partner will result in a longer buyout period, your gain will be much larger when you finally do leave. But whatever structure you choose, the valuation technique is the same.

By now, you should understand the most common techniques for establishing a selling price. Assuming you still feel the timing is appropriate for a sale, and sell price calculations yield a satisfactory return, it's time to move on to the next step—getting your company ready for sale.

5

Clean Up the Mess

Preparing the Company for Sale

NOW THAT YOU'VE DECIDED WHAT YOUR COMPANY IS WORTH AND WHAT TO ASK FOR it, it's time to begin the multiple–step process of actually selling it. Unfortunately, as I pointed out to a group of small businessmen who were attending a symposium on changing careers, "You can't just open the doors and expect a Buyer to walk in." There is a well–defined selling process that must be followed in every business sale. Some choose to make it an informal process and stumble through each of the steps without conscious effort. To be certain of selling your property in the fastest and most effortless way possible, and to ensure that you will receive the most favorable price and terms at the negotiating table, you should carefully follow a formal, well–thought out selling plan as illustrated in Chapter 2.

Regardless of whether you are selling a law practice, an insurance agency, an auto repair shop or a large manufacturing or distribution company, the selling steps and the sequence of events are the same. They are also the same under any structure of the sale: open market sale, merger, sale to a successor, a partnership, a public stock issue, or a sale to the management team.

Your particular needs and desires and your reasons for the sale will, to a large extent, control both the speed and the structure of the sale. If you must have cash quickly but the national economy is in the doldrums, probabilities are high that you will not get a very equitable price for your business. On the other hand, if you are willing to keep a minority equity interest in the business for a period of time, the price could probably be higher. If your business can demonstrate a recent trend toward higher growth and better profitability, it will sell a lot faster than if it is experiencing a decline in earnings—or even a stable condition. In any event, the same selling principals apply regardless of the specific condition the business might be in or what your particular needs might be.

THE MECHANICS OF SELLING

In Chapter 2, a typical Selling Plan was constructed using the MAKE MONEY FILTER CORP. as an illustration. There were nine steps to the selling process:

1. Evaluate the timing.
2. Calculate a selling price.
3. Examine tax implications.
4. Clean up the company.
5. Prepare an Offering Prospectus.
6. Locate a Buyer.
7. Negotiate the deal.
8. Assist the Buyer in arranging financing.
9. Negotiate and write the Buy/Sell Agreement.

It was also mentioned that, in most cases, the new owner will request your assistance in making a smooth transition of ownership. Of course, to minimize the hurt to employees and customers you would want to do this anyway.

The first three steps have already been completed. Requirements to notify all employees, customers, and other affected parties of your intentions to sell, and the methods to accomplish this, have also been examined. Now it's time to take a look at the rest of the housekeeping chores to get the company ready for sale so that you can then get on with writing your Offering Prospectus and begin searching for a Buyer. The items you still need to do to get the company ready include:

1. Putting key employees in place.
2. Resolving all contingent liabilities including:
   a) pending lawsuits for and against the company,
   b) outstanding tax disputes,
   c) unsettled insurance and pension claims,
   d) employee grievances,
   e) union contract disputes.
3. Fix up the facilities, including:
   a) painting the building,

b) repairing or replacing machinery and equipment,

c) implementing a housekeeping program,

d) building inventory stocking shelves or bins,

e) getting new office appointments, if needed.

4. Clean up the books: receivables, payables, accruals, annual audits, and contracts and agreements.

5. Take a physical inventory.

6. Implement a public relations campaign to improve the company's image.

PUTTING KEY EMPLOYEES IN PLACE

Almost all companies have continuing personnel turnover for one reason or another. Someone gets a better job offer, somebody else retires or comes down with a long–term illness or just gets mad and quits. Or someone isn't performing and you need to replace him. Whatever the reason, all employees, including key managers, are becoming increasingly mobile and your roster of management and key employees probably has at least one vacancy, maybe more, right now.

If a prospective Buyer is satisfied with the financial performance of your company, he will normally next look at the management team, or in a smaller company, the key employees. What key people are necessary to run the business smoothly? Will he need to replace or add people soon after he takes over, or will there be qualified managers on board and functioning the day he walks in the door? Are some of the key people your relatives or close friends who can be expected to leave shortly after you do? Will there be adequate coverage in those technical areas that he might be weak in? After all, he'll need to count on these key employees to run the business during the transition period at least. He certainly won't know much about the business the day he takes over, and somebody will have to keep it purring along while he ascends the learning curve.

One of the cleanest small companies I have ever tried to sell as an M & A consultant was a government subcontracting business that manufactured metal parts for the aerospace industry. It was profitable, on a good growth curve, and had excellent personnel. Although there were only 20 employees, six of them were key to the operation and were the only ones with the skills capable of performing their specific jobs without supervision. All were long–time employees and the owner left them alone to run their own autocratic functions. We brought the company to market in mid-March and by the end of May had finished negotiating the Buy/Sell Agreement. Both Seller and Buyer anxiously awaited a June 15 closing. Then, four days before the scheduled closing, catastrophe struck.

The Seller, who was a bit of a tyrant in his management techniques, blew up at one of these six key employees. The employee in question happened to be the CNC (Computer Numeric Controlled) milling department supervisor and the only employee who could perform the machine set-ups in a timely fashion and still meet the quality specs of the principal customer, Lockheed Corporation.

Ned walked out of the door by midday and his department came to a screeching halt. Nothing moved through the milling department. Of course, the Buyer got wind of the trouble and immediately called the Seller. "What's going on over there. I just heard that Ned quit and all production has stopped."

"No problem," replied my client. "I'll have another supervisor on board by tomorrow night and everything will be back to normal."

"It better be, or the deal's off. I'm not buying a company without its key production supervisor."

The new supervisor turned out to be incompetent and the deal never closed. My client didn't get another opportunity to sell until six months later, and by then economic conditions had changed and he had to settle for only 80 percent of the price he had negotiated that spring. All because of the loss of a key employee.

So fill whatever open management positions you might have, but especially in highly technical areas where a Buyer is unlikely to have the specific expertise of your employees. A new owner can always replace a controller or find a new personnel manager, but the two areas where he will miss your expertise more than any other, and therefore desperately need your key employees, are in the production of the product or service and the selling of it. If you have disgruntled employees in these areas replace them now, fill those vacancies, and try to keep everybody happy by practicing some merciful management through the selling period. A little preventive maintenance with people can go a long way toward a successful sale.

CONTINGENT LIABILITIES

Every business accumulates unresolved problems over the years. The accounting fraternity frowns on recording these problems on the books as liabilities because they might get resolved without you owing anybody anything. That's why they're called contingent liabilities. Resolving these problems should begin immediately and, if at all possible, clean them up before you ever place the company on the market—but certainly before closing.

One of the big fears of any Buyer is that after he takes ownership of the company, unresolved contingent problems will become real liabilities. Some skeleton will come out of the woodwork and he'll be stuck with the settlement. This is why a good acquisition lawyer for the Buyer will insist on Seller representations guaranteeing that there are no such matters pending, but should they appear in the future, the Seller will be responsible.

To avoid prolonged negotiations over Buy/Sell Agreement language, I always recommend to my selling clients that before the business is put on the market, clean up whatever contingencies might exist—if at all possible. Sometimes it is not possible. For example, if there is a pending lawsuit coming to trial in eight months, it is doubtful the judge will move the trial forward for the convenience of the Seller. Of course, a settlement might be attempted and the matter cleaned up that way, but even that is not always possible. There are generally six types of contingent liabilities that should be resolved:

1. Federal, state, and local tax audit adjustments

2. Insurance claims

3. Employee lawsuits against the company

4. Customer/vendor payment disputes

5. Pension or profit sharing plan claims

6. Union contract grievances or negotiations

Unsettled tax claims by the IRS are particularly troublesome because of the far reaching powers the Service has in placing liens on company property. I realize it is not easy to get the IRS to move very quickly; however if such contingencies continue into negotiations, either the Seller will lose considerable advantage in price and terms, or the deal will never finalize. This happened recently involving the sale of a small printing company.

My client, who wanted badly to buy the print shop, negotiated a price consistent with what the business could produce and everyone seemed happy. It was an asset sale and the Buy/Sell Agreement produced few problems. There was a disputed claim, however, from the IRS concerning unpaid payroll taxes. Even though the case was still awaiting a court date, the IRS put a tax lien against the machinery and equipment. To comply with the Bulk Sales Laws, IRS approval was required to settle this claim at closing date.

Nobody was concerned about the likelihood of this occurring and all parties marched forward to the closing date. One week before closing, however, the Seller's attorney notified all parties that the IRS had not yet made a decision whether to allow the settlement under the proposed conditions or not—and probably wouldn't make a decision for another six months. The deal died and both sides were out the legal fees. In addition, my client lost valuable time and money during his due diligence process. Fortunately, no outside financing was involved so at least bank submission fees were saved.

Resolve Legal Disputes

No one wants to buy someone else's headaches. You really have only two choices in dealing with outstanding lawsuits against the company: either settle them before the closing, or make an adjustment in the sell price for an estimated settlement.

If you opt for the second alternative, you will probably need to give up far more in price than what you could settle the suit for now. A knowledgeable Buyer will not want to gamble on losing cash to a suit of your doing, so he will be ultra conservative in assessing what the damages might be and then demand that much of an adjustment to the sell price. Of course, you might be able to negotiate a deal whereby you take a downward adjustment in price at closing, and if the settlement plus legal fees is resolved at a lesser number, the Buyer pays you back the difference. But this is risky. The Buyer has no incentive to try to reach a more favorable settlement and as long as the total cost doesn't exceed the price adjustment, he's safe. So if you do end up with this kind of an arrangement, don't count on getting anything back.

The other alternative is much more satisfactory: settle the dispute before closing. At least by doing it this way, you'll know you have made the best deal possible and won't need to rely on the Buyer to carry on where you leave off. Sometimes, reaching a settlement before closing is not possible. In this case, you're stuck with the price adjustment, but by all means, try for a settlement, even if you pay more than you think you should.

If there are outstanding lawsuits that you have initiated, the matter is somewhat easier to deal with. In this case, you have the choice of negotiating an estimated settlement—less remaining legal costs—as an addition to the sale price, or, more common, simply exclude the lawsuit from the deal and pursue settlement on your own after the close. Either way, however, it will make the deal more complicated, and a sale is complex enough without adding unknown factors.

Far and away, your best bet is to clean up everything before putting the company on the market. Your second choice should be to clean everything up before closing, even if it means postponing the closing for a while. Most Buyers are willing to wait a reasonable time period for you to dispose of these bothersome matters as long as you don't take forever.

Settle Insurance and Pension Claims

Just as with IRS tax adjustments and outstanding lawsuits, any insurance or pension plan claims either in dispute or outstanding because of foot-dragging on the part of the insurance company or the pension trustee, must be resolved before closing. If not, the same kind of adjustments or post closing paybacks will need to be negotiated; and that just adds more complexity to the deal. The best principal to follow if you want to make a sale at the earliest possible time and for the best price is: **keep it simple for the Buyer so he doesn't need to worry about your problems along with his own.**

Union Contract Disputes

I have yet to find a Buyer willing to walk into a new company where there is trouble brewing with the union. Now I don't mean the normal grievances that continually go on between any collective bargaining unit and company management. What I am talking about are serious strike issues, a contract about to expire, or a contract in the process of being renegotiated. You must finish any of these open union matters before closing a deal. Even better, resolve major issues before the company is even put on the market. The reasons should be obvious. If union leadership knows that the company will be sold in the near future, the natural tendency will be for the negotiating committee to believe they might get a better deal from the new owner than from the present management. When a new owner comes on board, he won't know enough about the background of labor/management relations to be able to negotiate very hard; and besides, he won't dare risk a strike as soon as he takes over.

I was negotiating the sale of a midsized manufacturing company with approximately 450 employees, 350 of which belonged to the IAM bargaining unit. The company was discreetly offered for sale in February, and the union contract was coming up for renegotiation the following January. That gave me a full year to close a deal before contract deadline. For some reason which I still cannot define, I failed to follow my own advice about notifying the employees early in the process about my intentions to sell. Instead, I opted to try to find a Buyer without disclosing my intentions to anyone—a drastic error in judgment. The timing for the sale was just about perfect, and in a very short time I found a viable Buyer and negotiated a cash deal, but with one proviso. For his own business reasons, the Buyer did not want to close the deal before December.

That was all right with me, except it left me with an enormous human relations problem: what was I going to do about the Union contract? Could I possibly keep the deal quiet during the Buyer's due diligence and then stall until December? I thought I could, and away we went.

Everything went all right until October. The union had been pressing for pre-negotiation meetings and the management negotiating team was anxious for my decisions about their strategy. I played along, knowing full well that when the deal closed in December, the Buyer would most likely structure his own negotiation strategy and this would put the management negotiating team at a tactical disadvantage. About the middle of November the IAM representative and the shop steward stormed into my office. "What are you trying to do Mr. Tuller, break the union?" "What are you talking about," I cringed, knowing full well what was coming.

"We just heard that you're selling the company to a guy who has a record of trying to break unions. Don't think you'll get away with this. We're calling a strike vote at midnight on December 31 when the contract runs out."

I tried to pacify them but to no avail. Now I had only one choice open. I had to tell the Buyer of the impending strike—which would probably kill the deal, and I had to face up to announcing my intentions to sell the company to all of the employees. Neither of which was very appealing!

When I told the Buyer, he immediately refused to close in December, but did agree to reschedule the close to February 15, providing I could get the new labor contract signed and in place by that time with a settlement of key issues at no higher cost than we had discussed earlier.

I then went to the employees and tried to explain what had happened, why I was getting out, what kind of a Buyer was coming in, and what it would probably mean to the employees themselves. Fortunately, after the initial shock wore off, most of them were supportive and there was a period of genuine cooperation between nearly everyone except for the union leadership, who were still adamant about a strike vote on December 31.

They finally convinced me to sit down and negotiate a new contract in December, but not with as favorable terms as I had anticipated. When the Buyer learned of the settlement cost, he became disillusioned and backed out of the deal.

I was forced to start looking for a new Buyer all over again, and this time around, the economic timing wasn't as favorable as a year earlier. All of this happened because I ignored the human relations principle to keep employees informed. If I had done that in the beginning, I am sure I could have negotiated a more favorable contract settlement and wrapped up the deal by mid-December.

Therefore, try to get union contract negotiations and any major employee disputes out of the way before you put the company on the market. It's a lot cleaner and much easier on your nerves.

FIXING UP THE FACILITIES

Unless you could get it at a distress price, you certainly wouldn't buy a house with the paint peeling, walkways disintegrating, built-in appliances not working, or a leaky roof. A Buyer also won't want your company if he sees these same conditions. One of the first things a Buyer looks for when he visits your facility is the general appearance and housekeeping. Whether you own a manufacturing plant, a warehouse, a laboratory, a store, or just an office, if it looks unkempt and in need of repair—or even cleaning—most Buyers will be turned off. Or if not turned off, they'll never pay you top dollar for the business, no matter how good the financial statements or industry position might be. I have always advised my buying clients to keep a sharp eye out for a messy facility or sloppy housekeeping during their visit because if a Seller doesn't care about the little things, chances are high there will be some major problem down the road. That was the advice I gave Jack and Mary when they looked at a small country inn they were interested in for the first time.

Jack had recently retired from his corporate position and he and his wife Mary decided to start over again by buying a small country inn in Massachusetts. We reviewed the preliminary financial data and the price looked about right. They were enthusiastic and ready to begin the due diligence investigation when I suggested they should take the time to stay at the inn for a weekend and see how it was run. They did, and the following Monday Jack called. "I'm sure glad we took your advice, Larry. Even though the numbers made it look like a good deal for us, after we spent three days and nights fighting off the roaches and rats we wouldn't set foot in that place again if it were the last place on earth! I've never seen such a dirty place. Nothing worked, paint peeling from the walls, and the kitchen was filthy." Five years later, the inn still hadn't sold.

So go ahead and spend the money to fix your place up. Even if you're leasing the property, either get the landlord to paint or ask him to let you do it. And get the pieces of equipment that haven't worked for years out of the door to the junkyard or else get them repaired to working order. Straighten out the inventory. If you need new storage racks, get them installed.

Put ashtrays or butt cans around so your employees don't drop their ashes or cigarettes on the floor. Remodel the restrooms to make them sparkle. If your employees eat in, get the lunch room freshened up. Put in some new tables and chairs, or get some new furniture for your reception room. If you don't have one, hire a janitor to keep the floor swept.

These things all cost money, but then so does having your house painted and driveway repaved before you sell it. Fixing up the facilities is well worth both the cost and the effort. If you don't, you might not be able to sell at all— just like the country inn.

CLEANING UP THE ACCOUNTING RECORDS

Just like the facilities, over a period of years, even with annual audits, the accounting records of most businesses tend to become jumbled and messy. This will turn the Buyer off just as fast as seeing a dirty facility. What do I mean by jumbled and messy books? Let's look at some examples.

Ahman sold oriental carpets in his small shop outside Philadelphia. With most carpet prices at least $3,000, nearly all sales were on open account. When he tried to sell the business, the Buyer argued that the receivables were worth only 50 percent of what was on the books because half of them were over six months old. Ahman tried to explain that this was standard for his type of business and they were still collectible. The Buyer said "No", and the deal died. Ahman should have either agreed not to sell the receivables and collect them himself, or written them off before the Buyer came in.

June ran a crafts store but was a terrible bookkeeper. She consistently forgot to record vendors invoices for her purchases and paid the bills only when a supplier threatened to cut her off. The store was very profitable and in a good location so when she put it on the market, there was no lack of Buyer interest. Every time a Buyer examined her books, however, he found her trade payables recorded at only about one-fourth of what they should be for her size operation. The threat of unrecorded liabilities frightened most Buyers off, and it wasn't until she hired a full–time bookkeeper to get her payables in order that she was able to close a deal. Even if you are on the cash basis of accounting for your business, when it comes time to sell, spend the money to have a qualified accountant get your books set up on the accrual basis so that a Buyer can at least see what he is buying!

Robert owned a small plant that assembled a key component for flight simulators for the U.S. Navy. Government contract accounting permitted him to record the jobs on a percentage of completion method which, in his operation, involved extremely complex calculations recognizing a variety of accrued expenses. My Buyer client and I spent six weeks trying to verify the calculations because Robert refused to record the accruals in his company books and insisted on keeping them on work sheets. Government auditors apparently could follow the trail, but we couldn't, and in the seventh week, my client withdrew from the deal. Even if you don't need a complete set of accounting records to run your business, if you expect to sell, you better get everything recorded in acceptable accounting fashion—including all liabilities and accounting accruals.

As seen in Chapter 4, the cost of having a CPA do annual audits of your accounting records is well worth the cost when it comes time to sell. You'll need the audits anyway for most banks, and certainly if you expect to make a public stock offering some day. Most Buyers are highly skeptical of financial statements not prepared by a qualified independent accountant. On the other hand, certified audited statements will be scrutinized far less than internally prepared records.

The final accounting area to clean up is not really accounting at all. When the Buyer begins his due diligence investigation, he will want copies of all outstanding contracts and agreements—of any kind. Because most businesspeople tend to file these documents away in a variety of places once they are executed, it would be a good idea to gather them all up in one place in anticipation of a Buyer's request to see them. Some contracts might be with your lawyer, some filed by your secretary, others are probably in someone's desk drawer or at home, or hidden away with other files. Agreements with employees or vendors might be oral or taken down in note form, but they should be formalized in proper legal format. Sales contracts and vendor long–term purchase orders might be several years old and, if you are like most small businessmen, long forgotten. They need to be resurrected and even re-drafted if no one can find the originals. For your own protection as well as the Buyer's, it's essential to account for, and turn over, all contracts and agreements supporting the operations of your business. Remember, you'll probably have to warrant in the Buy/Sell Agreement that this has been done, as we'll see in Chapter 11.

TAKING A PHYSICAL INVENTORY

Depending on the type of business you have and whether you opt for an annual audit, you might or might not regularly take a physical inventory of your materials and supplies. Many retail businesses use cyclical counts throughout the year. Manufacturers usually take a physical inventory at year end. Service businesses will often keep track of expensive supplies by perpetual inventory records. Most government subcontractors in the aerospace industry **never** take keep track of their inventory, much less take a physical count!

A Buyer wants to know what he is buying, however. Whether its a stock sale or an asset sale, but especially in an asset sale, he will want to be sure that amounts recorded in the books represent materials actually present in the facility. Some owners of small retail businesses tend to forget all about this when they try to sell the business as did Ted and Billy.

Ted and Billy owned a lumberyard catering to the do-it-yourself trade. Because of the small quantities and special cuts of materials in a normal sale, their yard looked a mess. Lumber and auxiliary materials were everywhere and it was impossible to tell how much inventory they really had. But having a full time controller on the payroll, the accounting records were immaculate. He kept computer–based perpetual inventory records of every nut and bolt and piece of lumber. He knew exactly what they owned.

Eventually, I located the ideal Buyer, anxious to make a cash deal and willing to use a multiple of five times cash draws plus actual cost value of inventory and equipment. It was almost too good to be true and the partners were elated. There was only one hitch, the Buyer wanted a list of all equipment along with cost invoices (no problem for the controller) and a physical count of all inventory and supplies. Ted and Billy closed down one weekend and everyone pitched in to count. When all of the lumber, auxiliary materials, and supplies were added up, the shock came. The total was only $50,000—60 percent less than what the controller had in his perpetual records. The deal finally closed, but the partners still believe they were somehow cheated out of $40,000 for the "lost" inventory.

So, if you are not in the habit of taking regular, physical inventory counts and reconciling the totals to your other records, start now. Don't let the Buyer tell you how bad your records are.

A Clean-up Checklist

As you have probably surmised by now, I am an inveterate believer in checklists—for almost anything. I put together the checklist shown in Fig. 5–1 some time ago to ensure no key elements in getting a company ready for sale are forgotten.

DEVELOPING GOOD RELATIONS

Developing a good reputation in the industry and in the community ends up being one of the most difficult and time consuming steps in preparing for a sale. Many entrepreneurs prefer to keep a low profile and leave public imaging to the more flamboyant. Many don't even recognize how much value a good reputation can be to the company. And others, through arrogance and disdain, intentionally ignore community affairs and industry participation. From the viewpoint of a smart Buyer, however, a company well thought of in the industry, and known for its concern and active support of both it's employees and community, is far more desirable than one nobody has heard of—or worse, one with a bad reputation. Any smart Buyer will thoroughly investigate the character of your employees, and the reputation of your company in the community and in your industry.

Both of these factors will have a major impact on your ability to get the maximum price for your business. It won't take long for a perceptive Buyer to determine if your employees, and particularly your management team are determined, happy, and of strong moral fiber, or, slovenly, discontented, and rebellious. The latter will certainly cause a Buyer to question the advisability of proceeding, at any price. Likewise, if your company is known throughout the industry, and particularly in your own community, as a well–run, high–morale business, with demonstrated caring and compassion for the less fortunate, it will go a long way toward enthusing the Buyer.

One way to ensure such a reputation inside and outside of the company is to take a stand and make a contribution toward solving the most insidious problem in American business today—the use of drugs.

The only way to stop the insane use of drugs is through education. If the denizens of industry would spend only a fraction of the funds on drug education that they currently spend trying to stop public and employee cigarette smoking,

Fig. 5-1. Use this checklist to ensure you haven't forgotten any key elements of preparing your business for a sale.

```
A CLEAN-UP CHECKLIST

Personnel                                    In Place      Open
A.  Department Heads
    Production                               _____    _____
    Sales                                    _____    _____
    Marketing                                _____    _____
    Advertising                              _____    _____
    Contracts Administration                 _____    _____
    Finance                                  _____    _____
    Personnel                                _____    _____
    Engineering                              _____    _____
    Application Engineering                  _____    _____
    Quality Control                          _____    _____
    Data Processing                          _____    _____
    Legal and Administrative                 _____    _____

B.  Foremen:

    1. _____          _____    _____

    2. _____          _____    _____

    3. _____          _____    _____

    4. _____          _____    _____

C.  Other Key Employees

    1. _____          _____    _____

    2. _____          _____    _____

    3. _____          _____    _____

    4. _____          _____    _____

D.  Copies of:
    1. Group Health Insurance Plan           _____    _____
    2. Group A D & D Plan                    _____    _____
    3. Group Dental Plan                     _____    _____
    4. Group Life Insurance Plan             _____    _____
    5. Pension Plan including three years' tax returns
       and actuarial reports                 _____    _____
```

(Fig. 5-1 continues)

	In Place	Open
6. Profit Sharing or Bonus Plans	_____	_____
7. Incentive Programs	_____	_____
8. Current Union Contract	_____	_____
9. Others	_____	_____

Legal	**Resolved**	**Open**
A. Lawsuits Against Company		
1. EEOC suits		
a. _____	_____	_____
b. _____	_____	_____
c. _____	_____	_____
2. EPA suits	_____	_____
3. Wage & Hour suits		
a. _____	_____	_____
b. _____	_____	_____
c. _____	_____	_____
4. Vendors		
a. _____	_____	_____
b. _____	_____	_____
c. _____	_____	_____
5. Customers		
a. _____	_____	_____
b. _____	_____	_____
c. _____	_____	_____
6. Workman's Compensation		
a. _____	_____	_____
b. _____	_____	_____
c. _____	_____	_____

(Fig. 5-1 continues)

	Resolved	Open
7. Others		
a. _____	_____	_____
b. _____	_____	_____
c. _____	_____	_____
B. Lawsuits By the Company		
a. _____	_____	_____
b. _____	_____	_____
c. _____	_____	_____
C. Outstanding Tax Claims:		
1. IRS	_____	_____
2. State	_____	_____
3. Unemployment Compensation	_____	_____
4. Other	_____	_____
D. Unsettled Insurance Claims	_____	_____
E. Unsettled Pension Claims		
a. _____	_____	_____
b. _____	_____	_____
c. _____	_____	_____
F. Employee Grievances		
a. _____	_____	_____
b. _____	_____	_____
c. _____	_____	_____
G. Union Disputes		
a. _____	_____	_____
b. _____	_____	_____
c. _____	_____	_____

(Fig. 5-1 continues)

(Fig. 5-1 continued)

Facilities	Completed	To Do
A. Building Exterior		
B. Building Interior		
C. Roof		
D. Parking Lot and Walkways		
E. Broken Equipment		
F. Obsolete Equipment		
G. Clean House Program		
H. Storage Bins/Racks		
I. Reception Furniture		
J. Carpets		
K. Windows		

Accounting Records	Completed	To Do
A. Computer systems completed		
B. Aged Trial Balance of Receivables		
1. Resolve old accounts		
C. Aged Trial Balance of Trade Payables		
1. Resolve past due balances		
D. Analyze Accruals		
E. Update Pension Liability		
F. Update Depreciation Schedules		
G. Monthly Internal Financial Statements for three years		
H. Manpower Reports		
I. Current Production Reports		
J. Orders and Order Backlog Reports by Month for three years		
K. Annual Audited Financial Statements for three years		
L. All taxes current		
1. Federal Income		
2. State Income		
3. Sales Tax		
4. Use Tax		
5. Property Tax		
6. Franchise Tax		
7. Payroll Taxes		
8. Other Taxes		

(Fig. 5-1 continues)

(Fig. 5-1 continued)

Contracts and Agreements	In Hand	To Get
A. Union Contract		
B. Pension Plan Agreement		
C. Sales Reps Contracts		
1.		
2.		
3.		
D. Leases		
1. Equipment		
2. Building		
3. Autos		
4. Other		
E. Customers		
1.		
2.		
3.		
F. Vendors		
1.		
2.		
3.		

Current Physical Inventory	Completed	To Do
A. Supplies		
B. Raw Materials		
C. In-process Materials		
D. Finished Goods		
E. Reconciliation Sheet		

there might be enough money to curb the tide. If the top executives in the airlines industry—a very visible industry in American business—would worry as much about stopping the use of drugs in their places of business and educating the children of employees in the deceptive and criminal use of drugs as they do about smoke–free airplanes and glass–partitioned offices, this great country might continue to be great 20 years from now.

As long as our business leaders, including owners of small businesses, continue to think that drug education is someone else's worry and responsibility, hundreds of millions of young minds will be destroyed. You, as an entrepreneur, can begin this crusade. Care enough about your employees and business associates to become active in fighting the drug mobsters. Implement drug education classes on company time. Negotiate with union leadership to require drug testing of employees. Conduct sessions on drug education in your local school system. Keep writing letters and articles to your local newspaper, congressman and others. But do something!

The business owner who demonstrates this kind of caring will surely have higher employee morale and a smoother road toward selling his company than one who sits back and does nothing.

Jack and Marie owned and operated a small real estate agency in the Philadelphia suburbs. Both were in their fifties and, for some time, had considered selling their business and buying a small resort inn in New England.

One night their two sons, both in their late twenties, were killed when the car they were riding in was hit head-on by a local teenager high on cocaine. Although devastated, Jack and Marie felt that they owed the community an honest effort at trying to curb the use of drugs in the local high school. They used nearly all of their savings to fund an independent foundation to operate a midway house to help teenage drug addicts kick the habit.

Over a three–year period, the couple's efforts were well publicized in the local newspapers. When they finally put their real estate agency up for sale, a Buyer stepped forward within two weeks and the deal closed in 60 days.

I met the Buyer later and asked what had prompted him to act so rapidly. "Very simple," he replied. "Anybody who cares as much about people as Jack and Marie do must be honest, and anybody that devoted to the community must be highly thought of. I knew I could trust what they told me about the business and I knew their reputation would carry over after the sale to give me time to establish my own customer base. And I was right on both counts!"

Although I am certainly not a public relations expert, I have worked with several clients in developing meaningful public relations programs at very little cost. Although perhaps not applicable to all businesses, the following nine steps, if worked in unison, seem to do the job for most small and midsized businesses.

1. Become active in the chamber of commerce or community planning board or one or two civic organizations (Kiwanis, Lions, etc.).

2. Support local school functions and make donations of your products or services wherever possible (athletic events, school sales, school fund–raising drives, parades).

3. If you are in a smaller community, run for a local political office.

4. Develop a program of sending articles about your company and your employees to the local newspaper.

5. Teach an adult education class (if such a program is offered in your community).

6. Take out advertisements in local news bulletins (school events, community promotions, political rallies).

7. Hold an open house at your place of business at least once each year and invite community political, education, social, religious, and business leaders. Be sure to include members of the press.

8. Donate space in your facility for meetings of social organizations (Boy/Girl Scouts, support groups, other youth groups, Amnesty International).

9. Organize and sponsor public health conferences, drug and alcohol rehabilitation programs, and senior citizen forums.

You probably won't be able to do all nine steps, but the more you can keep your company's name and your name in the public eye as a concerned member of the community, the more and better public relations you'll have. Remember, it doesn't cost much to be a good and caring citizen, and the benefits can be substantial.

Industry recognition takes a bit more effort but is still possible in a relatively short period of time. Chairmanship of trade association committees, contributions of articles and ideas to trade publications, innovated product or service introductions will all contribute toward your improved industry reputation. But the best and surest way to become known in the industry is to become known as a company that produces a top–quality product or service, deals honestly and truthfully with vendors and customers, and who will stand behind their product or service—no matter what. Sears is a perfect example of a company building a reputation for delivering quality products simply by guaranteeing customer satisfaction—forever. Just last week, I returned a wristwatch I had purchased from Sears 10 years ago. Without any haggling at all, or even proof of purchase, the local store gave me a new watch. This is why I continue to buy from Sears.

Once you have begun to get your company cleaned up and are developing a good public image, the next step is to get the Offering Prospectus, prepared and then go find that elusive Buyer.

6
Another Business Plan?
Preparing the Offering Prospectus

"AN OFFERING PROSPECTUS! YOU MUST BE KIDDING. I'M NOT PLANNING TO GO public. All I want you to do is sell my company."

"I know, I know, Peter. But how will the buyer know what you have for sale if you don't have a sales brochure? When your salesmen call on customers they always carry full–color product literature with them. You know how the customer always wants to see pictures of your products, drawings of how they are made, how they are used, and so on? Well, it's the same thing with your company. That's all an offering prospectus is—a package of information about your company to be given to qualified Buyers. Nothing more, nothing less."

Whether you are selling a medical practice or a manufacturing company, you will need some type of sales document to describe the business. Although many small business owners try to get by with a one– or two–page descriptive memo, this only delays the sale. A Buyer needs all of the financial, marketing, personnel, and facilities information about your business before he can make a decision, so you might just as well put it all together in the first place and use the document as a sales tool.

The offering prospectus, in its simplest form, is a sales brochure (to give to prospective Buyers.) It is a package of narrative numbers and photos that describes (in the most glowing terms,) as much about your company as possible. It should include sections on the following subjects:

- A description of the company, including ownership, business activities, and a five–year strategic plan.
- The offering price and terms.

- The history of the company.
- A description of products, markets, and distribution channels, including a five–year sales forecast.
- An organization structure, with profiles of key management personnel.
- A description of real estate and listing of machinery and equipment.
- Financial statistics for the previous three years and a five-year pro forma financial forecast.
- Photos of facilities, products, and people.

A private company offering prospectus is similar to one that is prepared for a public stock offering but serves an entirely different purpose. The latter must comply with a myriad of Securities and Exchange Commission (SEC) regulations and procedures, qualify the validity of any forecasted financial statistics, and do everything possible to convince the investor of the high risks he will take if he chooses to invest in the company. The public stock issue prospectus acts as a warning to the investor of the hazards of buying the stock. On the other hand, a private sale offering prospectus is a selling tool and need not comply with SEC regulations. The accuracy of the forecasts can be verified personally by the Buyer. As a selling tool, it points out the benefits of investing in your company, not the hazards.

THE MAKE MONEY FILTER CORP. PROSPECTUS

Take a look at the offering prospectus for our hypothetical company, MAKE MONEY FILTER CORP. It is structured to show the best picture of the company. It will be a properly bound document with a tastefully designed cover that tells the buyer why this company is the best buy around. The Buyer should feel that if he passes up this deal it will be a major mistake. Remember, when putting the prospectus together that the "look right" is just as important as the "be right," maybe more. The first step is to prepare an outline of the contents of the Prospectus:

MAKE MONEY FILTER CORP
Chicago, IL
OUTLINE
OFFERING PROSPECTUS FOR THE SALE OF 100% OF
THE COMMON STOCK

A. Description of Company
   1. Current ownership

    2. Prior ownership

    3. General business description

    4. Five–year strategic plan

B. Offering Price and Terms

C. History of Company

    1. Prior to current ownership

    2. Since current ownership acquisition

D. Description of Products and Markets

    1. Product uniqueness

    2. Market size—domestic and export

    3. Market share

    4. Distribution channels

    5. Five–year sales forecast

    6. Package of sales literature

E. The People Who Make it Happen (Organization)

    1. Organization chart

    2. Personal profile of management team

    3. Marketing organization

    4. Manufacturing and engineering organizations

    5. Financial organization

    6. Bargaining unit

F. Production Assets (Facilities)

    1. Real estate

    2. Machinery & equipment

G. The Numbers (Financial)

    1. Three–year, audited financial statements

    2. Five–year pro forma financial statements

H. Photos

Although the prospectus resembles the business plan used in acquisitions, there is a major difference. A business plan is prepared for financial institutions and must be written conservatively, in language that bankers can understand. An offering prospectus is compiled as a sales tool for other businessmen, and therefore written with flare and style. Put your best foot forward and don't worry about being conservative. The potential Buyer attaches his own risk factors. Tell the world what a great company you have: how it is one of a kind, the best company around, and nobody, short of a fool, could turn down the opportunity to buy such a gem. Be creative, inventive, and optimistic, but at the same time, cover the same salient features found in the business plan.

The Company Description

The company description section should include three parts:

1. A history of the ownership of the company.
2. A brief description of the company's business.
3. Comments about your strategic plan for the future.

If you started your own company, then the year of start–up and any changes in ownership shares since the beginning should be enumerated. If you purchased a company, then ownership prior to acquisition, as well as the current ownership structure, should be described. Be certain to specifically identify what is for sale, particularly if there are two or more interrelated companies or locations or if you own real estate personally. For our hypothetical company, MAKE MONEY FILTER CORP., this introduction would be as follows:

> All outstanding shares of the company's stock are currently owned by Acquisition, Inc., a closed corporation, formed five years ago for the express purpose of acquiring 100 percent of MAKE MONEY. John E. Joe owns all of the outstanding shares of Acquisition, Inc. The parent company is not included in this offering.

> Acquisition, Inc. acquired MAKE MONEY FILTER CORP. in 19XX from Mark P. Curtain, a sole shareholder, who, 10 years earlier, purchased the company from Big Boy Parent, Inc. Probably the most profitable company of its size in the residential, metal water–filter industry, MAKE MONEY FILTER controls a significant share of the domestic market, and has been successful over the years in protecting its envious position from both the market leader and other competitors. The company is currently poised to take advantage of a potential burgeoning market for midsized metal filters and has structured its sales force and pricing policies to recognize this unique opportunity.

Get the idea? Don't be afraid to toot your own horn—that's the only way to sell. You can't say anything untrue, but you can certainly use the proper adjectives and superlatives to attract attention. Sure you're optimistic, you're supposed to be: it's your company.

> A recently completed, five–year strategic plan calls for an annual growth rate averaging 15 to 25 percent. Some of this growth will occur in existing products with existing customers, however, the company plans a

massive advertising campaign next year that will attract an entire new segment of customers. As a result, the company expects to make significant inroads on the market share of its nearest competitor.

The strategic plan also calls for the introduction of three new families of products over the next five years, making the company the market leader in this specialized market niche. A final factor contributing to this outstanding growth curve is the introduction in just two years of a worldwide export program using the worldwide marketing network of a noted export trading company.

How's that for a sales pitch? It uses salesmen's language, and even though these are real plans, they are just plans. The predicted results might or might not occur, but the possibilities alone should whet the appetite of even the most jaundiced Buyer. Remember, a strategic plan is not an operating plan. Instead, it reflects the strategy a company expects to employ to reach its goals: nothing more, nothing less, but it sounds good!

By this time, a prospective Buyer should be chomping at the bit to get his hands on MAKE MONEY FILTER. He wouldn't even be reading the prospectus if he wasn't already 50 percent sold. Your M & A consultant would not have released the prospectus in the first place to anyone who wasn't a genuinely interested and financially viable Buyer. That's one of the benefits of using a consultant for a Buyer search, as will be seen in the next chapter. It keeps this proprietary offering prospectus out of the hands of tire kickers and competitors.

Offering Price and Terms

The price and terms section sets the stage for further negotiations and must answer four questions:

1. What is for sale—assets, common stock, real estate?

2. What is the asking price?

3. What are the terms: all cash, part cash and part notes, stock, or a hybrid combination?

4. How long will the offer remain open?

Remember, everything is negotiable. If you are adamant about a price or specific terms of sale and won't negotiate anything less, make the announcement here. If you don't state that the asking price or terms of payment are firm, the Buyer will assume he can negotiate something better. If either or both are negotiable, then the prospectus should state the best case parameters. You can always come down, but it is next to impossible to negotiate upward.

For MAKE MONEY FILTER, the price and terms are negotiable, and this section would be written as follows:

All outstanding common shares of the company are offered for sale at a total price of $15 million cash at closing. This must be a stock sale and counteroffers for the purchase of some or all of the assets of the business will not be entertained. Current and projected earnings, as well as the value of the business assets, easily support this price. The offer to sell at this price will be available to a qualified Buyer until November 30, 19XX, at which time it will be withdrawn from further consideration.

That's all you should say about price and terms. The pace of negotiations has been established by taking a stand on a stock sale and a termination date, but leaving price and terms open to negotiation. By stating these conditions firmly, the first round of negotiations is already completed. It is now up to the Buyer to come back with variations of this offer. He must try to figure out how much you're willing to give away in terms and how firm you are on price. This puts him in a guessing game, which is not a very strong position.

History of the Company

In the history section, include a complete historical description of the company since its founding. This description should mention:

- Major changes in product lines or markets.
- Additions or disposals of facilities.
- Company name changes.
- Growth trends.
- Major management changes.

For an older company, product lines or major markets might have changed over the years. Perhaps new product introductions obsoleted original offerings or foreign competition caused a realignment in distribution channels, or the beginning of an export program alters major customer markets. All of these major changes should be highlighted here.

Over the years, additions to original plant and offices might have occurred, or perhaps the company opened new plants in different locations, or unused land was sold or new properties acquired. Entire new businesses might have been acquired or divisions divested. These are all important historical events to be included in this early section of the prospectus.

Growth trends relative to the industry should be emphasized. A Buyer is always interested in how a company has performed against its competition. Major changes in management or management philosophy over the years, and the impact of any major variations in industry or government regulations, should also be covered.

The following history section in the MAKE MONEY FILTER prospectus illustrates how to address these items:

MAKE MONEY FILTER CORP. was founded in 19XX as a result of a merger of the Wire Frame Products and the Water Gasket divisions of Big Boy Parent, Inc., a publicly traded (AMEX) company located in Kansas City, Missouri. Big Boy organized MAKE MONEY as a highly autonomous subsidiary and chartered the company with the mission to become the market leader in mid-sized, residential, metal water filters. The newly formed company never got off the ground and three years later, under a reorganization program, Big Boy sold the company to Mark P. Curtain who (10 years later,) sold it to Acquisition, Inc., after bringing the Company from $2 million in sales to nearly $20 million. During this period, the company gained a reputation in the industry as a quality producer of competitively priced products, but not very creative in introducing new marketing strategies or product designs. Prior to current ownership, the company experienced an annual sales growth of about 3 percent, which approximates the industry average.

In 19XX, Acquisition, Inc. acquired the company. Since that time, MAKE MONEY has experienced a five–year average annual growth rate of over 10 percent against the industry average. Truly a remarkable record in a relatively mature industry. This growth was achieved by introducing innovative marketing techniques, meeting market demands for new products, and developing an outstanding management team acknowledged as the best in the industry. The company is poised to take the next giant leap forward to become the industry leader.

Granted, you can't embellish historical events very much, but if you have done a good job, why not blow your own horn? After all, part of the pricing formula will involve an arbitrary assessment of what the company can do in the future and that is, to some degree, predicated on what it begins with when the new Buyer takes over. So let him know about your superior marketing strategy and management talent. It can't hurt, and it will probably add a few dollars at the negotiating table.

Products and Markets Description

In the products and markets section, you can either make or break the deal. Every company, whether manufacturing, financial services, personal services, retail, or wholesale, has something unique about it. A Buyer wants to know what makes your business superior to others. What is unique about the products you sell or the services you perform. All dentists are not alike. Each endeavors to build his own business to be better than, or different from, other practices. Every law practice has something unique to offer clients, whether it is expertise in a specialty field of law, a record of winning cases, or an outstanding professional reputation. Every video store has developed some sales or promotion gimmick to bring in more business—two for one sales, weekend specials, VCR rentals, and so on. Every manufacturer tries to exploit those product variations and modifications that make his products superior to his competitors'.

Include in this section all of the aspects of your business that make it better than another, or unique in its products or services. Continue to emphasize what an outstanding opportunity your company offers a prospective Buyer. The following points should be covered:

1. Competitive advantages.
2. Creative advertising, promotions, or sales incentives.
3. Unusual distribution techniques.
4. Management philosophies different from industry norms.
5. State of the art equipment and processes.

MAKE MONEY FILTER has several unique features, as can be seen in the following:

The company is one of only three major competitors designing and manufacturing metal water filters for in-line filtration systems between the well and the residence. In addition, a few small product lines are sold for industrial uses. A research and development program to develop filtration systems for small water utilities is leading the industry to innovative new products. MAKE MONEY is the only company that services such a broad market. Major product lines consist of:

1. Single Filters—3″ and 6″
2. Double Filters—6″ and 10″
3. Single Filter Systems
4. Double Filter Systems

Smaller product lines consist of off-sizes in the same engineering configuration.

MAKE MONEY has designed proprietary flow configurations for specific use in highly porous terrain that is susceptible to toxic contaminate proliferation. These systems applications, both single and double, give the company a unique competitive advantage in a rapidly growing market niche. To date, there have been no other systems introduced to this market that are as effective as the MAKE MONEY filter systems.

The company uses creative advertising and promotion techniques to keep customers informed of new product and service innovations. In 19XX, an ingenious automated display at the national trade show brought praise from customers and competitors alike.

As will be seen in the facilities section of this prospectus, the company uses state-of-the-art, computer–controlled quality assurance equipment in its production lines, some of which were designed by its own engineering department.

This will certainly give the Buyer something to chew on. He probably thought one filter is pretty much like any other, but now he knows better! If he buys MAKE MONEY, he will have a state-of-the-art product line and facilities and a leg up on all competition.

Success in Marketing

Five factors should be included in the marketing section:

1. Market size.
2. Market share.
3. Marketing techniques.
4. Pricing structure.
5. The historical record of sales growth by product line.

The Buyer is looking for some assurance that the past year or two are not flukes and that the business does in fact possess a record of continual growth. Recent increases in market share can be a very strong selling point. On the other hand, if sales have been relatively constant or even declining, this must also be disclosed. A deal that blows up half way down the road because the Buyer suddenly discovers a decreasing market share has little chance of being rejuvenated. If the prospectus can explain such a decrease, however, there could still be strong Buyer interest to proceed. MAKE MONEY did not have such a decrease, and the following portrayal makes the point:

> The company sells principally to domestic markets, although in the past few years a new export marketing program has been imminently successful. Domestically, the products are traditionally sold through plumbing wholesalers and distributors but recently an increasing number of Single and Double Filtration Systems are marketed direct to large drilling and plumbing contractors. With a premier distributor network nationwide, MAKE MONEY services plumbing contractors, large plumbing supply houses, national hardware centers, municipal procurement offices, and industrial users of plumbing supplies.
>
> The company's estimate of current domestic market sizes and shares for its major product lines is as follows:

Product Line	Market Size	Market Share	Prior Year's Sales
6″ Single	$58,000	25%	$14,000
3″ Single	$230,000	50%	$115,000
6″ Double	$5,750,000	40%	$2,300,000
10″ Double	$11,500,000	30%	$3,450,000
Double Systems	$115,000,000	12%	$13,800,000
Single Systems	$230,000,000	4%	$9,200,000

Domestic sales of other products and export sales account for the difference from reported sales figures.

The major growth over the past five years has been realized in a doubling of market share for Single Systems and a 20 percent increase in market share for Double Systems. The strategic plan calls for a continued increase in market share of both Single and Double Filtration Systems over the ensuing years through a massive advertising campaign, a sales incentive program, and the introduction of new, high–tech products. Export sales should also expand markedly as the anticipated marketing and distribution program is finalized through an export trading agent.

Not only can the Buyer see what a great job the company has done in expanding market share, but by reintroducing the strategic plan, his attention is directed toward the future, not the past. The future is really what you want to sell, because that's the basis upon which the price premium will be negotiated.

Future Sales Growth

Here's your chance to discuss those plans and programs you would implement if you were to keep the business. The future sales growth section should include:

1. Improving market share strategies.
2. Competitive pricing strategy.
3. Sales promotion schemes.
4. Sales department organization.
5. Distribution changes.
6. Sales literature.

The MAKE MONEY FILTER strategic plan has all of these ingredients:

The strategic plan discussed in an earlier section of the prospectus emphasizes a strengthening of the residential water filter markets overall in the next five years. The company does not plan to rest on its laurels, however, and merely ride the industry curve (which has averaged 3 percent per year for the past decade). Rather than being content to expand at this rate, the company plans to implement a major advertising campaign and sales incentives to effectively close the gap between it and the market leader. New product introductions and additional emphasis on export sales will further enhance the company's position. As a result of these planned moves, MAKE MONEY has forecasted the following sales growth over the next five years:

($000)

Product Line	Year 1	Year 2	Year 3	Year 4	Year 5
6" Single	16	17	19	20	21
3" Single	130	150	170	200	220
6" Double	2,600	3,000	3,600	4,200	4,700
10" Double	4,000	4,600	5,400	6,200	7,100
Double Systems	15,100	17,400	20,000	22,500	24,000
Single Systems	10,300	12,000	13,600	16,400	19,100
Other	1,000	1,000	1,000	1,000	1,000
Export	500	2,000	3,000	4,000	5,000
Total Sales	33,646	40,167	46,789	54,620	61,241

Although an ambitious program, if the steps as outlined in the strategic plan are implemented in a timely fashion, this sales forecast should be achieved or bettered over the five year period.

Terrific, there's that optimism again, and it's done without inferring any guarantee that these events will occur. It also illustrates the company's planned marketing strategy, not the expected financial results. As a Seller, these are your objectives, and although they might differ from the Buyer's, you can't be accused of misleading anyone by using this approach.

The final item to include in the products and markets section should be a complete set of sales literature. Pricing sheets are unnecessary but any brochure that has pictures or drawings of the products, or of the facilities, for that matter, is very important. A picture is worth a thousand words.

Personnel

The personnel section will be more extensive than many would expect. Remember, you are selling an opportunity for the Buyer to meet his profit and cash objectives, not just a group of assets, and such an opportunity arises through creative marketing, product strategy, and people. You have already disclosed the market and product stories, now it's time to sell the people. There should be five parts to this section of the prospectus:

1. A discussion of the organization structure.
2. A complete organization chart.
3. Personal profiles of key employees.
4. Comparisons of head counts for three years.
5. Discussion of labor relations.

Everyone is interested in the people aspects of a business. A smart Buyer knows that his bankers must be convinced that nothing in the personnel area will prohibit or diminish his chances for success. This is the place to bring the organization together into a homogeneous operating structure.

Although it can be painfully laborious, try to draw a formal organization chart for the entire company, complete with boxes, titles, and management names. A formal box chart is easier understood than a less formal listing, tabulation, or descriptive narrative, and can be all encompassing. Fortunately, there are some very inexpensive software programs on the market today that can draw these charts automatically on your personal computer.

Personnel profiles of key managers' background and experience are an important adjunct but should not take the place of a formal organization chart. These vitae include not only the manager's experience with your company, but previous affiliations as well. Education and special talents should be emphasized.

Even though you might have used an organization chart from time to time, you have probably never had occasion to compile one. Composing an organization chart to give a potential Buyer a full picture of the organization and the interaction of one department with another can be tricky. This section of the MAKE MONEY prospectus illustrates an easy way to draw a compact organization chart:

> The management team at MAKE MONEY is organized along traditional functional lines except in the marketing organization, which utilizes the product manager concept. A product manager is, in effect, the manager of his own small business, which consists of finite product lines (except that he has no equity interest, of course). His responsibilities include not only sales volume but the profitability of his lines. Consequently, he has an inherent interest in booking orders that will result in the highest profit margin, not necessarily the highest sales volume. He also monitors the manufacture of his products, including timely deliveries at the highest quality and lowest cost. The company currently uses three product managers: Distributor Filters (Single and Double), Filter Systems (Single and Double), and Export. A functional organization chart of the management team and the balance of the company personnel is as follows:

I will omit an organization chart in this narrative, but for your real prospectus this is where you would present a complete one in box format, that shows boxes for each of the salaried personnel. Within each department, there would be a description of the number of people in each of the hourly labor activities. It is not necessary to draw a box chart for the hourly workers. For a company as small as MAKE MONEY FILTER there should be enough room on one sheet of paper to have one box for each of the salaried personnel. The hourly personnel head count for each function can then be included under each supervisor. Within each box the following information about the individual should be included:

- Function
- Title
- Name
- Tenure
- Salary
- Exempt/non-exempt

The following is an example of what the box should look like for a department manager:

Marketing
Vice President
J. E. Jones 10 yrs. — $60,000 (E)

For a shop foreman or similar employee use the following format:

Machining
Foreman
M. A. Royce 16 yrs. — $28,000 (E)

	# of People
(N/E)	
Grinders	15
Mill Workers	7
Lathe Operators	5
Helpers	6
Tool Makers	3
Total for Dept. 36	

You might need several pages to build an organization chart. In this case, use one page for the top management structure and department managers and the following pages for each department. The quantity of paper is not important: the quality and completeness of the charts are. Personal profiles of each of the key managers, including data on their education, work experience with MAKE MONEY FILTER and elsewhere, along with their ages, are included in the Appendix to this Prospectus.

A brief documentation and head count of historical and current manpower for both salaried and hourly employees follows the projected personnel additions and deletions each year as reflected in the strategic plan pro forma financial statements.

Labor Relations

A summary description of the historical and current state of labor-management relations will suffice in the labor relations section. Have relations been amicable or have there been work stoppages and/or strikes? What is the average tenure in the hourly ranks? What is the demographic curve of the work force? Is there a union contract? If so, a brief description of the salient features should be included, however, details about contract terms should not be discussed. The complexity of most labor contracts is too great for an offering prospectus. Once again, at MAKE MONEY, a brief description of labor relations would be appropriate:

> The company employs approximately 250 hourly workers who are members of an IAM bargaining unit. There have been amicable relations with the union and no strikes to mar the relationship. Union leadership is cooperative and most grievances are settled at either the first or second step proceedings.

These few facts about union relations are sufficient. The mere fact that there is a union will scare off some potential Buyers. There's no sense in aggravating what could be a sensitive issue in the Buyer's eye by being too elaborate.

Production Assets

The importance of the facilities section is directly dependent on the type of business being sold and the extent to which it either owns or occupies real estate or equipment. A medical practice might lease office space, but might have a substantial amount of diagnostic equipment. A retail store might lease its facility and have nothing more than a few cases or freezers. A manufacturing concern, however, might own its production and office real estate, and a significant amount of machinery as well.

This section covers both real estate and machinery and equipment, whether owned or leased. It should clearly describe the following conditions relative to both real and personal property:

1. What is owned and what is leased.

2. Recent appraised values.

3. Maintenance policies.

4. Brief description of buildings.

5. Significant new additions or disposals.

The real estate segment should include a brief description of the premises, age, and condition of buildings, and a summary of lease terms if applicable. Plot maps can be made available for a Buyer's inspection, but do not have to be included in the prospectus. Photos are helpful to give the Buyer a perspective of the layout.

A listing of all of the machinery and equipment included in the deal can be presented as part of the appendix. A statement about the maintenance policy and the age and condition of the items would also be helpful. The Buyer wants to be assured that the equipment necessary to continue the business is not falling apart.

If you personally own either the real estate or some of the equipment independent of the company, and not included in the company's Balance Sheet, you should disclose this here. If you want to include these assets in the sale, they should be included in the narrative. In the case of MAKE MONEY FILTER, this section is very straightforward:

> The company owns all of the real estate occupied by the manufacturing plant (130,000 sq. ft.), warehouse (15,000 sq. ft.), and administrative offices (15,000 sq. ft.). The buildings are approximately 25–years old and maintained in excellent condition throughout. Major renovations have been made when required over the years. A plot map is available in the offices of the company for inspection by a qualified Buyer. A real estate appraisal five years ago resulted in a fair market value of over $3 million for the land and buildings.
>
> With the exception of some minor maintenance vehicles and office equipment, the company owns all of the machinery and equipment in use. A preventive maintenance program has been in effect for many years resulting in machinery being upgraded to current requirements, as needed. Five years ago, a qualified appraiser valued all machinery and equipment at a fair market value in excess of $4 million. Since that time, new additions of state-of-the-art CNC (Computer Numeric Controlled) machining centers and other machinery total over $4.5 million.
>
> A listing of all machinery and equipment included in the sale can be found in the Appendix to this prospectus.
>
> The following are some recent photos showing the manufacturing plant, the office and warehouse facility, and some of the machinery and equipment.

That's about all there is you can say about the facilities—just enough to let the reader know that you value the hard assets at more than what the books show, and to let him see what the place looks like.

The Numbers

The financial section of the prospectus is divided into three distinct parts—one estimated and two factual. The five–year forecast is often included first. This tends to get the reader thinking about the future (instead of dwelling on the past), which is the whole thrust of the prospectus. The sub-sections are:

1. Financial statistics from the five–year strategic plan, together with assumptions used.
2. Restated three–year historical income statistics.
3. Three years of audited financial statements.

Both historical financials and pro forma forecasts should clearly identify how much you have withdrawn from the company and how much you plan to take in the future. This "owner's draw" should identify not only salary and bonuses, but major fringe benefits, such as life insurance premiums, automobiles, planes or yachts, and personal living expenses charged to the company. A Buyer wants to see what the company has done without your draws and what it could do in the future. He can then judge his own take accordingly.

A genuinely interested Buyer can obtain complete financial statements, both actual and forecasted, at a later time and therefore the prospectus should include only highlighted statistics of the three prior years and the forecasted five years and should include:

· Sales
· Operating profit
· Income taxes
· Net profit

If relevant to the business, balance sheet items can also be included, such as receivables, inventory, and capital expenditures. Take a look at the MAKE MONEY financial section:

Five Year Forecasted Financial Statistics

The company's five–year strategic plan indicates a doubling of sales from last year. As discussed earlier, this phenomenal growth will be achieved by a combination of the following:

1. The introduction of new products and product lines to capture an increasing share of the application systems market.

2. National advertising campaigns highlighting the increasing need for purified water and directed at both plumbing contractors and residential users.

3. Sales incentives to manufacturers' representatives and distributors.

4. The introduction of an innovative export marketing program for Third World countries.

5. A healthy industry.

Profits will range from 8.5 percent of last year sales to 10.2 percent in year five of the plan. At the conclusion of this growth period the company will be positioned in the industry to take advantage of what will then be a growing trend toward diversification of materials used for filtering water. It can then invest the necessary funds to add machinery to manufacture these new composite structures. The following are the pertinent statistics from the strategic plan:

MAKE MONEY FILTER CORP.
STRATEGIC PLAN FIVE YEAR FORECAST OF INCOME
($000)

	Year 1	Year 2	Year 3	Year 4	Year 5
Sales	33,646	40,167	46,789	54,520	61,141
Operating Profit	4,714	6,107	7,333	8,792	10,016
Owner's Draw	381	381	381	413	413
Adjust. Prof.	5,095	6,488	7,714	9,205	10,429
Income Taxes	2,038	2,595	3,086	3,682	4,171
Net Profit	3,057	3,893	4,628	5,523	6,258
% to Sales	9.1%	9.7%	9.9%	10.1%	10.2%

Note: Owner's draw consists of salary, bonus, payroll fringes, and other fringes.

Three–Year Actual Financial Statistics

The following table includes the same adjustments for "owner's draw" to restate the prior three years actual income. In addition, debt service for the original acquisition debt of the present owner has been eliminated:

MAKE MONEY FILTER CORP.
RESTATED INCOME STATISTICS FOR THE PRIOR THREE YEARS
($000)

	First Year	Second Year	Third Year
Sales	27,830	30,056	30,958
Operating Profit	3,139	3,562	3,799
Owner's Draw	325	310	365
Acquisition Interest	500	350	200
Adjusted Profit	3,964	4,222	4,364
Income Tax	1,585	1,689	1,746
Net Profit	2,379	2,533	2,618
% to Sales	8.5%	8.4%	8.5%

Annual Audited Statements

Annual audited financial statements for the three prior years are included in the Appendix of this prospectus.

The whole idea in this financial section is to continue to whet the Buyer's appetite without going into volumes of numbers, tables, and statistics. If really interested, he can get all of the details during his due diligence phase. There's no need to be too explicit at this time. Tables 6-1 through 6-4 at the end of this chapter illustrate the complete historical and proforma financial statements used in the MAKK MONEY prospectus.

Be absolutely certain to include only the truth about historical events. When the Buyer performs his due diligence he will work from the audited statements and federal tax returns to arrive at the same statistics you have presented. Don't try to fool him now or you will definitely be embarrassed later on.

Forecasts can take a slightly different slant, however. These projections represent your objectives if you were to continue to own the company, and you make no claim of their authenticity or reliability. This is part of the "caveat emptor" for the Buyer. He must prepare his own forecasts to include his own best estimate of the future. Always remember that the offering prospectus is a sales tool and should convince the prospective Buyer to go forward with the deal, nothing more.

Photographs

Nothing attracts a potential Buyer more than a portfolio of professionally prepared photographs. The old adage that a picture is worth a thousand words certainly holds true in selling a business. The more photos included in the prospectus, the higher the probability of rapidly attracting a Buyer.

A professional photographer should know how to put together an eye-catching presentation that tells the story of the company in pictures. It should include applicable photos of:

- Management team
- Inside the manufacturing plant
- Larger pieces of equipment
- Inside the office
- Inside the warehouse
- Employees working at their jobs in each of these locations
- Aerial view of real estate
- External view of office building
- Examples of each of the product lines
- Representatives of major customers and vendors, if possible

These photos should be bound in a hard cover book with a cover page done in display type. The right look can do a real selling job and open the door to many potential Buyers.

SUMMARY

Every offering prospectus is different and must be constructed to reflect the particular business. Whether the business is large or small; in manufacturing, retail, or service trades; a sole proprietorship, partnership, or corporation, a well–conceived and attractively presented offering prospectus will enhance the sale. All prospectuses should include the 10 basic sections illustrated above:

- Description of business
- Offering Price and Terms
- History of the Company
- Analysis of Products or Services
- Portrayal of Market
- Potential for future growth
- Personnel organization
- Description of facilities
- Financial statistics
- Photos

The entire thrust of the offering prospectus is to give the potential Buyer an easy way to determine what an investment in this company can do for him.

What it did for you was interesting, but he is more concerned about the next five years than its history. Write with enthusiasm and optimism. If you have difficulty writing, hire a professional. An English teacher, a journalist, a freelance writer, some consultants, or an ad agency can all do the job at fairly reasonable rates. If there are factual negatives, and if they are relevant, then of course they should be revealed. But try to keep the document as upbeat as possible. Just like selling a product, once you entice the Buyer in the door, you should be able to close the sale. The prospectus should be sufficient enticement.

Finally, spend the money to have the document typed and bound profes-

TABLE 6-1
MAKE MONEY FILTER CORP.
Five-Year Pro Forma Statements of Income
($000)

	Year 1	Year 2	Year 3	Year 4	Year 5
Sales	33,646	40,167	46,789	54,520	61,141
Cost of Sales	24,562	29,242	34,062	39,691	44,450
Gross profit	9,084	10,925	12,727	14,829	16,691
% to sales	27.0	27.2	27.2	27.2	27.3
Operating Expenses					
Selling	1,120	1,268	1,444	1,824	2,036
General & Admin.	2,100	2,150	2,200	2,263	2,489
Depreciation	800	900	1,000	1,100	1,200
Other	50	100	100	100	100
Interest Expense	100	100	150	150	150
Bonuses	200	300	500	600	700
Total operating exp.	4,370	4,818	5,394	6,037	6,675
Profit before taxes	4,714	6,107	7,333	8,792	10,016
Add backs:					
Owner's salary/bonus	225	225	225	250	250
Fringes	156	156	156	163	163
Total add backs	381	381	381	413	413
Restated profit	5,095	6,488	7,714	9,205	10,429
Income taxes	2,038	2,595	3,086	3,682	4,171
Restated net profit	3,057	3,893	4,628	5,523	6,258
% to sales	9.1	9.7	9.9	10.1	10.2

sionally in book form. If you don't have the artistic talent, hire a small ad agency to design the cover sheet and put the book together for you. It will cost a few dollars, but in the long run it's worth every penny you spend. If you don't look like a professional, no one will treat you as one. With offering prospectus in hand, its time to go after that elusive Buyer.

TABLE 6-2
MAKE MONEY FILTER CORP.
Restated Actual Statements of Income
For the Three Previous Years Ending December 31
($000)

	19x1	19x2	19x3
Sales	27,830	30,056	30,958
Cost of Sales	20,372	21,941	22,599
Gross profit	7,458	8,115	8,359
Operating Expenses			
Selling	1,067	1,264	1,220
General & Administrative	1,742	1,929	2,130
Depreciation	700	700	700
Other	10	10	10
Interest Expense	600	450	300
Bonuses	200	200	200
Total operating expenses	4,319	4,553	4,560
Profit before taxes	3,139	3,562	3,799
Add Backs:			
Owner's salary & bonus	225	175	225
Fringes	100	135	140
Acquisition Interest Expense	500	350	200
Restated profit	3,964	4,222	4,364
Income taxes	1,585	1,689	1,746
Restated net profit	2,379	2,533	2,618
% to sales	8.5	8.4	8.5

TABLE 6-3
MAKE MONEY FILTER CORP.
Comparative Balance Sheets
As of December 31, 19x1, 19x2, and 19x3
($000)

Assets	19x1	19x2	19x3
Cash	300	350	100
Short Term Investments	1,625	1,200	–0–
Accounts Receivable	4,649	5,086	5,100
Inventory	4,800	4,990	4,800
Prepaid Expenses	10	10	75
Total current assets	11,384	11,636	10,075
Land & Building	1,200	1,200	1,200
Machinery & Equipment	10,269	11,269	12,669
Vehicles	122	122	122
Total fixed assets	11,591	12,591	13,991
Accumulated Depreciation	(7,891)	(8,591)	(9,291)
Net fixed assets	3,700	4,000	4,700
Other Assets	175	200	150
Total assets	15,259	15,836	14,925
Liabilities			
Short Term Bank Notes	1,300	1,500	1,000
Accounts Payable	1,000	990	1,000
Accrued Expenses	1,050	1,100	1,000
Total current liabilities	3,350	3,350	3,000
Long Term Note Payable	2,400	1,600	–0–
Total liabilities	5,750	5,190	3,000
Net Worth			
Common Stock	500	500	500
Retained Earnings, begin/year	8,125	9,009	10,146
Profit	1,884	2,137	2,279
Dividends	(1,000)	(1,000)	(1,000)
Retained Earnings, end year	9,009	10,146	11,425
Total net worth	9,509	10,646	11,925
Total liabilities and net worth	15,259	15,836	14,925

TABLE 6-4
MAKE MONEY FILTER CORP.
Comparative Statements of Income
For the Years Ended December 31, 19x1, 19x2, and 19x3
($000)

	19x1	19x2	19x3
Sales	27,830	30,056	30,958
Cost of Sales	20,372	21,941	22,599
Gross Profit	7,458	8,115	8,359
% to sales	26.8	27.0	27.0
Operating Expenses			
Selling	1,067	1,264	1,220
General & Administrative	1,742	1,929	2,130
Depreciation	700	700	700
Other	10	10	10
Interest Expense	600	450	300
Bonuses	200	200	200
Total operating expenses	4,319	4,553	4,560
Profit Before Taxes	3,139	3,562	3,799
Income taxes	1,255	1,425	1,520
Net Profit	1,884	2,137	2,279
% to Sales	6.8%	7.1%	7.4%

7

Who Is Going to Buy It?

Locating a Buyer on the Outside

ONE OF THE SELLING RULES SOME PEOPLE HAVE TO LEARN THE HARD WAY IS: DON'T try to locate a Buyer exclusively by yourself unless you have unlimited time, unusual patience, and uncanny objectivity. Use professionals. In what I call the "Case of the Raucous Robots," a professional consultant-turned-entrepreneur forgot this very critical rule.

"What am I doing wrong? I want out in the worst way but I've been looking for a viable Buyer for months and I'm no closer now than when I started."

Harry had been in the merger and acquisition (M & A) consulting business for more than 10 years when he made the decision to start a small robotics importing and assembly company. This terrific little company had grown remarkably in three years. His product line of robots was specifically designed for hazardous duty such as disarming bombs, entering smoke–filled structures, and handling dangerous chemicals. The market timing was perfect for such a start-up, and by the end of its third year, the company was grossing over $3 million in sales. But now Harry was bored and, once again, the timing was right, but this time to sell.

As a consultant, Harry never had difficulty finding Buyers for a profitable, well–managed business. Now, however, when it came time to sell his own business, he was having disastrous results. "I assume you've tried all the normal sources, Harry?," I queried.

"Yes, I've tried the network, the Journal, my employees—you know, everything both of us have done for years."

"Well, it seems to me you have two problems. You know that trying to sell your own business never works. It's the same as selling your own house. You'll always believe it's worth more than the market does. Second, your business serves such a minute market niche and involves such a high tech product that there probably aren't too many people out there who even know what you're talking about when you say you make hazardous–duty robots much less able to run such a business. If you want me to, however, I'd be happy to help you find a Buyer. Maybe I can apply some objectivity to your valuation and selling price at the same time."

"It's all yours, friend. I've tried everything I can think of and still I come up short. Maybe you'll have some new ideas."

For a Buyer to give full value to such a business, he would need to know it intimately and be able to see future market potential. Because there were only a handful of other firms in the world that produced similar products, the likelihood of interesting one of them as a Buyer was remote. So I took a different tactic. Instead of looking for a Buyer, I looked for a general manager, willing to work for Harry for a period of time—say six months—to learn the business, and then buy Harry out.

Between the two of us, we located just such a successor. Harry executed an employment contract with him along with an agreement to sell the business to him. The price would be determined by an independent appraiser. The general manager worked out fine and within seven months Harry sold his business and was back in the M & A consulting business.

There's more than one way to find a Buyer, although no common pool of Buyers exists, ready to step forward when you're ready to sell. Each sale requires a different approach. But don't ever try to sell the business yourself. As with the "Case of the Raucous Robots," you'll always overvalue or undervalue your own business. Even more important, the time you spend searching for a Buyer takes away from your primary task of running the business profitably. The fees a qualified agent charges for this service are really quite minor compared to the results he can attain.

Finding the right Buyer for your business can be difficult and time consuming. The structure of the sale will largely determine where to look for a Buyer. Therefore, to reduce the parameters of the search, think in terms of internal and external Buyers. Let's look at how to source external Buyers first. Methods for locating an internal Buyer are explored in Chapter 8. An external Buyer is anyone outside of your business and can be classified into:

1. Individuals or companies looking for a purchase in the open market,
2. Corporations interested in expanding their business through a non-cash merger deal, and
3. The investing public.

AN OPEN MARKET SALE

Locating a Buyer in the open market shouldn't be too difficult, right? With all the people answering *Business Opportunity* ads in the *Wall Street Journal* every day and banks continually advertising about how much they want to loan money, there must be thousands of Buyers in the marketplace interested in buying your business.

Maybe, but in most cases, for every 100 lookers there might be one legitimate Buyer. And for every 10 legitimate Buyers, maybe, just maybe, one of them will be capable of raising the financing to make the deal.

An all too common misconception of business owners is that the asset they own (their company) is the hottest property around. They can't imagine why everyone else doesn't agree with them. Unfortunately, the majority of would-be Buyers look for a needle in a haystack—that just right deal—and the odds are that your company won't be that needle. The market of serious, financially viable Buyers is very small, and the supply of companies for sale is quite large.

Some small percentage of employees currently working for someone else will someday become entrepreneur business owners. Some small business owners will want to expand. A few large corporations might be interested in your company for diversification. But the combined total of these Buyers is the complete market you'll be trying to sell to. That number is not very large to begin with and when the time comes to sell your company it shrinks dramatically. A combination of the following sources will generally yield the greatest penetration of the Buyer market:

- Merger and acquisition consultants
- Business brokers
- Lawyers and accountants
- Bankers
- *Wall Street Journal* ad
- Customers/vendors
- Personal contacts

M & A Consultants

Merger and acquisition consultants are in business to sell a business, buy a business, or merge or combine a business with another company. Their coverage of the entrepreneurial market is usually very broad and they generally know, within specialized industries or regions, which larger companies are actively searching for additions to their product lines or industry groupings.

Some M & A consultants take on a Buyer search for a contingency fee, which means no fee is paid unless a deal closes with a Buyer introduced by the consultant. Others work off a retainer. M & A consultants generally charge a fee based on the Lehman Scale formula. The old Lehman Bros. firm developed a formula some years ago as follows:

5% for the first $1 million of sell price
4% for the second $1 million
3% for the third $1 million
2% for the fourth $1 million
1% for the fifth $1 million
½% for the excess over $5 million

Obviously, you'd rather engage a consultant who charges contingent fees, however, many reputable M & A consultants, fearing months of wasted effort if you aren't serious about selling, will not undertake an engagement without a monthly retainer. This retainer, ranging from $4,000 to $10,000 per month, can usually be offset against the Lehman Scale fee at closing. If you plan to use a consultant charging a retainer, this fee should be included in your selling plan. It is cash out of your pocket not recoverable unless and until you actually close a deal. Having been an M & A consultant for a number of years, I strongly suggest that if your company does more than $2 million in annual sales, or if you are selling a professional practice, that you use this type of an arrangement. It will get you a Buyer faster and it will be the most helpful of any of the following alternatives. Yes, it is costly, but it is also the fastest and surest way to close a deal. Not only will the consultant do the Buyer search for you, but he can also be invaluable in assisting in valuing your business and during negotiations.

One warning about M & A consultants, however. There are many people calling themselves consultants who actually are nothing more than hucksters. No licensing is currently required as with real estate agents, and therefore, there is little or no control over the qualifications of M & A consultants. Several trade organizations have attempted self regulation and the best seems to be the National Association of Merger and Acquisition Consultants (NAMAC). Membership demands fairly rigid standards and the number of members per geographic region is limited. If you decide to use an M & A consultant and pay a retainer fee, try to get a reference from someone who has used the consultant for a sale. If that fails, try this organization for a member in your area. Even if he belongs to NAMAC, however, he still might not be the best for you, and the interviewing process described a little later is your only sure bet.

Business Brokers

Business brokers are exactly what the name implies—firms that list businesses for sale, then advertise them for sale to the public. They are very similar to real estate brokers but not licensed. The fee is normally contingent on closing, payable at closing, and usually, but not always, paid by the Seller not the Buyer. The amount of the fee ranges from 10 percent of the purchase price to a modified Lehman Scale formula. A business broker will not usually investigate the businesses he lists but will rely entirely on data given to him by you, the Seller. Valuation of the business is usually left completely up to you, and although a reputable broker will make suggestions, he is generally either not qualified or not interested in spending much time analyzing the business to determine marketability. There are plenty of charlatans in this business so if you really want to use this avenue, beware. There are also many reputable business brokers who can be extremely helpful in selling very small businesses. Business brokers handle mostly local businesses in retailing, wholesaling, restaurants and bars, service firms, and some small manufacturing and assembly companies. They are listed in the yellow pages of any city telephone directory. Stay away from those who advertise in big city newspapers, however. They usually list so many small businesses that they don't have the time or make the effort to help promote the sale of any one.

From years of buying and selling companies for myself and as a consultant, if I've learned anything, it is to be extremely careful in dealing with any consultant or broker. What you see is not always what you get, and once you have committed to a broker or consultant it will be costly and time consuming to change down the road.

How to Select the Right Consultant/Broker

Because of the lack of uniform licensing procedures and the high percentage of incompetent people holding themselves out as M&A consultants or business brokers, I strongly suggest interviewing as many as possible before you make a selection. Be sure to complete the following questionnaire at each interview.

Questionnaire for M&A Consultants and Brokers

1. Is he listed in the telephone directory (it's amazing how many are not!)?

2. Has the Better Business Bureau and the chamber of commerce ever heard of him?

3. What professional organizations does he belong to?

4. How many deals did he close in the past 12 months? (If less than three for an M&A consultant or seven for a business broker, go elsewhere.)

5. Get the names of Sellers of at least three deals he has closed in the past year. Actually talk to these references.

6. Get the names of Buyers from at least three deals he has closed in the past year. Actually talk to these references.

7. Get at least two references for banks financing deals he has closed. Actually talk to them.

8. Has he ever closed a deal involving a company of similar size and industry to yours?

9. How does he plan to locate a Buyer? Networking? Advertising? Personal contacts?

10. How long does he estimate it will take to find a Buyer? To close the deal? If he says less than 180 days, forget it and look elsewhere.

11. Does he insist on an exclusive listing? He should!

12. What information does he want from you other than your offering prospectus? (He should want your bank and trade references.)

13. What is the fee arrangement? Compare this to the others you interview. Brokers should all charge about the same. M & A consultant fees might vary, but never pay more than the Lehman Scale.

14. What type of contract will he want you to sign? It should be inclusive and should guarantee how much time he will spend on your deal—five days per month, one week, four months, or whatever. If he refuses to commit his time, go elsewhere.

If he is not articulate and well groomed, or if you sense any lack of business etiquette or honesty, walk away. Charlatans are either very smooth or very rough. Either way, by answering the above questions and observing his actions you should be able to make a fair assessment.

LAWYERS AND ACCOUNTANTS

It would seem that lawyers and accountants would come into contact with many individuals wanting to become entrepreneurs. A tax advisor assisting a client in tax planning and return preparation sees the client's income and investments every year. As income grows, the client needs investment advice to minimize his taxes. It would be a natural for his tax advisor to recommend buying a company, turning it into an "S" corporation and using the depreciation as a tax shelter. Therefore, it would seem that lawyers and accountants would be an excellent starting place to locate a Buyer.

Accountants yes, lawyers no! I have received valuable Buyer leads from practicing CPAs who seem to be attuned to advising clients about investment strategy. I have never had much luck in getting good solid leads from lawyers, however. I think the reason is that lawyers pride themselves on client confidentiality and are somewhat ambivalent about passing information on about a client, particularly financial information. Also, I don't believe they really want to get involved in this type of endeavor.

I related the following anecdote in *Buying In* and it applies equally well in the case of locating a Buyer as in sourcing a Seller.

I was becoming frustrated that my attorney friend never gave me a lead for either Buyers or Sellers. When questioned, he replied, "Well, you've given me many referrals for legal work and I've given you many referrals for consulting work, which is the way it should be. I'm a lawyer and you're a consultant. But just like you don't help me research a brief, I don't help you perform your search." There is no way to win that argument.

Bankers

The investment banking community can be a fertile source of Buyers and some of the smaller houses might even be potential Buyers themselves. Because investment bankers and venture capitalists are practically indistinguishable, they should be looked upon as one source.

Commercial bankers, however, are usually dead-ends, perhaps because they are not really businessmen and therefore don't see the opportunity of directing a customer in the direction of buying a business. Or maybe there is some real or imaginary conflict of interest. Exceptions can arise, however, and it certainly can't hurt to let your banker know of your intentions. He might come up with a few contacts leading to viable Buyers. Nothing ventured, nothing gained.

Wall Street Journal Ads

Journal ads are a very good source of Buyers already in the market. Many are individuals looking for a small company to acquire and many are tire kickers, not financially viable to make an acquisition and not really serious about taking the plunge (dreamers). Nevertheless, nearly everyone looking for a business to buy or sell reads the Journal, at least once a week.

Every Thursday in the "Business Opportunities" section there are two to three pages of: (1) businesses for sale, and (2) Buyers who are anxious to acquire. Once in a while, you'll see a corporate search or divestiture, but most are individuals and single–owner businesses. Buyers of varying degrees of capability are looking for deals at any given time. Many use M & A consultants and business brokers who place ads in the journal on their behalf, so you might very well make a valuable contact here. But be alert to the shyster! He advertises here also. Don't sign any fee agreement or contract with a broker or a consultant without first checking references and going through the interview process.

Journal ads can be of greatest help if you are selling a small retail or service business and then it is certainly worth a try. I have used it as a good source many times and continue to scan the *Business Opportunities* section on Thursdays.

Customers and Vendors

Customers and suppliers are often overlooked as potential Buyer sources, and they shouldn't be. Here are potential Buyers on your back doorstep just waiting to be asked. Not that all customers or all suppliers will be interested, but odds are high that at least one or two would be. In addition, you should be able to identify fairly easily which ones are financially viable.

A client came to me several years ago to help him find a Buyer for one of the divisions in his metal fabricating company. This division produced sheets of a carbon–based composite material used to manufacture a variety of products in the sporting goods industry—golf clubs, canoes, tennis rackets, and bowling pins. The rest of the company manufactured metal components and sold to the aerospace industry, so this division was a poor stepchild. Even though it was extremely profitable, with a good cash flow, it didn't fit with my client's long–term growth strategy.

The first place I looked was within the customer base. Here were many companies, all using the same composite materials manufactured by the division. It seemed to me that achieving at least a small amount of vertical integration might be very appealing to a CEO of one of these companies. The division was small with sales of just over $3 million, and I thought a larger customer might be able to absorb the business into one of its own operating divisions, which would make the actual transaction much cleaner and faster to bring to close.

I contacted six of the larger customers, three of whom were divisions of large, multinational conglomerates, and received positive responses from two of the three big boys and one of the midsized companies. All were interested in exploring the possibility and one, let me call it ABC Corp., had actually considered making a pitch to buy the division four years earlier.

We put together an offering prospectus and made a proposal to ABC Corp. After very brief negotiations, we struck a deal. Within four months, from start to finish, my client had disposed of his maverick division by merging it with ABC Corp. in exchange for publicly traded stock of the parent, at what he considered a very fair price. The president of ABC Corp. was jubilant to have a captive source for his raw material. Most important, ABC Corp. was a people–oriented company and the employees were all retained by the new owner. They actually received an upgraded insurance and pension benefits package. Management of the parent was so familiar with my client's business that no operating changes were necessary. Here was one of those very rewarding deals that, through a merger, everyone came out a winner.

Personal Contacts

Ex-business associates and friends can be a terrific source of leads, maybe even be a Buyer. So don't overlook all of those contacts you made during your years as an employee or when you were in school. Remember those discussions you had with your compatriots about some day owning your own business? Maybe one of them is ready to try it now. Customers, vendors, business friends and acquaintances, school chums, perhaps trade association contacts, are all valuable leads. Their combined source of leads might surprise you, and they'll be thrilled to hear from you. I have never met a person yet who was not willing to at least try to be of assistance if asked. No one has ever said, "I wouldn't help you even if I could!," but maybe the time will yet arrive. A personal telephone directory of business cards picked up over the years can also be fertile ground for Buyer leads.

A good friend, and an M & A consultant, related the following true story to me some years ago involving a client, Ned J. and the difficulties he was having in selling his business. The company was small, about $2 million in sales, and manufactured only one product designed and patented by Ned. The product was a complex optical lens that, when used in certain types of lighting environments, refracted light rays to project extraordinarily clear images. Although the market was very small, consisting almost entirely of Department of Defense agencies, he was the sole supplier. Ned was almost 70–years old and wanted to retire. With no one to succeed him he was now looking for a Buyer on his own. Having virtually no success in his search, one day Ned mentioned the problem to his consultant friend.

"The problem isn't that people aren't interested. There are a lot of people who want to buy my company. But none of them could run it. The business is too technical and there are continuous configuration changes in every order. In order to do the technical part, you need to be an optical engineer from the old school. They don't teach this stuff in the classroom anymore. You just have to know it from years of experience."

"How about business contacts over the years. I know you keep all of your old business cards. Isn't there someone there who would be qualified?" That night Ned dug through all of his old cards. He claims he has never thrown out a business card or an address or telephone number and supposedly has drawers full of them from all over the world. About two in the morning, he came across the name and number of an old friend with whom he had attended a technical institute in Germany some 50 years ago. He immediately picked up the phone and called his old school chum in Munich.

"Well sure," replied the German. "I've been teaching optics at the Institute for 30 years now, and I know of several ex-students who would be qualified to handle the technical side of your business. I don't know if they are interested in buying a business though, and I certainly don't know if they would want to move to America, but I'll ask for you."

Within a few weeks, two ex-students of the professor traveled to America to negotiate a deal, and in another 90 days, Ned was free to pursue his retirement plans. Being a pack rat does help once in a while.

A MERGER

Most small business owners never think of a merger as a way to get out. Believing the merger game is reserved for the big boys and too complex a maneuver for a small business, the possibility of becoming part of a larger parent corporation never enters their minds. This disinterest is not surprising given the lack of publicity for mergers of small and midsized companies.

Yet, in competitive industries, mergers with a competitor or a company that wants to expand into your industry is often the only viable scheme for getting out. It does work, and I have used this method for clients several times, as in the case of the client making composite materials. Of course, the trick is to find the right parent, with the right price/earnings ratio and the right trading volume. If the suitor is a public company, eventual complete liquidation of your interest is easier, although merger with a private firm also works. Merging professional practices, however, has been recognized for some time as a viable answer. In the fields of law, medicine, dentistry, accounting, architecture, and even consulting, sole practitioners are increasingly exchanging their practice for an ownership interest in a larger firm as a means of retirement planning.

The technique is really very simple. It merely involves a payment of parent company stock or ownership interest instead of cash. Other than that, most mergers are as straightforward as any other type of sale. Once you locate a suitor, just follow these steps:

1. Establish a price for your company using one of the valuation methods described in Chapter 4.
2. Determine the value of the parent company. In the case of a publicly traded corporation, the published P/E ratio establishes the value. In privately owned businesses, one of the methods from Chapter 4 can be used.
3. A simple division of the negotiated selling price of your company by the value per share of the parent determines how many shares of the parent you receive.
4. Part of the contractual agreement should be a method for you to sell your shares in the parent company back to the parent at agreed upon prices and times in the future.
5. A transfer of shares is made and you are now a shareholder in the parent company.

Most mergers involve the continuance of the Seller in a management role, either with his old company or with the parent. It is also quite common for the Seller to assume a seat on the parent's Board as part of the deal. If you do continue on in a management or Board capacity, be sure to negotiate an appropriate employment contract as part of the deal, including getting out provisions.

Now that you understand how a merger is done, the next step is locating a viable candidate to merge with. Some sources of merger candidates are:

1. Competitors
2. Customers
3. Vendors
4. Industry trade associations
5. *Wall Street Journal* ads
6. M & A consultants
7. Ads in industry publications
8. Ads in other business publications

The case of Bobby F. illustrates how a trade association was used to accomplish this end. Bobby and I had been friends for a long time and I also did some turnaround consulting work for him shortly after he acquired a small but thriving engineering design company servicing the telecommunications industry. Bobby was a good manager and he built the company into a highly reputable and respected force in a small market niche of this industry.

One day, Bobby's wife called saying that he had suffered a stroke three days earlier and, although it looked like he would pull through, the doctor was pessimistic about his ever returning to the active management of his business. She had no interest or skills in the business and asked if I would give some thought to the best way for Bobby to get out without suffering the huge financial loss of a distress sale. She was also concerned about the effect on the employees and requested me to try to figure out a way to satisfy Bobby's needs and still save their jobs.

The solution was obvious. Merge his company into a public parent for an exchange of stock. This would give Bobby a chance to control his income stream through the trading of the parent's stock and the receipt of dividends, and most of the jobs could probably be saved. The only problem was where would I find a merger candidate with adequate management talent to run Bobby's business. And it had to be done fast to save the existing customer base.

If merger seems a viable alternative for you, there are a number of questions to be considered before seriously seeking a merger partner:

1. Do you need cash right now?
2. Do you want to treat the proceeds of sale as a long–term investment?
3. Do you want to remain active in your business for a period of time?
4. If you do want to remain, can you put up with the rules and regulations of a large company?

The first step is to decide whether you want to merge with a public corporation with traded stock or a private company. Both have advantages and disadvantages and your cash-out requirements will determine which one you choose.

If you need to cash-out as soon as possible after the merger, choose a publicly traded company. Generally, the larger the better. Because there are SEC regulations governing the disposal of stock by an insider, obviously, the bigger the parent, the less likely you'll be considered an insider and subject to these regulations. A person owning 100,000 shares of a corporation with 15,000,000 shares outstanding will not be an insider, but if the company has 1,000,000 shares outstanding, he would be. Detailed explanations of SEC regulations would require a full book, so if you need to know more about this area, I strongly suggest you consult with a good SEC lawyer or accountant.

On the other hand, if you don't need to get your cash out quickly, and would rather treat the deal as a long–term investment with potential for appreciated value later on, then you might choose a private suitor. There are usually a number of private companies (competitors, customers, or vendors) who would be happy to buy your company to further expand their market or as a means of vertical integration. Companies are also more apt to consider this means of expansion if they can pay for it with their stock rather than cash.

If you go the private route, however, be sure to insist on contractual clauses enabling you to cash in your stock holdings at defined pricing formulae and at specific time periods. If you don't, you'll be stuck with another getting out problem worse than what you have now.

As for my friend Bobby, a phone call to the home office of his trade association yielded a list of eleven member firms engaged in similar engineering design work. Calls to the presidents of these firms resulted in four interested parties and meetings were held to discuss the possibility of a merger. Of the four, one was particularly interested and seemed to have extremely competent management talent. This company happened to be publicly owned, and with the concurrence of Bobby and his wife, we arrived at a satisfactory valuation of Bobby's company. A deal was negotiated exchanging all of the stock in Bobby's company for 10,500 shares in the public company, and within three weeks, a letter of intent arrived. The deal closed quickly after that and both Bobby and his wife were satisfied with the result. I was lucky and they were lucky. There aren't too many merger deals that culminate that fast!

Psychologically, mergers can be much less painful than an outright sale. At least with a merger, you usually remain either with your old company or with the parent corporation for a period of time, then gradually phase out. By retaining stock ownership in the parent company, in a way, you really haven't sold out completely, and this also tends to mitigate feelings of loss. The transition of clients/customers to the new parent is always much smoother than with an abrupt change in ownership.

A PUBLIC OFFERING

Under certain circumstances, you might get the best results by selling through the circuitous route of making an initial public offering of stock (IPO). Though not feasible for very small retail, wholesale, or service businesses, and certainly not for professional practices or other small personal services companies, given the right type of business and the right economic environment, you can get a higher return through a public offering than any other route. What are the types of businesses and economic conditions most conducive to an IPO?

The company must be large enough to have professional management. A one–doctor medical practice would not qualify, but a medical clinic specializing in cardiovascular diagnostics and treatment could afford a business manager, controller, equipment engineer, and so on.

It must sell a product or service that has a rapid potential for sales growth over the next five years. A company making cast–iron kitchen ranges doesn't stand a chance but one manufacturing high–intensity computer controlled cooking devices would be warmly received.

The company must have three years of continually increasing sales and profits and be able to project a continuation of this growth over the next five years. Although there have been a number of IPOs to raise seed money for start-up companies, particularly in the rapid growth high–tech industries, a successful IPO for an existing business does require a profitable history.

The national economy should be upbeat. While it is true that some IPOs are successful in a downturn economy, or even in a recession, probabilities of achieving a satisfactory sale are heightened considerably by an optimistic investing public.

Making an initial public offering of stock is a very tricky business. It is also expensive. But it can be an effective way of getting out. As with any other method, planning is essential. The requirements for a successful initial stock issue clearly dictate that the planning process must begin much earlier than required with other alternatives. To make a successful IPO:

1. The company must have three years of audited financial statements (two years if the issue does not exceed $7.5 million and you can register it as a small issue using a Form S-18). Be sure to have the audits performed by a nationally recognized CPA firm because this will carry more weight in the investor's eyes. Annual audit fees from a Big 8 firm can run the gamut from $10,000 to $100,000 or more, depending on the size of your company and the complexity of the audit.

2. Your business should be growing in sales and profits at a steady rate over the preceding three years.

3. Your management organization must be competent and all key management positions filled and stabilized. Key members of the management team should have visible credentials carefully packaged in personal resumes held ready and available.

4. You should develop a strategic operating plan for five years out and have it ready in good presentation format. This will be part of the stock issue offering prospectus.

5. Your company's annual sales should be at least $10 million to attract interested investors.

6. If you don't have a good relationship with your friendly banker, get it straightened out. Do some public relations work. It's important to have the banker on your side during the entire public issue process.

7. If possible, develop an advertising campaign to make your company more visible in the public eye. Embark on a solid public relations program. By the time the stock issue comes out, many potential investors will already know of your company and its reputation in the industry.

8. If possible, develop some new products or services that have some zing to them. They will catch the investor's eye as potential growth opportunities for the future.

9. Try to secure some well known people as outside members of your board of directors. Directors who are well known to the investing public can be invaluable for the right look in a prospectus.

The Industry

Your specific industry is especially significant. It is a lot easier to interest investors in an initial issue of a company in a glamour industry such as computers, medical technology, diagnostic equipment, or electronic control devices than in a more mundane industry such as nuts and bolts manufacturing. Just because you don't happen to be in a high–tech industry, however, it doesn't mean you won't be successful with an IPO, it just makes it harder.

The Stock Market

The current status of the stock market is crucial. There are good times for an IPO and there are bad times. The good times are not always when the market is at its peak, but when it's on an upward curve. If an IPO sounds attractive to you, coordinate your plans with current stock market performance as well the financial results of your own company.

The whole idea of going public as a means of getting out is based on the assumption that after the offering, the trading market in your stock will be active enough and at sufficient price levels so that you can liquidate your stock holdings for cash over a relatively short period of time.

The SEC

SEC regulations control what you can do from the legal side, both in making the initial offering and in cashing in once the stock is traded. SEC regulations are extremely complex and require expert interpretation. If you're thinking about an IPO, the first thing to do is hire an advisor with expert experience in SEC filings who can guide you through the maze of legal and tax regulations. The filing of an SEC registration statement is also very expensive. Attorney fees can run upwards of $75,000 to $100,000 or more. Then there are accounting fees, printing costs, filing fees, and a host of other costs easily totaling over $250,000. The cost alone might be enough to discourage smaller companies from trying an IPO.

The Offering Prospectus

Chapter 6 discussed the mechanics of preparing an offering prospectus for the private sale of your company to a single buyer and the emphasis was on using it as a selling tool. The strategic plan, descriptions of markets, products, organization, and facilities were flavored with optimism and superlatives. The future growth and profitability were predicated on planned advertising campaigns, incentive promotions, new marketing strategies, and confident new product introductions.

A prospectus for an SEC filing is not a selling tool, except in the broadest sense. This prospectus must comply with stringent SEC requirements of full disclosure and must be worded so that the potential investor will be fully cognizant of the risk he takes when buying the stock. The categories describing the company are the same, but the words must be cautious rather than optimistic. Usually, to avoid several rewrites and added expense, the best idea is to ask your accountant, SEC lawyer, and underwriter to become intimately involved in its preparation. It's costly, but at least they know what words are acceptable or unacceptable to the SEC.

The Underwriter

You could underwrite an offering yourself and save some added costs, but I would strongly advise against such a move. A qualified underwriter has the marketing expertise to know what stock will sell at any given time and what an acceptable price per share would be. Because they are in the business, underwriters generally know what investors will be interested in your stock and know how and where to market the issue.

Underwriters generally charge a commission of 7 to 10 percent of the offering price. Most firms will also want some kind of kicker—warrants or options—to give them the opportunity to buy your stock at a favorable price.

Although an IPO can be costly, time consuming, and risky (you might spend all the money on expenses and still not be successful in selling the issue) it can get you out of your business. It might take a while to sell off your holdings in the public market, but if you're patient, you can probably make a much larger gain through this method than any other. Nevertheless, for most Sellers one of the other ways of getting out is generally preferable, either through an external Buyer or by a sale to an insider, which is examined in the next chapter. If you want to stay in the business and use the issue to raise operating capital, that's an entirely different matter. This book deals only with getting out.

OTHER SOURCES

I have never had much success with the sources listed below, but I have included them here for completeness:

- Local newspaper advertisements
- Commercial finance companies
- Insurance agencies
- Real estate agents
- *New York Times* advertisements
- Unsolicited mailings
- Trade associations

So these are the ways to find an external Buyer. They don't all work all of the time or for all types of companies. There are cycles in sourcing Buyers just as there are business cycles. If you are trying to sell a profitable business in a glamour industry when the economy is booming almost any of these sources will result in at least some Buyer interest. If your business is not unique, however, or if the business cycle is down, or if you are in financial difficulty, then no matter which sourcing strategy you employ the business will be hard to sell. If you find yourself in this situation, perhaps a sale to an insider—a partner, employee group, or specified successor—might make more sense. In the next chapter, you'll see how to structure a sale to an insider.

8

Insiders Are Safer

Selling to an Internal Buyer

"Better to deal with the devil you know
than the devil you don't know."

AN INTERNAL BUYER COMES FROM WITHIN THE COMPANY. HE CAN BE AN EMPLOYEE
or an employee group, a designated successor, or a partner. Selling a business
to an insider requires a different approach than selling to an external Buyer.
Because his qualifications are well known to the business owner, extended payment terms involving Buyer paper and contingency earn outs—described fully
in Chapters 9 and 10—are most common. Contractual documents, though just
as important, are generally more informal and, at times, loosely constructed.
Bankers assume, right or wrong, that an insider, already involved in the business
can run the company better than an outsider and, therefore, are more eager to
provide financing. Finally, keeping your finger in the pie during the payout period
makes the psychological impact of leaving much less intense.

SELLING TO EMPLOYEES

Increasingly, owners of small and midsized companies are turning to their
employees when the time comes to move on. Almost without exception, there
will be one or more employees interested in exploring the possibility of buying
your company. Being honest with employees right up front when you finally
make the decision to get out inevitably stimulates such interest. For Don and
David, selling to their employees was the only sensible thing to do.

Don and David were equal partners in a medical clinic started six years earlier. The clinic employed four medical doctors, three technicians, eight nurses, and two secretaries. When the partners started fighting about growth opportunities, both realized it was time to get out of the business. Their squabbling had driven off many patients and the four doctors who ran the clinic in the partners absence believed they could do a better job than either Don or David. They approached the partners with an offer to buy them out if Don and David would help them finance the deal. The partners elated, agreed, and within a year, the clinic had new owners.

There are three different groups of employees that might be interested in a management buyout, or MBO for short:

1. A key employee such as a vice president or a general manager.
2. A small group of employees such as the management team.
3. All of the employees.

For obvious reasons, this is fertile territory. Most employees yearn to have their own business. All employees are concerned about someone else buying the company and either being fired, or not being able to work for the new boss. Consequently, the security factor is present. Omnipresent pride leads many employees to believe they could run the business better and more profitably than the current owner. And last, when it comes time to finance the sale, bankers will bend over backwards to assist an MBO, although they might not be interested at all in an outside Buyer.

In almost any company, employees jump at the opportunity to become the boss. Most lack the ambition, determination, or financial resources to either start or buy a business. If you offer them the chance to own the very business they have helped manage, however, most will grab it at once.

In many cases, unable to sell their company on the open market for a fair price, owners have turned to employee groups and at prices satisfactory to both parties. This is particularly true of businesses that do not have a very good profitability track record. Especially when external market forces are detrimental to a sale or in personal service businesses. When an owner–manager retires or dies suddenly, an MBO can save the day. Remember, employees have an inherent interest in seeing the company stay alive and usually ban together to effect a management buy out rather than lose their jobs. There are risks in a management buyout, however. An employee might be an expert in his particular functional activity, but be unable to manage an entire business. An employee, or a group of employees, usually will not have the resources to make a cash deal.

The probabilities are high that you will need to carry some amount of Buyer paper or agree to an earn out contingency schedule. Consequently, you must be confident that one or more of the buyout team has the ability to manage the entire business. Furthermore, if the group opts for external financing, a financial institution will insist that an employee or employee group prove management experience before lending acquisition funds. Therefore, before agreeing to an MBO, make sure that one or more of the buyout group has been trained in all management aspects of the business. This training process can be started at any time and can be done overtly with the agreement of the employee or covertly to test several employees.

The type of training program is up to you. Certainly, as a business owner, you know what it takes to manage your company. Hiring the management team yourself, or at least having worked with them for several years, you must know who is intellectually capable and who is not. In any event, by participating in a well, thought-out management training program, the potential Buyer will be viewed more favorably by bankers when it comes time to apply for an acquisition loan and the takeover will be that much smoother.

An MBO can also be financed another way, which in recent years has gained favor with employees and financial institutions. It's called an ESOP, Employee Stock Ownership Plan. Although pioneered by large corporations, an ESOP might be equally appropriate for any company with two or more employees.

Management Buyout Through an ESOP

An ESOP is nothing more than an employee profit-sharing plan instituted by the moguls of the IRS to ease the tax burden on the employer corporation and the financial institution lending money to the ESOP. Conceived several years ago as a method for employees to acquire equity ownership in their own company, ESOPs have developed as a viable mechanism to finance MBOs.

An ESOP benefits the corporation and the bank financing the takeover. The corporation can *deduct* contributions to the plan from taxable income, and the lending institution can *exclude* interest earned on loans to the ESOP from its taxable income. To qualify, corporate contributions must be either:

- Paid in cash directly to the participants.
- Paid to the ESOP and subsequently distributed in cash to the participants within 90 days after the plan year ends.
- Used to repay an ESOP loan.

Clearly, a very attractive arrangement. The employer gains by funding equity in the ESOP as an employee benefit with pre-tax dollars. The employees benefit by earning an equity share of the company while simultaneously building a vehicle to eventually acquire the entire company. And the bank earns tax-free income. No wonder ESOPs are so popular! There are restrictions, however, that you should be aware of:

1. Company contributions to the ESOP must be allocated to each of the participants' accounts, and this allocation must be made on the same basis as the pro rata share of each participants annual compensation to the total compensation paid.
2. Compensation in excess of $100,000 annually is excluded.
3. All participants must have non-forfeitable rights.
4. Employer securities must remain in the ESOP for seven years, except for:
   a. Death, disability, separation from service, or termination of the plan, in which case securities can be withdrawn by the participant.
   b. Transfer of a participant's employment to an acquirer corporation.
   c. Disposition of the selling corporation's stock in a subsidiary when the participant continues employment with the subsidiary.

Notwithstanding these minor restrictions, an ESOP offers a tax–free method for the corporation to provide additional employee benefits, and it gives the employees a viable vehicle to effect a management buyout. Employee Stock Ownership Plans have become very popular over the years and are probably the most effective way of financing an MBO.

An ESOP is a creature of the IRS and a thorough understanding of the mechanics of setting one up and then using it as an acquisition medium demands sophisticated tax knowledge, which is far beyond the scope of this book. If you are seriously interested in using an ESOP, contact your tax accountant or tax attorney for more information and advice.

SELLING TO A SUCCESSOR

Any business owner should want to provide for the continuity or dissolution of his business in the event of sudden death or disability. Someone must be available to make decisions on a day–to–day basis or decide how to dispose of the business. This is a most critical consideration, and yet one that very few people are willing to take seriously. Entrepreneurs seem to think they will live forever. Selecting and training a successor provides the solution to the problem and the selection process can be started immediately.

Why worry about succession in a book about getting out? Because once you have a trained successor, you have a Buyer already in place when you're ready to leave, voluntarily or otherwise. Successors can be found in three places:

· The owner's family.
· Employees of the business.
· Outside of the company.

Most owners prefer to turn their business over to a family member as a gift, as part of their estate, or for financial consideration. It's a lot cleaner, faster, and easier to control than bringing in an outsider or selling to an employee, and there might also be tax benefits. Family succession does present unique problems, however. More than one family member might want to run the business, and you don't want to get caught playing favorites. You might need or want financial compensation for the business, while the family member feels it should be a gift. The potential successor also might believe in significantly different management practices. Any number of problems can arise when you to decide to sell to a family member. If this method seems feasible for you, I suggest you read *Challenges to Wealth* by Amy Domini, Dow Jones-Irwin, 1988, for a detailed explanation of the pros and cons of family succession.

Many business owners don't have the luxury of selling to a family member, however. They must find a successor either among their employees or on the outside. In both cases, after agreeing to a buy out price, a workable contractual agreement becomes the key to a mutually beneficial takeover. To structure a contractual agreement with a designated successor, whether from the outside or an employee, follow this 10-Step Succession Program:

Ten–Step Succession Program

1. **Defining the Purchase Time**—Whether the successor buys the business all at once, or in increments over a period of time (eventually resulting in total ownership), this time period must be succinctly defined.

2. **Setting Penalties for Failing to Meet the Time Schedule**—Penalties for procrastination must be sufficient to ensure that the successor will fulfill his contractual obligation to buy. These should be monetary penalties and might be deductions from salary, forfeiture of company stock, increase in total purchase price, or otherwise equally severe sanctions.

3. **Requiring a Cash Down Payment**—At the time of executing the agreement, the successor should be required to make some cash down payment to show good faith. It should be within his financial means but high enough to encourage him to fulfill his contract. This down payment would then be non-refundable in the event of breach.

4. **Defining a Training Program**—A specific training period is mandatory to be certain of the successor's capabilities to run the business.

5. **Defining Duties During Training**—The successor must hold a specifically defined job during the training period, the performance of which can be measured.

6. **Performing to Sellers Satisfaction**—The Seller must be the sole judge of the successor's performance during the training period, and the decision to proceed with the succession must be his alone.

7. **Including a Hold–Harmless Clause**—If the successor buys increments over time, the owner must be held harmless from all liabilities arising from breach of contract during the buyout period.

8. **Successor Collateral**—If the deal involves deferred payments after the owner leaves the business, the successor should provide security for future payments using his stock holdings in the company plus additional collateral other than company assets, such as his house or personal investments.

9. **Maintaining Confidentiality**—Until the successor accumulates more than 50 percent of the company's stock, he needs to execute and abide by a confidentiality agreement with the owner covering all company business, trade secrets, processes, and customer lists.

10. **Including a Seller Escape Clause**—The owner must be able to break all contractual obligations to sell if he is not satisfied with the successor's performance, at least until the successor owns more than 50 percent of the stock. If such agreements are breached, all stock should be returned to the owner in exchange for payments made, except for the non-refundable down payment.

Regardless of the form of the contractual agreement, finding a successor willing and able to buy you out at a specified time in the future can be extremely difficult and time consuming. One way to locate a successor and then structure a workable buy out agreement was implemented several years ago by a midsized manufacturing company in which I held a 50 percent interest. Though it would never work for a very small company, variations on this theme can be adapted to any business with at least 30 employees.

Each of us owned half of the outstanding stock of the holding company, and we realized that if either partner were to die or become disabled, the remaining shareholder would not want to continue in the business alone. We had to find some means of guaranteeing a quick getting–out position for the survivor. Furthermore, we both agreed that three to five years would be sufficient time to turn the subsidiaries around and both of us would then want to get out anyway. Planning for succession began immediately.

We decided to hire management personnel who would agree to take over the parent company within the next three to five years. Each manager had to be willing and able to make a capital contribution within the first year. Our goal was to find at least two, preferably three or four, employees who would take over the company as a joint effort. Eventually, we did fill two of the four management positions with individuals we had known through previous business connections. We structured the following deal:

1. Bob would be responsible for all marketing activities and Joe would handle the operations of the parent company and each of the acquired companies.

2. Bob and Joe were required to invest $5,000 each in common shares before the beginning of the second year.

3. Both would draw a monthly salary and be entitled to an annual bonus if operating profits exceeded a set amount.

4. A stock option plan was established for the parent company and Bob and Joe were each granted options to purchase up to 25 percent of the outstanding shares at prices equal to the book value at the time of exercising the option. The options could be exercised anytime during the ensuing three years.

5. Deductions from monthly salary or annual bonus amounts could be used to fund the option purchases.

6. At the end of three years, Bob and Joe would use leveraged funding by refinancing the parent company to purchase the remaining shares from us at a price equal to a predetermined book value, plus a premium for goodwill.

Everything went smoothly until near the end of the first year. Then Bob informed us that he could not raise the $5,000 and he was not very enthused about taking over the company two years hence anyway. Other business interests were beginning to materialize and, in fact, he would like to break his contract with us to follow up these other interests. Joe, in turn, became uncertain about proceeding on his own and unless we could find another person to join him, was not interested in buying the company by himself. The best laid plans went awry, even with two people we had known for many years!

Left high and dry, we were forced to find and train new successors. This time, we tried a new approach. We decided to abandon the parent company concept, hire an entrepreneurial general manager at each of the operating companies, and write employment contracts to cover succession and eventual buyout. Terms of the contracts for each general manager were as follows:

1. The general manager would receive a monthly salary plus earned units of a new Class B, non-voting stock.

2. He would also earn an annual bonus and additional Class B units if the predetermined profit was met.

3. If he remained an employee for the full, two–year period, the accumulated total of earned Class B stock could be converted to voting stock at book value and would equal 25 percent of the outstanding shares.

4. To exercise his conversion rights, he must purchase at least an additional 25 percent of the outstanding voting shares at a price equal to the greater of book value plus a 20 percent premium, or 10 times average earnings over the two–year period.

5. If either of us were to die or become disabled during the two–year period, the two general managers, or one if there was only one remaining at that time, would purchase the deceased or disabled person's share of the company with the proceeds of key man life insurance. The remaining shareholder would continue to own his share of the company and have the majority vote on the board of directors until the end of the two–year period, at which time the above provisions would kick in.

If both of us should die or become incapacitated during this period, the plan wouldn't work. But that was a gamble we took, and with both of us still active, it turned out to be a good risk.

The scheme worked well, and at the end of two years, the two general managers ended up with a company of their own, which they were fully qualified to operate. The Employment/Buyout Agreement we used can be seen in Appendix B.

Planning for continuity and buyout should be of prime importance. If you own your company by yourself you can implement a program much easier than with a partner or two. No matter how complex the arrangement might be, however, a succession and buyout plan will bring peace of mind and provide a smooth transition of ownership.

Selling a business to a designated successor is such a clean, harmonious, and satisfactory way to get out that it is becoming almost commonplace in many personal services businesses and professional practices. The benefits of providing an introductory and training period to meet and get to know the clients, customers, or patients, usually overshadows undesirable contractual complexities in buy out agreements. The transition upon retirement can become so smooth that hardly anyone will notice you slipping away. On the other hand, if you have a one–man business, employing and training a successor might not be economically feasible, and you will have to find another way out.

SELLING TO A PARTNER

Sole practitioner doctors, dentists, lawyers, accountants, consultants, investment advisors, and owners of other highly personal or unique businesses, find getting out through a partnership works best.

You might have been a lone eagle when you started the business or acquired your company, but now that it's time to sell, wouldn't it be convenient to have a partner already in place to buy your interest? Well, it's not too late to start planning for this transfer,—assuming you don't have to get out quickly.

"There's no way for me to sell this business on the open market. If a stranger tried to service my clients they would all go to another analyst. I certainly can't afford to hire someone as a successor."

Mercer Abdul was a securities analyst who had started a very small but highly profitable business 10 years ago selling investment advice and securities portfolio management to wealthy individuals. He looked forward to retirement in about six years and sought my advice in planning for a getting out program. This was a ready–made situation for a partnership. A personal friend of mine working for E.F. Hutton happened to be looking for a way to get into his own business so I introduced him to Abdul, and within 90 days a partnership was formed. Mercer Abdul eventually sold his share to his partner and retired to New Hampshire.

Customers of a manufacturing company buy the product regardless of who owns the company. In a personal service business, however, the customer buys the service because of his confidence in the person providing it. It's not easy to sell this type of a business because goodwill is the only business asset, and without the previous owner, there might not be any goodwill. If you have a business such as Abdul's, which cannot be sold in the open market and where training a successor is not economically feasible, a partnership might be the only practical way to solve the problem. There are definite advantages to using a partnership:

- There's no need to search outside for a Buyer.
- It makes an easy transition because the customers, clients, or patients already know and have confidence in your partner.
- There is no requirement for the Buyer to perform an extensive due diligence investigation.
- Payment terms can be easily arranged over a period of years.

Unfortunately, there are also some negatives:

- Locating the right partner can be difficult.
- People change, and what was once a good personality fit might turn sour over time.
- Once the partnership is formed, disagreements can arise over the price or terms of buyout.
- Goals and objectives of the two partners might become divergent.

Even with these negatives, a partnership can be the best answer. There are some tricky issues to deal with right in the beginning, however, such as:

1. How do you locate the right partner?,
2. How do you structure a partnership agreement to ensure the buyout is successful and still give you a way to break the partnership if it doesn't work out?
3. How can the buyout be financed?

Finding A Partner

Five good sources for locating partners are:

1. Previous business contacts—an ex-boss, co-worker, or others.
2. Old school friends and affiliations.
3. Customers, competitors, and vendors.
4. Word–of–mouth advertising in the industry.
5. The previous Seller from who you bought the business.

Over the years, several of my clients have located partners in each of these ways, and I have personally located partners for my own businesses using all except the fourth source. A good friend, however, was successful in reaching a potential partner by giving a speech at a trade seminar where, while on the podium, he announced his search. After the meeting, he was approached by no less than 12 people wanting to be considered for the partnership!

Previous business contacts are an excellent source for a potential partner. Maybe one of your old bosses would be interested in joining you, or somebody you worked with when you were an employee. Perhaps an old school chum would be a perfect match, particularly if you have both pursued similar careers. And don't overlook the possibility of an employee working for a customer, competitor, or vendor. Although his boss might not like the idea, these fertile breeding grounds can often produce potential partners. For most would-be entrepreneurs, a partnership offers a chance to eventually get their own business which they otherwise couldn't afford or wouldn't have the courage to try on their own.

If the "getting–in" terms are flexible and you are not pressed for a quick evacuation, the right partner can be found. It certainly is one of the cleanest ways to go, with the fewest contingent problems after you leave, most likely the best price offer, and psychologically satisfying.

Another Way To Find A Partner

Most acquiring entrepreneurs never think about selling back to the previous owner of the business, but the following anecdote illustrates that it can work. A number of years ago, I found myself in a difficult getting–out position. One of my first acquisitions was a financial services company located in a small town in the Midwest. The Seller had started the business 10 years earlier and built it into a viable competitor in its market. He sold the company because he was bored with the day–to–day activities and wanted to try something new—a true entrepreneur! We closed the deal and parted on the best of terms.

The company prospered and volume doubled over the next three years. I was making money and having fun. In the fourth year, however, there appeared to be little opportunity for future growth, short of acquiring additional businesses to add to the customer base, and I began planning a getting–out position.

Because I remained in contact with my predecessor over this period, I learned that his new business was not doing well and he was becoming dissatisfied. I think he also missed his old clients, many of whom were his good friends. It occurred to me that I might have the solution to both our dilemmas. "What would you think of coming back into the business as an equal partner and buy out my remaining interest in a year?," I asked Pat one day.

"Hey, that's an interesting idea. How much would you want for it?" We agreed on price and terms and within two months I had a partner and a method to get out. We operated profitably for the next year and parted good friends.

Buyer and Seller don't always part friends, however, and it is even more unusual for the Seller to want to buy back at a later date. Or is it? I have since learned that my situation was not unique. Assuming original acquisition negotiations are amicable, there is no reason not to remain friendly with the previous owner. After all, you get to know each other pretty well during the long acquisition period. If he gets out for reasons other than retirement or poor health, he very often welcomes the opportunity to get back into the business at a later date, unless, of course, he has committed all of his funds and efforts to some other business.

Structuring a Partnership Buy Out

An ill–conceived partnership agreement can destroy an otherwise workable arrangement for getting out. Remember, you're not looking for a long–term relationship, only a Buyer for your business. For many years, I have recommended what I call my "Eleven Rules of Partnership" to all of my clients who opt for a partnership for getting out.

Eleven Rules of Partnership

1. **Price**—Agree to a fixed price in the beginning. Avoid moving formulae based on financial performance.
2. **Time**—Establish a fixed date for the complete buyout and fixed intervals for incremental shares of ownership.

3. **Terms**—Determine specific terms of payment and transfer of shares. Leave nothing to chance.

4. **Cash Contribution**—Except in rare cases, your new partner must make some capital contribution in the beginning.

5. **Escape Clause**—Leave the door open to break the partnership if you become dissatisfied with your partner's performance.

6. **Early Buyout**—At a price significantly higher than the sell price, have a buy out clause in the agreement for your partner to buy your share in total if you should die or become disabled before the sale is completed.

7. **Background**—Choose a partner with a technical background either similar to yours or the complete opposite.

8. **Honesty**—Check character references—bank, neighbors, prior employers, school, family, church, and so on. Any blemish on his honesty disqualifies him.

9. **Financial Integrity**—Check credit references, personal financial statements, police records, even tax returns if you have suspicions. Look for bankruptcy history.

10. **Authority**—Remain in command until you leave the business completely.

11. **Compatibility**—Like each other. There is nothing worse than being in partnership with someone you don't like!

Financing a Partnership Buy Out

A number of methods are available to finance a partnership buy out and which one you choose will depend on the needs of both partners. For example, if your new partner does not have the cash to actually buy a share of the business now, structure a deferred payment plan. He can pay for his share out of his earnings during the transition period. Other possibilities of structuring terms of payment include:

- A promissory note with a multiyear payout.
- A combination of cash payments out of the partner's share of profits and a promissory note.
- No cash payments, other than a down payment at inception, as long as you continue in the business, with a full cash payment for the entire business when you leave.

The third method is generally the easiest to sell to a prospective partner. Because he will be unable to borrow against his share of the business assets (a bank will not split assets for collateral), the only source of funds would be from his own savings. Most people do not have access to substantial liquid funds and therefore, demanding a large cash payment, will significantly narrow the market of potential prospects. Also, many people might be willing to risk time and effort but not much cash to learn your business.

This method will usually work out best for you too. It gives you time and the opportunity to determine the qualifications and human relations expertise of your new partner before actually turning over the entire business to him.

If for some reason you agree to a partnership without a down payment, insist on a clause written into the partnership agreement stating that, if you are not satisfied with your partner's performance, you can terminate the arrangement at any time and take the company back.

The Partnership Buy-Back Agreement

Last, if you do bring a partner into your business, even for only a short period of time before you get out completely, be sure that your lawyer executes a Partnership Buy-back Agreement, which will provide the details for a buy out in the event of your death or disability while you are still active in the business. I have found the following language inclusive and workable, though a bit cumbersome, as most legal documents are:

ARTICLE II
DEATH OF "Jones"

2.1 *Death of Jones.* In the event of the death of Jones, the Corporation shall purchase and the legal representatives of his estate shall sell, at a price determined by Article III, all but not part of the shares of Stock owned by Jones on the date of his death.

ARTICLE III
PURCHASE PRICE AND PAYMENT

3.1 *Determination of Purchase Price.* The purchase price for all of the Stock subject to this Agreement shall be determined as follows:

(a) **Stipulated Value.** The purchase price for the Stock owned by Jones shall be equal to $_____or such other value as may from time to time be established by resolution adopted by all Shareholders of the Corporation (such $_____value or the value later established is herein referred to as the "stipulated value"); provided, however, that if Jones' death occurs more than 18 months from the date of this Agreement, and if no such resolution has been agreed to in writing by Jones within the 18 month period preceding the death of Jones, then the purchase price for such Stock shall be determined in accordance with the following paragraph (b).

(b) **Alternate Value.** Given the conditions of (a) above, then the purchase price of Jones' Stock shall be equal to the stipulated value last established pursuant to paragraph (a) of this Section 3.1 plus or minus, as the case may be, the increase or decrease in the book value per share of the Stock from the last day of the fiscal year immediately preceding the date on which the stipulated value was last determined to the last day of the fiscal year immediately preceding the date of Jones' death, multiplied by the number of shares of Stock owned by Jones which are subject to this Agreement. The book value per share shall be computed by the CPAs regularly retained by the corporation and in accordance with generally accepted accounting principles on a consistent basis and shall include all adjustments, which in the opinion of the CPA's are necessary for a fair statement of the results of operations of the Corporation for the interim period. In determining such book value, there shall be excluded the amount by which the proceeds of any life insurance on the life of Jones which are payable to the Corporation exceed the value of any such insurance policy as carried on the books of the Corporation prior to Jones' death.

3.2 **Payment of Purchase Price.** The payment of the purchase price for any stock purchased under this Agreement shall be made as follows:

(a) **Initial Payment.** In the event of the death of Jones, the Corporation shall pay to the legal representatives of Jones' estate for application upon the purchase price of stock owned by Jones the total net proceeds, if any, of life insurance upon the life of Jones payable to the Corporation up to but not to exceed the total purchase price therefore as determined in accordance with this Article III. Such initial payment shall be made on or before the later of (1) the date upon which the Corporation receives such insurance proceeds as the designated beneficiary and (2) the 30th day following the date on which the accountants determine the value of the Stock (if a stipulated value is not then in effect). If no such insurance on the life of Jones is paid to the Corporation, then there shall be no initial payment, and the entire purchase price shall be paid in the manner provided in the following paragraph (b).

(b) **Balance.** (i) the Corporation shall pay to the legal representatives of Jones' estate that balance of the purchase price (herein called the "Balance") represented by the amount (if any) by which the aggregate price of the Stock exceeds the amount of the initial payment under paragraph (a) above, in not more than 40 consecutive equal quarterly installments of principal, plus accrued interest thereon, commencing on the first day of January next following (1) the date of Jones' death if a stipulated value is then in effect, or (2) the date on which the valuation of the Stock is determined pursuant to Section 3.1 hereof if no stipulated value is in effect at the time of Jones' death. The amount of the unpaid balance outstanding from time to time shall bear interest at the rate of 9% per annum which shall be payable semiannually with installments of principal, and such interest shall accrue from (1) the date which is 30 days from the date of Jones' death if a stipulated value is then in effect or (2) the date on which the value of the Stock is determined pursuant to Section 3.1 hereof if no stipulated value is in effect at the time of Jones' death, and,

(ii) The obligation to pay the balance and interest due thereon shall be evidenced by a duly executed promissory note payable to the order of the party or parties from whom the Stock is purchased, containing the aforesaid terms and such other terms as are customary for such instruments, including the right of prepayment, in whole or in part, without penalty, from time to time.

The complete Buy-back Agreement as well as a sample Partnership Agreement are included in Appendix C for your reference. The payment to your estate can be covered by key man insurance in the event of death, but I don't know of any insurance available that covers a lump–sum payment on disability. Therefore, this part of the Agreement should provide for a deferred payment schedule over a period of years and secured with a first–position interest in the outstanding common stock of the company. It's not a foolproof assurance of payment, but it's better than nothing.

A partnership is similar to a marriage. If both partners do not have the same goals and objectives, moral standards, and caring and compassionate attitude toward others, there will be insurmountable problems in running the business. As in a successful marriage, where there is a lot of give and take by both parties, so there must be in a partnership. Finally, remember that, just like a marriage, getting in is much, much easier and less costly than getting out.

Whether you choose to sell to employees, a successor, or a partner, an insider sale generally works much smoother and faster than selling to an outsider. Because most insider sales are structured with deferred payments over a period of years, you will be able to keep apprised of the progress of your business. This alone eases the psychological burden of selling. If you can see your baby grow, the severity of the loss is diminished. It will also provide a stream of income for your retirement years.

9

Cash or Promises

Financing the Sale

"RAISING MONEY TO BUY THIS BUSINESS WAS HARD ENOUGH. WHY SHOULD I NOW worry about financing its sale? That's the Buyer's problem, not mine!"

"That may be. But if you really want to sell instead of just playing the game, you better be prepared to offer financing assistance. Very few small Buyers have the knowledge to arrange financing on their own, and you know that most don't have the resources to make a cash deal."

While some Buyers might have the sophistication and banking connections to arrange their own financing, your chances of a quick sale at a satisfactory price are enhanced if you are willing to enter the financing loop. If you're serious about selling, then you should be willing to help in whatever way you can to bring the deal to a satisfactory and quick closing, including helping the Buyer to arrange outside financing. Also, if you really want to maximize the selling price, you better be prepared to negotiate some type of deferred payment plan as well. Whether selling to a successor, a partner, employees, or on the open market, bank financing will go smoother if you're willing to defer some of your receipts to later years. This is all part of the negotiations. Now that you have seen some options for structuring the deal, and how to find the Buyers, it's time to take a look at some concrete negotiation tactics.

NEGOTIATING STRATEGIES

While there are many variations in negotiating strategy, the "Rule of the Four "Ps" seems to bring the best results:

143

1. Know the *people* who you will negotiate with.
2. *Plan* your strategy in advance of negotiations.
3. Exercise your *perceptive* judgments, and don't be afraid of your intuition.
4. Be *patient*—silence is golden.

Anyone who has negotiated on my side of the table has heard me preach the Four "Ps" many times, and if you have already seen my earlier publications or have heard me speak on this topic, I beg your indulgence. The Four "Ps" are necessary for successful negotiations. Yet, many times, people forget one or more of them. So if you have heard my sermon before, skip over this section and go on to the financing alternatives.

Know Your Opponent

As the Seller, you have a distinct advantage at the negotiating table. You know the business and the Buyer doesn't. But that doesn't in any way negate the first rule of knowing your opponent. Years ago, I kept a small notebook in my pocket and, as I held preliminary meetings with a potential Buyer, would jot down his personal characteristics as I saw them unfold. To hasten the process, I now use a small checklist—which fits in the same notebook—to refer to before the next negotiating session. Figure 9-1 shows the checklist I use.

By this time in the selling process, you and the Buyer will probably have been together at least a couple of times, so you should have a feel for his personality. Is he aggressive or passive? Is he methodical, argumentative, creative, a detail man? Does he like the good ole' boy approach or is he a dark, gray suit and button–down–collar kind of man? It's important to observe these characteristics because they'll guide you in your tactics. If he is aggressive, let him rant and rave until he gets tired. If he is methodical, have three or four indisputable facts ready to throw out on the table. If he's a good ole' boy, maybe you should negotiate at the corner diner over lunch.

At times, the Buyer might elect to be in the background during negotiations. He might feel inadequate in dealing with financial data, or realize that he has little talent in the persuasive arts. For whatever reason, many Buyers use their legal counsel, accountant, or an outside consultant as the negotiator. It's important to know just who will be across the table from you in order to plan the appropriate strategy. Obviously, if you are negotiating with an accountant, you'll want to base your strategy on sound financial accounting principles as much as possible and be prepared to defend your valuation calculations from an accounting perspective.

On the other hand, if the Buyer elects to use his lawyer, I strongly advise bringing along your own legal counsel. Lawyers are notorious for arguing with a layman even when there isn't anything to argue about. As long as lawyers get

	Very	Somewhat	Never
Company _____			
Name _____			
Title _____			
Personal	_____	_____	_____
Aggressive?	_____	_____	_____
Passive?	_____	_____	_____
Neutral?	_____	_____	_____
Self-confident?	_____	_____	_____
Sneaky?	_____	_____	_____
Honest?	_____	_____	_____
Business Acumen	_____	_____	_____
Broad knowledge?	_____	_____	_____
Narrow minded?	_____	_____	_____
Technical?	_____	_____	_____
Financial?	_____	_____	_____
Salesman?	_____	_____	_____
Legal?	_____	_____	_____
His needs	_____	_____	_____
Cash now?	_____	_____	_____
Retirement?	_____	_____	_____
Keep active?			

Fig. 9-1. Getting to know the buyer well in advance of the negotiating process allows you to plan an effective strategy. This checklist of personal and business characteristics covers most of the items you should try to identify.

paid by the hour rather than by what they accomplish, I'm afraid we businessmen are doomed to listen to argument after argument at the negotiating table. You certainly don't want to be outmaneuvered at this point, so bring your own counsel and let him advise you when to back off and when to fight. But beware, don't let the two lawyers negotiate with each other. Lawyers are trained to advise, not to make business decisions. Two lawyers having fun arguing can cost a lot of money! In addition, be sure to bring your tax advisor. Outflanking the opponent on tax issues is a favorite ploy at the negotiating table.

Plan Your Strategy

Planning is the essence of negotiating strategy. Before you ever enter the negotiating room, know what your hard points are and which you are willing to give on. Decide how to maneuver your opponent into thinking your idea is his idea. Concern yourself with the tactical steps you will take and in what sequence. And most important, make sure that you control the pace, tempo, and sequencing of the negotiation. Know what the numbers are so you won't get out-flanked with your own financials. You might even want to bring your controller or CPA along.

One of the best methods for planning a negotiating strategy is to outline, on paper, your strong points and weak points and another outline estimating the same for the Buyer. Compare the two outlines and any matchups—your strong versus his weak—can be disposed of very quickly. Items that are strong for both of you are the points that need to be negotiated with vigor. Use Fig. 9-2 to help you plan your negotiating strategy.

Also, make a judgment of what you feel the Buyer is really after. Can he afford to do the entire deal with cash? Does he have that kind of financial backing? Your consultant should know. If you do need to take back Buyer paper, what is his credit record? Is he reputable, and if so, will he give you bank and character references? If not, you better make it all cash. These are some examples of the kind of questions and planning to be done before negotiations begin. Each case is different, but the principle of planning is the same. Always do your research and construct a planned strategy before entering negotiations.

Trust Your Intuition

Be perceptive and trust your intuition. You wouldn't have been able to make the acquisition in the first place or to start your own business without a fairly keen intuitive sense. Negotiations are usually based 10 percent on fact, 40 percent on bluff, and 40 percent on intuition. Trust your intuition to tell you when a point is won. Know when the sale is made and don't negotiate yourself out of a deal like Barbara did.

Barbara loved to debate, and negotiating the sale of her small bookkeeping practice was more fun than she had had in years. The Buyer finally agreed to nearly all of her demands and was ready to sign the contract, but Barbara couldn't let go. She felt she had to make her last point about closing before Christmas rather than in January. Though intuitively she knew she should shut up, she couldn't stop negotiating. Sick of arguing such a moot point, the Buyer left the negotiating table and the deal fell through.

Negotiating Points	———— Me ————		———— Him ————	
	Strong	**Weak**	**Strong**	**Weak**
1. **Price**	————	————	————	————
2. **Terms**				
All cash	————	————	————	————
Deferred—				
Buyer note	————	————	————	————
Earn out	————	————	————	————
Contingency	————	————	————	————
3. **For Deferred payments—**				
Collateral	————	————	————	————
Interest rate	————	————	————	————
Payment schedule	————	————	————	————
4. **Closing date**	————	————	————	————
5. **Employment contract**				
Period of time	————	————	————	————
Salary	————	————	————	————
Fringes	————	————	————	————
Getting out provisions	————	————	————	————
6. **Non-competing covenant**				
Amount	————	————	————	————
Period	————	————	————	————
Area	————	————	————	————

7. **Other options** _____

_____

_____

_____

Fig. 9-2. Planning a negotiating strategy is essential to a successful sale. Use the data you collected from using Fig. 9-1.

You'll need all of the help you can get from your intuition during negotiations, so don't be afraid to trust your instincts. Most of the time you'll be right.

Patience is Golden

Patience, the golden virtue, is the one characteristic most entrepreneurs don't have. At the negotiating table, patience can win more points than any other tactic. Patience is the antithesis of pride. In sports, the best offense is often a good defense, and that's what patience is—a good defense. That's about all there is to say about this "P," except to relate the story of my first, major contract negotiation where I learned the value of patience. A case where ignorance was truly bliss.

I was a young controller trying to work my way up the corporate ladder and had been assigned to the negotiating team to handle upcoming labor contract talks. Being a number cruncher, I never expected to be required to say anything at the negotiating table except to assess the financial effects of proposals put forth by both sides.

As we faced the union committee across the table, I was mesmerized with the rapid give and take from both sides. It became impossible to follow the tactics of either side. The talks continued off and on for six weeks and I began to wonder how these people were ever going to reach a conclusion. We never seemed to finalize any of the points on the table. Just a lot of shouting and arguing about minor contract language. Finally, the talks got around to the economic issues, with the union demanding an increase of 15 cents per hour, and our side offering four cents. The vice president of manufacturing, who headed up our negotiating team, was very weak in juggling numbers in his head and, as the talks became more heated and the alternatives on the table more complicated, he became visibly agitated.

We adjourned for a recess and while out, the vice president turned to me and said, "Larry, you're the numbers expert. When we get back, I want you to lead the discussions and get this thing off dead center". He had to be joking! What did I know about negotiating, I was only a controller. As we were seated once again at the table, I opened the discussion by distributing a complicated new calculation involving pension contributions, group insurance, and wage rates that I had been hypothesizing in my spare time. It was quite complex, and even I had difficulty following the economic implications over a three–year period. As I distributed the sheets of paper I commented, "Gentlemen, this is the fairest combination we can come up with. It's even better for you than what you have proposed." (Which of course, it wasn't!)

The union negotiator read through the calculation, threw the paper down on the table, and started shouting and pounding the table, chastising me and the company for even suggesting such an outrageous offer. I really didn't know what to say next, so I just sat there and listened. He ranted and raved and carried on for half an hour. Finally, he ran out of steam and there was dead silence. I said nothing, because I didn't know what to say, and he said nothing. After five minutes of silence, which seemed like five hours to me, the union negotiator began squirming in his chair. "Don't you have anything else to say?" he finally exploded. "No," I replied, and another five minutes of silence followed. By this time our vice president was getting uneasy also and was just about to interject something when the union said, "OK, we'll discuss it in committee and if we agree we'll take it to a vote".

That part of the negotiation was settled, and all because, out of ignorance, I had the patience to wait and say or do nothing, just listen!

The Sin of Pride

Pride is not one of the Four "Ps" because they are positive approaches. Pride is a big negative! Yet most negotiators have an abundance of pride. According to Webster's New World Dictionary pride is "an overhigh opinion of oneself, haughtiness, arrogance." I believe pride is one of the most harmful personal characteristics anyone can have in business. Pride is competitive. It gets in the way of sound logic and reason so that the only important goal is to win. Pride even precludes the possibility of merciful management. It makes it impossible for the entrepreneur to exercise care and compassion in his dealing with other people. Pride can prohibit love and understanding, which are important to the success of any entrepreneur—or anyone else for that matter.

Many times, people fail in business because they are afraid to admit they were wrong, or because they could not bring themselves to ask for other people's help. They can become so consumed with the overpowering need to win that it doesn't matter who they hurt or how many people suffered.

Pride at the negotiating table is disastrous. How many times have two parties sat down to work out differences only to find that one, or both, is more interested in winning than in reaching an equitable solution? How many times have you known in your heart that the proposal submitted by your opponent was the right solution for everyone concerned yet you could not accept it because it wasn't your idea? That's pride coming through. So even though there are really five "Ps" in the negotiating process, only four are worthwhile practicing. The fifth can only destroy.

Throughout the negotiation process, keep in the back of your mind: "Bulls make money, bears make money, hogs make mud." Don't be a hog!

FINANCING ALTERNATIVES

Once the price and terms of sale have been negotiated the next step is to assist the Buyer in arranging outside financing. A little later, I'll use our hypothetical company, MAKE MONEY FILTER, to illustrate how a financing package might be put together, but first let's take a look at some of the more common financing alternatives.

Excluding the exchange of stock in a merger or the issuance of public stock through an IPO, both of which are explained in Chapter 7, there are five principal ways of financing a sale:

1. All cash at closing
2. Buyer paper
3. Partial sale
4. ESOP
5. Earn Out

Which one is used is determined almost entirely by the structure of the sale and the identity of the Buyer. If you are selling your company on the open market and the Buyer is a stranger, then all cash at closing is probably the preferable method. If the Buyer has outside collateral, however, you might be willing to consider part of the price to be paid with Buyer paper.

A partial sale, where the Seller retains either a minority or majority share of the company, has its own peculiarities. An ESOP can only be used for a management buyout (described in Chapter 7) and, therefore, I won't belabor the point here except to point out some pitfalls. An earn out is merely when the Buyer pays for the company out of its own earnings (a form of profit-sharing) after he takes possession.

There are many variables in financing a sale, and the needs of both the Seller and the Buyer, the type of company, outside collateral, macro economic conditions, and the attractiveness of the business all have major impacts. Let's take a look at each of these methods.

Cash

Very few, if any, individual Buyers ever have sufficient cash to use their own funds in making an acquisition. Therefore, most deals that require cash at closing are financed, in part at least, by outside sources. The Buyer can use a variety of sources to accomplish this end, and certainly, it is his responsibility to choose which sources are best, not the Seller's. Still, it can't hurt you, as a Seller, to understand some of the financing resources available in the marketplace. It has probably been several years since you last looked at what was available and things do change, usually quite rapidly.

Types of Debt Financing

There are many sources of debt financing ranging from commercial finance companies to venture capital houses and a host of variations of secured and unsecured, primary and secondary, mezzanine, and equity sources in between. The glossary lists definitions for all of these financing terms. Which type of financing the Buyer chooses will depend, to a large extent, on the type of acquisition and the amount of his equity contribution. All financing has a cost, ranging from the most secure loans with very little leverage, the least cost and no share of ownership, unsecured equity investment with substantial ownership participation; to high leverage secured loans at a significant interest rate and stringent operating covenants. The cost of money will be a significant factor for any Buyer and can determine how the debt will be structured.

Investment Banking

Large investment banking houses such as Donaldson-Luftkin-Jennrette, Salomon Bros., PaineWebber, and Bear Sterns, to mention just a few, and a host of small investment bankers, have emerged as the principal financiers of many large and small acquisitions during the eighties. As the stock market turned bullish and the P/E ratios continued to climb, investment banks found that equity participation offered a promising investment opportunity. Acquisition Buyers learned quickly that with the high prices demanded by Sellers, earnings and cash flows were not sufficient to service large amounts of long–term debt. Consequently, the traditional debt markets dried up.

Investment banking firms have been able to buoy the acquisition market in the face of these high prices because investors continue to be optimistic about the American economy. How long this will continue is anyone's guess, however.

The traditional principles of valuing a business and the danger of buying at high P/E ratios have been severely violated by investment banking manipulations. Sooner or later, this irrational investing must stop and the house of cards built by investment bankers fall just as surely as the wave of high–leverage deals made in the early part of the eighties resulted in a rash of bankruptcies a few years ago. Many entrepreneurs listened to advertising from the asset–based lenders and acquired companies with all debt financing and little or no equity of their own. The nation's bankruptcy courts are now loaded to overflowing by them.

Typically, an investment banker will take the lead in arranging a diversified financing package. A commercial bank for the operating line, and an asset–based lender for long–term secured financing will normally participate because of the reputation of the investment banker. The balance of funds required to make the deal comes from the investment banker himself, in the form of mezzanine financing, equity contributions, or both. He will take a percentage ownership in the company in exchange for his equity contribution. This share can range anywhere from 15 percent to 75 percent. He will also probably want to be a board advisor. There have been several instances where an advisor has been invaluable in giving professional advice on operating policies in specialized areas of the industry where he has considerably more expertise than the business owner.

Small investment banking houses tend to specialize in particular industries or types of product. The DJS Group in New York, for instance, looks favorably on deals involving waste disposal facilities. Other small houses have their own niches in the money markets.

Venture Capital Firms

At times, it's hard to tell the difference between venture capital firms and investment banking houses, because they both provide equity, mezzanine, and sometimes secured financing. They are also lead sources in assembling a financing package. Historically, the major difference is that venture capital firms provide financing for start-up or first–or second–stage developing companies and investment banking houses provide financing for established companies.

In the seventies, the emergence of high–tech companies commanded the attention of venture capital financial institutions, and massive funds were invested in these industries. A true venture capital firm is not particularly interested in a fixed return on its money, but prefers to take an equity position in anticipation of taking the company public within the foreseeable future. Through a public issue, it can recoup substantial investment appreciation. A venture capital firm will always want a share of equity of the company and many times a controlling interest.

These firms serve a special need in the financing marketplace. Many times, a small company cannot raise funds anywhere else because of little or no collateral and their earnings records won't support substantial cash flow projections. This type of deal is the riskiest for the financier and therefore, his reward for taking the risk must be substantial.

Finance Companies

Commercial finance companies or asset–based lenders, as they like to call themselves, such as ITT Capital, Security Pacific Capital, or Fidelity Capital, will usually make acquisition loans only on hard–asset security such as real estate or equipment and machinery. Recently, however, they have been taking more receivables and inventory as collateral. Usually, they will lend for five to seven years at an interest rate of prime plus a significant point spread. They require a first position on all of the hard assets of the business and, if another bank has the operating line, probably a second position on working capital assets. The advantage in using asset based lenders, assuming there are hard assets to secure, is that they usually require less equity contribution on the part of the Buyer and therefore, are willing to do more highly leveraged deals. The disadvantages are the high cost and the extreme difficulty in working with these institutions. Experience has shown that finance companies will, without hesitation, interfere with the management of the operating business at the first sign of trouble.

Asset–based lenders love to have the Seller carry some portion of the sell price in Buyer paper. They feel this ties the Seller to the deal and if the going gets tough, he will step in and bail out the company and the bank. The moral here is clear. Be extremely cautious of taking back Buyer paper if a Buyer finances part, or all, of the deal through a finance company. You could end up with the company right back in your lap and with substantial debt to pay off. Asset–based lenders make loans nobody else wants. For this reason alone, if your deal involves either a partial sale, or requires you to carry Buyer paper, and the Buyer finances through one of these institutions, you should consider backing off and looking elsewhere for a Buyer.

Finance companies do serve a market niche, however. There have been a number of highly leveraged deals that have turned out very well. As long as there is no way that you can be coerced into coming back into the company, or in any other way be liable in the event of default by the Buyer, then it doesn't make any difference to you how the Buyer does his financing.

Commercial Banks

Commercial banks are somewhere in the middle of the financing spectrum. Deregulation of the banking industry has allowed commercial banks to offer a hodgepodge of services. Most large commercial banks have finance company subsidiaries. Several also have investment banking divisions.

Generally, however, commercial banks are the primary source of working capital funding, which is secured by receivables and inventory. Many times, it can be helpful to the Buyer if he can continue with the same local bank used by the Seller for his operating line. It certainly can't hurt to volunteer an introduction to your own friendly banker. It might even speed things up.

BUYER PAPER

The phrase "Buyer paper" refers to a promissory note from the Buyer or an executed contractual agreement identifying specific amounts to be paid by the Buyer to the Seller on specific dates. Payment of the note is not dependent on any business occurrence or condition. It is simply a promise to pay specific amounts on specific dates. The payment terms can be structured as monthly, quarterly, annually, or with a balloon payment at the end. It can be for any length of time—three years, five years, or longer. Of course, the note must carry an interest rate to avoid IRS constructive receipt provisions. Financial institutions view Buyer paper with glee. It gives them the assurance that the Seller is comfortable with the financial projections and the Buyer's credibility. There are three reasons why it might be both reasonable and desirable to negotiate a portion of the selling price using Buyer paper:

1. To increase the selling price.
2. To defer receipt of payment to reduce income taxes on the sale.
3. Because the assets of the company do not support leveraged financing.

If one of these reasons doesn't apply to your specific case—and of course, assuming you are selling the entire company—stay away from a Buyer's promise to pay in the future. The reason is simple. If the Buyer defaults, it will be costly, time consuming, and generally a horrendous bother to try to collect. Which introduces the biggest problem of all with taking Buyer paper: What collateral can the Buyer provide that is not already pledged to the banks?

Any financial institution providing acquisition financing is going to want all of the Buyer's and the business' assets as collateral for the loan or as collateral for personal guarantees. In addition, they will demand a first position. So what does that leave the Seller? At best, a second position to the banks in the event of default, and the likelihood of collecting under these circumstances is remote.

With an honest Buyer and a profitable business, however, the likelihood of default diminishes, in which case, Buyer paper might be a good way for you to increase your cash take out of the deal. But beware, Buyer paper of any kind is fraught with danger. If you do take it, make sure it is for the excess part of the sell price—above and beyond that which you really must get—so that if you don't collect, at least you will have received the cash you wanted as a minimum.

A PARTIAL SALE

Partial sales can get very tricky and involve all kinds of unusual provisions that mitigate everything I have said so far about cash at closing and Buyer paper. A partial sale involves the sale or transfer of part of the interest in a business, usually to a partner you have brought in, a successor you have trained, or a group of employees in a management buyout. The concept is simple, but the mechanics are difficult. Because the number of variations are limited only by a person's imagination, a list of steps to follow or a set of rules to get the job done is impractical, but the following scheme has worked several times to finance a sale to a designated successor. To set the stage, let's first assume that:

1. A year ago, you hired a new vice president of marketing to train for one year in the overall operations of the business so you could name him as your successor and sell the company to him.
2. If at the end of one year, you felt he was ready to take control, you would sell him 10% of the company for book value and step down from active management.

3. You would keep a seat on the board for another three years and during that time, he would purchase an additional 15 percent of the company each year, so that, at the end of the three–year period, he would own 55 percent and you would go off the board.

4. At the end of another three years, he would purchase the remaining shares of the company to give him total ownership.

5. Book value of the company after his one year of training was $4 million, his salary was $100,000 per year, and you set up an incentive plan for him to earn an additional $50,000 each year if he met the annual operating plan profit goals.

Those are the facts. Now, how is this new man, we'll call Joe, going to raise the funds to buy you out? Let's do some calculations. If book value is $4 million, and that's the price for all of the shares, then 10 percent (the amount Joe will buy after his first year of training) will amount to $400,000. Furthermore, each of the next three years he will need to come up with 15 percent, or $600,000, and three years after that, he will need another $1.8 million, assuming the book value remains about constant. That's a lot of money for one person to raise, so we'll structure the deal as follows:

A. At end of training year:

Joe will borrow against the cash surrender value of his life insurance policy	$30,000
Joe will contribute from savings	25,000
Reduction in salary from $100,000 to $50,000	50,000
Year end incentive bonus	50,000
Total cash paid	$155,000
You take a promissory note from Joe, at 10% interest, payable in six years, secured by 10% of common shares of the company	245,000
Total Purchase Price for 10%	$400,000

B. For the next three years:

Reduction in salary from $100,000 to $50,000 × 3 years	$150,000
Year–end incentive bonus $50,000 × 3 years	150,000
Total cash paid	300,000
Three promissory notes from Joe, at 10% interest, payable separately in five years, four years, and three years, respectively	1,500,000
Total purchase price for 45% interest	$1,800,000

C. At end of sixth year:

Joe will borrow against the assets of the business to
purchase the final 45% and to pay off the Promissory
notes and interest —

Debt to purchase additional 45%	$1,800,000
Debt to pay off first year note	245,000
Debt to pay off (3) three year notes	1,500,000
Debt to pay interest due on notes	750,000
Total bank debt for Joe	$4,295,000

After six years, Joe has now paid $4,750,000 for a company with a book value of $4 million, but only $25,000 out of his own savings. You have made a $750,000 premium over book and have deferred taxes, at least somewhat, over a six–year period. The bank is willing to lend Joe the $4,295,000 since they have now known him as the manager of the company for six years and have faith in his ability to perform. Your receivable from Joe has been secured by his stock holdings, so if he were to default on the payment of the notes at any time during the six years, you could reclaim the company and still have nearly $500,000 in your pocket. A good deal for all parties.

This is merely an example of one way to use a partial sale to finance a successor. There are as many other ways as your creativity can come up with. Personal circumstances of the two parties usually determines the structure of the deal. Although it takes longer to liquidate your total holdings and get your cash, a partial sale is certainly an inexpensive, low–risk way to get out.

AN ESOP MANAGEMENT BUYOUT

Chapter 8 illustrates the use of an ESOP in a management buyout. Little needs to be added at this time except to alert you to the often complex arrangements necessary to establish and fund an ESOP. Contrary to popular literature on the subject, ESOPs are not for everyone. The biggest drawback is the funding requirements. Merely forming an ESOP isn't enough. The employer company must also fund the Plan. Usually this funding must be made in addition to existing employee benefit programs, and thus, ends up costing the company incremental cash. Then of course, the Seller is paid for his company with his own money with which he funded the ESOP in the beginning! So before you venture down this road, be certain to get clear advice from your legal counsel and your CPA.

EARN OUTS

An earn out is simply an agreement to take a portion of the selling price each year for a fixed period of time out of the earnings of the company after the Buyer takes over. Most earn out plans are contingent on the level of profits a company earns. No profits, no payments.

Sometimes, an earn out agreement will have minimum, fixed amounts to be paid in the event the profits drop below certain levels or the total payments might be cumulative, so that shortfalls in poor years are added to payments due in good years. There are any number of structures an earn out agreement might take.

Because of these variations, there is no set formula for structuring earn outs. Payment of the total price depends on how well the company performs over the earn–out period, therefore, you probably should insist on participation in some manner in the policy and/or management decisions during this period. One way is to execute an employment or consulting agreement with the new owner as part of the closing documents. You might also keep your hand in the business by taking an active role as a board member, although currently unattractive liability considerations attached to board membership make employment or consulting contracts preferable.

In spite of its contingency nature, an earn–out sale can be a most attractive method if you don't need immediate cash and are willing to continue in the business, at least for a while. If you do negotiate an earn out, be sure to incorporate the following provisions in the Buy/Sell Agreement or in subsidiary closing documents:

1. A payout period of no longer than five years.
2. Minimum payments each year in the event profits fall below a specified level.
3. A total payout of a fixed amount if the company is resold or merged.
4. A fixed number of shares and value per share if the company goes public.
5. A definitive description of your responsibilities in the operations of the company.
6. A getting out position, at your option, with a fixed payment in case of an emergency.

With these provisos, you should be protected from mismanagement by the Buyer and still benefit from good management or windfall gains.

Because of the extreme hazards in collecting on an earn–out deal, particularly if you sell to a large corporation, the entire next chapter will illustrate how **not** to write an earn–out agreement. The true story of John Bioto, founder and sole owner of Pla-Day Preschool Products, Inc. will be analyzed as an example of how dangerous such deferred payments can be and illustrate the dangers of taking deferred payments from a large corporation with a poorly written contract. Before going on, however, let's go back to our hypothetical company, MAKE MONEY FILTER, and take it through negotiations and the financing phase of its sale.

NEGOTIATING THE MAKE MONEY FILTER SALE

In Chapter 4, several valuation methods were calculated yielding significantly different valuation amounts, ranging from $5 million to $30 million. To be realistic, we have thrown out the top and the bottom values and have arrived at a going-in price of $15 million, cash at closing, with a drop–dead bottom number of $11.7 million. The future cash flow method and the net asset value calculation provide the best outer limits within which to negotiate. The Seller, John E. Joe, and the potential Buyer, both of who have legal and tax advisors, proceed to try to reach an accord.

Obviously, the Buyer argues strongly for the liquidation value. He professes shock that a number like $15 million could even be suggested! He argues that he has no confidence in John's strategic plan or forecasts. The prior year's cash flow was only $1,259,000 and, at a five times multiple, that isn't nearly enough to cover more than $5 to $6 million. If the company fails, he must be able to recoup his investment through liquidation, and with a liquidation value of $5,600,000, that's about all he can afford to pay. In addition, his bank will only loan on liquidation value and if the bank feels that is the maximum value of the company, why should he feel any different.

John E. responds that the Buyer knew going–in what the deal was—$15 million cash. If he cannot afford this size company, but must borrow money to make the deal, then he shouldn't be negotiating. Now is a good time for John to pick up his papers and begin to leave the negotiating table! It always embarrasses the Buyer when the Seller claims he is not financially viable, and this is a good time to play the offended Seller. John argues that the company is a real steal at that price, which is based on the current stock market average P/E ratios. As a matter of fact, the price really should be $30 million, not $15 million.

In addition, John invested five years of effort and money in building MAKE MONEY to take advantage of the future, including almost $3 million invested in new equipment in the past three years and it was the $1.4 million in new equipment that caused the low cash flow last year. John feels he should be compensated for two things:

1. The amount of investment he has in the company, which is the net asset value or book value.
2. An amount representing part of the future earnings of the company which will occur because of his past investments, efforts, and skills.

Clearly, the negotiation of price could go on for a long time and probably will, so let me stop here and recommend an alternative for arriving at a fair price to both John and the Buyer. From a financing perspective, the Buyer should be able to raise $6 million from asset–based lenders and commercial banks. He should have another $1 million to $2 million of his own equity for a deal of this size, and he should be able to raise another $4 million from investment bankers without too much difficulty. This makes a price of $12 million cash. John is entitled to at least net asset value plus a premium for future earnings, and current P/E ratios should have some bearing on the price. Therefore, a price of $13.7 million should be reasonable. This leaves a spread of $1.7 million between what the Buyer should be able to raise and what John wants. This amount could be taken in Buyer paper, say over three years at 12 percent interest.

Considering P/E ratios, cash flow (historical and projected), net asset value, and liquidation value, the $12 million cash plus $1.7 deferred seems a reasonable price. It will yield a $7 million gain on John's original investment, and with his original equity of only $1 million, the return over five years is enormous. The one thing the Buyer insists on, however, is that John assist him in financing the deal because he had counted on a much lower price.

Financing the MAKE MONEY FILTER Sale

With John's help, the Buyer put together the following financing package:

	$ million
Buyer equity	2.2
Long term debt from asset based lender	6.3
Investment banker —mezzanine debt	2.0
—equity	1.5
Total cash at closing	12.0
Buyer paper	1.7
Total selling price	$13.7
Operating line	$ 2.0

Now that the MAKE MONEY deal is negotiated and financed, the only step remaining is to draft and negotiate the closing documents, which is covered in Chapter 11.

10
Getting Burned
The Earn–Out Contract

BECAUSE OF THE INCREASING USE OF EARN–OUT SALES CONTRACTS, THE GENERAL misunderstanding in the small business community about the pros and cons of entering into such an agreement, and the high risks of selling to a large corporation under such terms, a detailed example of the exigencies of this arrangement should forewarn you to look before you leap. This chapter contains an actual case history of a small business owner selling out to a large corporation while under financial duress and the mistakes he made in structuring the deal. The names and some of the detailed events have been changed to protect the identity of the parties, but the story is true and the salient ingredients of the Buy/Sell Agreement and the resulting events have been left intact. This chapter is included, not to sour legitimate earn–out contracts that are necessary to close a deal, or to discourage you from selling to a large corporation, but to wave a red flag about any promise to pay based on future earnings when you stay on as an employee to run your own company. A deal might look terrific when signed, but turn out to be a catastrophe when it comes to collecting.

THE COMPANY

Pla-Day PreSchool Products, Inc., was incorporated in the sixties to design, manufacture, and distribute children's toys and other learning products used by nursery schools and day care centers. The founder of Pla-Day, John Bioto, envisioned a need for such products as the population of preschoolers began to mushroom and more special training centers were established to care for them. He believed these youngsters could learn a great deal about life long

160

before entering kindergarten if teachers had the right tools to work with and could prepare them on an individual basis to face the trauma of large classrooms once they entered the regular school system.

When Bioto founded Pla-Day, he intended to design three types of pre-school learning tools: wooden put-together type toys, building blocks, and educational puzzles. He already had plenty of ideas from his previous employment and from raising three of his own children. John felt he knew what youngsters liked and what kindergartens lacked in educational toys. He also realized that the safe and sturdy construction of toys was a number one priority. Of course, they also needed to be quality products at prices nursery schools and daycare centers could afford. He set out to design a series of four, wooden pull–apart toys, two sets of various shaped wooden blocks, and two, five–piece wooden puzzles.

Over a period of seven years, John Bioto was successful in developing a specialized market niche through his unique designs and his uncanny aptitude for marketing. His products were used not only in nursery schools and daycare centers, but eventually found their way into many kindergarten classrooms around the region. The company grew to sales of nearly $5 million, and John was satisfied that he had done his best and was making at least some small contribution to the early education of children. In the trade, Pla-Day was known as a high–quality producer with an excellent reputation for customer satisfaction.

Then the bottom fell out. The economy went into a recession, the price of hardwood skyrocketed, and when the next annual order cycle came around, many of the Pla-Day customers made significant cutbacks in their order book. Bioto borrowed from his bank to meet the payroll and pay other bills, but he could see that unless something drastic was done, he would go under.

About a year later, with the recession deepening, Bioto found himself in deep financial trouble. Sales continued to plummet, over half of the work force was laid off, and his competition was beginning to design competitive toys accepted in the marketplace by large chain Buyers.

John didn't know what to do. He couldn't just close the doors, he owed too much money to the bank by this time. He also felt a responsibility toward his remaining employees, most of whom had been with him for many years. On the other hand, even though he had some great new design ideas for next season, he couldn't even afford the travel expense of attending the annual toy show in New York much less the cost of bringing his ideas to market. John was in a quandary. It seemed that he was dammed if he did and dammed if he didn't.

Fortunately, John Bioto had a friend who worked for a large conglomerate that was in the process of building its own toy division. John explained his problems over dinner one night and his friend suggested that he talk to this company and see if they would be interested in buying him out. He knew they had made several acquisitions of toy companies already, and that they were staffing–up to make more. Maybe John's line would fit right in! It was certainly worth a try.

John agreed, and the next day called the vice president development of the toy division of the conglomerate. Although the vice president didn't sound too interested on the phone, he said he would consider the possibility and get back to Bioto. That was about all John could do for the time being, so he continued to try to struggle along as best he could with the diminished market and work force, and the bills mounting.

Two months later, he heard from the conglomerate. It seems they were interested in talking to John about the possibility of buying his company but were in no particular rush. A date two weeks off was set for a meeting at their corporate office. Meanwhile, John kept struggling. The meeting was postponed twice, and by the time it finally occurred, Bioto was practically out of business.

He had laid off the remainder of his work force and was in the process of liquidating the small amount of inventory remaining when he finally got his meeting. It was almost too late now to save the company, but being a proud man, Bioto wouldn't give up and tried his best to interest the representatives of the giant corporation in buying his company.

THE BUYER

General Awareness Monet Enterprises, Inc. (GAME for short) was a New York Stock Exchange conglomerate that had been a leader in its original industry of food products for several decades. The company reported sales of nearly $1 billion the past year, and earnings per share were close to $3.10. Over the past 15 years, GAME had pursued other avenues to broaden its business base beyond its traditional markets, and the corporate structure now consisted of four divisions.

The Toy and Games (TAG) Division was a "Johnny come lately" into the corporate fold, and so far, GAME had made only three acquisitions for the division. TAG sales were only $75 million—about 5 percent of total corporate volume. The president of GAME was solidly behind this division, however, because he believed the future growth of the corporation had to be in diversified areas—not foodstuffs.

When Bioto first approached the vice president of Development for the TAG Division, R.T. Lescomb was not very enthusiastic. They had been having enough problems digesting the first three acquisitions without getting involved in another one right away. Also, the business was so small that even at maximum profitability, wouldn't contribute anything significant to division profits. He knew the corporate president, and the Board for that matter, were vitally interested in expanding the TAG Division as quickly as possible, however, so he didn't dare turn Bioto down cold. He calculated that he would string this guy along for a while and see what developed with a couple of other targets he was looking at. If they both fell through, then maybe he would take a serious look at Pla-Day.

Lescomb had done some checking on Pla-Day and recognized immediately what was happening. Another case of a great designer and good marketer who had ignored the financial side of the business. If Bioto had been willing to go a little slower over the past three years, he probably wouldn't be in trouble with his bank now. Bioto was just another impatient entrepreneur trying to conquer the world without adequate financing. Lescomb wondered if entrepreneurs would ever learn the virtue of prudence. He doubted it. At any rate, he felt that Bioto was a talented toy designer and the market niche he had chosen was certainly an interesting one. The only competition was from two, small Southern companies trying to break into this new market. If TAG decided to go ahead with the acquisition, Lescomb didn't see any serious threat from them.

The rest of the management team at TAG were all in their early forties. They were aggressive, professional managers who had been with the parent company GAME for several years. They had all known each other in other divisions and thus formed a close–knit group as the TAG division leaders. The president of the division, Roger Craig, had been in the marketing end of the foodstuffs business for more than 10 years and felt qualified to judge the appropriateness of marketing strategies and programs for any consumer–oriented product line. The rest of the TAG management team had also progressed up the corporate ladder in the food division and food services division through marketing, distribution, and engineering. Lescomb represented the financial side of the team.

This group of managers was hand picked by the president of GAME to develop the Toy and Game Division through its formative stages, and although none of the team boasted specific experience in the toy industry, he believed that, with their varied backgrounds, they could overcome this deficiency. The CEO firmly believed that this group of managers could make, and then manage, the appropriate acquisitions to bring to reality his dream of a major force in the toy industry. So far, the three companies acquired over the past 18 months were being integrated satisfactorily. Through a careful screening process, Lescomb had identified and subsequently negotiated the acquisition of three industry leaders: one making primarily board games, one in the design and manufacture of arts and crafts, and one small company making a specialized line of craft toys for elementary school–aged children. All were brought on board with a minimum of confusion, with prices paid at, or below, book value. Furthermore, there had been no cash outlay. All three acquisitions were for GAME common stock.

The primary criteria used by Lescomb in his acquisition searches and negotiations were that the target must be a leader in its market niche, have good design and marketing management, and a top management team or individual willing to stay on and run the company. He would prefer to look at companies doing at least $25 million in sales, but he realized that in the toy industry, because of market fragmentation, there were only a few firms of this size. The industry was served mostly by small companies. Such was the case with the newest target presented to him by John Bioto.

There were problems with the Pla-Day deal, however. The company was nearly bankrupt, and even though Bioto had done wonders in carving out a new market niche in preschool educational toys, he had slipped in recent years because of undercapitalization. TAG would have a major restructuring job to get Pla-Day back in the forefront of the market. Lescomb reasoned, however, that if he could get the company at a low enough price, and if he could structure the deal to keep Bioto in the saddle, it might work. Also, if he could manage to accomplish this with a small cash outlay, maybe Roger Craig would recommend him for a promotion! In R.T.'s mind it was certainly worth a try. And the fact that Pla-Day was located right down the street from the division offices meant it would be an easy acquisition to manage after closing. Even if Bioto did goof it up, Lescomb could keep a close watch over the operation and recommend remedial steps early on.

With this rationale, Lescomb decided to go for it, at least as far as trying for a no-lose structure for the deal. If he couldn't get that, he'd back off and look elsewhere for the next target.

THE DEAL

When R.T. Lescomb finally called Bioto and suggested a meeting to discuss possible price and terms, John was elated. He was almost at the end of his rope, but maybe there was still hope. Then the meeting was delayed and delayed. Each delay forced the company closer to bankruptcy. Bills continued to pile up and sales kept dropping. John was forced to watch his dream of a lifetime, a business born and bred with his own sweat and blood, his very own child, go down the drain. It was a heart-wrenching experience, and he was about to throw in the towel when Lescomb finally agreed to have the meeting.

The meeting was held on a Monday morning at the corporate office of GAME. A prepossessing arrangement for Bioto, but also a bit overpowering. It didn't take long for Lescomb to get down to business.

"We called this meeting, John, to determine if there's any possibility for TAG to acquire your company. We all know about your financial condition, and I think we all recognize that it's going to take a substantial amount of cash from our side to get Pla-Day back on its feet. About the only thing you have to sell is some equipment, a small amount of inventory, a building lease, which we really don't want anyway, and the name Pla-Day."

Bioto had not built his company from scratch by being afraid to negotiate, so he threw modesty to the winds and waded right in. "Granted, we're having some hard times right now, but Pla-Day has been the leader in the preschool educational wooden toy market for several years. My program of new toy designs for next season is already on the drawing boards and many prototypes have already been developed. The New York show is coming up in two months and I expect to book some substantial orders for these new products. The difficult period we're going through right now is only temporary, and by next year Pla-Day should be back on track again."

"But you've laid off almost all of your people, John. Even if you get the orders, which I think is doubtful, how are you going to produce the product with no people?"

"I had a lot of good, hard working people before this crunch hit," replied Bioto. "A few telephone calls, and I can have most of them back on the job within two weeks."

Lescomb wouldn't let go, "But all of your workers belong to the Teamsters Union. Even if you do get them back, you'll need to negotiate a new contract with the Teamsters. How do we know the demands won't be more than Pla-Day can afford?"

"I can take care of the Teamsters. Don't worry about that!"

Negotiations continued all day and again the next day. It appeared that TAG was genuinely interested or they certainly wouldn't spend all this time negotiating. But John Bioto couldn't seem to close the order. Every time he got close to reaching an agreement, Lescomb brought up his uncertainty about the future of Pla-Day: people, product design, marketing effort, equipment requirements, advertising campaigns, there was always something.

John realized he might be wasting his time, but he really didn't have any other choice. He must try to convince TAG to make the deal. He'd be out of business in two months without them!

Lescomb also knew that Pla-Day couldn't survive without TAG. Bioto had waited too long. As was true with so many of these proud entrepreneurs, he didn't know when to quit! On the other hand, the more they talked, the more Lescomb could see an advantage for TAG in getting this target. It would fit nicely with their other product lines. Advertising campaigns could be combined with the other three toy companies, and he was very impressed with John Bioto. Even though his aggravating independent thinking was characteristic of the typical entrepreneur, he was a good designer and marketer with an impeccable reputation in the industry. All R.T. needed to do was convince Bioto to stay on and run Pla-Day without taking much cash up front.

At the end of the second day of negotiations, Lescomb decided to bring matters to a head. "John, I've listened to all of your points for two days now. You want $3 million for the business. We don't think it's worth more than $500,000 in its current condition, and I recognize that you owe this much to the bank. You claim that your strategic plan calls for a recovery next year and then a sales growth of an average of 15 percent per year for the next four years. If that happens, I agree your company is worth more than $500,000, so this is the deal we would be willing to go with:

1. TAG will pay you $500,000 cash at closing, and you will use these funds to pay off the bank loan in its entirety.

2. We will give you another $500,000 worth of GAME common shares, at closing.

3. You will escrow the $500,000 worth of GAME shares with our financial representative for three years, but you will be able to draw the dividends.

4. We will give you a three–year employment contract as general manager of Pla-Day, with certain provisos that, if your performance isn't satisfactory to TAG, we have the option of terminating your employment. Your salary will be $75,000 per year, the same as you were drawing last year.

5. At the end of three years, if you are still general manager and have met the sales and profit forecasts in your strategic plan, you will receive your original $500,000 of shares from escrow, plus an additional $500,000 worth of GAME shares.

6. As an incentive, if the Pla-Day profit exceeds what you have forecasted for the combined three–year period, TAG will pay you 50 percent of this excess profit up to a maximum of $300,000.

7. This will make a total purchase price of $1,500,000 if you perform as you say you can and up to $1,800,000 if you can do even better than you planned.

8. You will execute a covenant not to compete with Pla-Day for five years from the date you leave the company.

I think that's a fair offer and, just so that you realize we are not playing games, if you don't accept these terms, we're no longer interested. There will be no further negotiations."

Although this offer was even better than he had hoped for, John Bioto stayed calm. "Let me think about it and get back to you".

"All right", replied Lescomb, "but we must have your answer in two days or the offer is withdrawn".

Bioto had already decided he would accept. He thought this was a terrific deal and he had really put something over on the Big Boys! Wow, $1,800,000 for his little company which was on the steps of the bankruptcy courts. He was exuberant. He had put the strategic plan together himself so he was totally confident that he could make it happen, so long as TAG would provide the financing. John called Lescomb back in two days and "reluctantly" accepted the offer.

Year One

By the time all of the due diligence investigations by the TAG acquisition team were completed, and the volumes of closing documents signed, Pla-Day sales had dropped to a paltry $50,000 per month. John Bioto was forced to lay off the balance of his factory work force. Now, his manufacturing manager, personnel manager, and himself were the production line. He owed the bank nearly $500,000 and, even though he had not purchased any new raw materials for six months, he owed the vendors over $50,000.

Then conditions began to brighten. After the closing, John paid off the bank and made a small dent in the vendor accounts. Of course, this left him with no cash payment to himself, but he wasn't worried. He was confident he could make it up over the next three years.

TAG opened an operating line for Pla-Day and, now with some funds to draw on, Bioto began hiring back his ex-employees. Most of those laid off in the past six months came back willingly. In the end, John was able to convince about half to take the gamble, which was enough people for him to get started. He also hired a controller and an engineer, although these two were not in the plan he had presented to TAG. The biggest people problem was with the union. He had not expected the Teamsters to give him any argument about a 10 percent reduction in wages and to work without a contract for the next six months. After all, look how many of their people he was bringing back! The union leadership didn't see it that way, however, and immediately began bargaining for a new contract and a wage hike. He finally had to compromise on a 5 percent increase this year and 8 percent each of the next two years, significantly higher than what he had planned on. But he still had confidence that he could make or beat the plan.

The next problem was to get sufficient new toy designs and prototypes made up for the New York toy show. Normally, he would have an entire new line to present, but now, because of the extended period it took to close the sale of his company, followed by the union negotiations, John could muster only a dozen or so new items, about half of what he usually had. His sales were climbing slowly as new materials were purchased and the workers came back to the production line, but not as fast as he thought they would. Apparently, most Buyers were still hurting from the recession and were not placing orders until the new lines came out.

Somehow, John eventually put designs and prototypes together for his new line and made it to the annual toy show. He was surprised to see that some new competitors had arisen in the past year. There were two other companies showing wooden blocks and wooden pull-apart toys. Their products didn't look as good as his, but they were certainly acceptable. Their prices were also substantially under his new price sheet. The recession had taken its toll and higher-priced, quality products were not making the mark they normally did at the show. Undaunted, John went home knowing he had his work cut out for him, but still confident he could pull off his strategic plan. His earn out from TAG depended on it, and he wasn't about to give up on that!

John immediately went to work to get his new line into production. He lost some key employees during the layoff and this began to hurt the production timing of the new runs. John ended up spending several weeks training new employees in line set-ups and in making new tools and dies.

He also began to have some difficulties in the marketing area. The new engineer hired specifically to help him in marketing was not working out. He was just too slow a learner and couldn't grasp the techniques of how to talk to the preschool administrators who generally passed on the purchase orders for new educational toys.

John was somewhat perplexed when his new controller informed him one day that on a year–to–date basis, production costs were running about 35 percent over plan and the operating line was nearly exhausted. Bioto asked why he wasn't informed of this earlier and the controller's answer was that he had been too busy filling in reports for the TAG home office to get a budget system installed and was operating mainly out of the cash book.

Here was something no one had warned John Bioto about before he made the deal with TAG—corporate and division reports—daily, weekly, and monthly; financial, sales, personnel, and purchasing. Furthermore, Roger Craig was beginning to get disturbed that Bioto was missing most of the weekly and monthly management meetings. A reprieve to get the company started and running was one thing, but to continue to have excuses on a regular basis was something else entirely. Well, John would just make room in his schedule someplace for these time-wasters. He had no choice.

During the rest of the year, Pla-Day continued to increase its monthly sales rate until by the end of year one, it looked like sales would come in at just under $2.8 million. John had forecasted $3 million, but $2.8 was close enough to give him heart. Profits were down, however. A combination of the higher wage rates demanded by the union and lower selling prices forced by recessionary market conditions held pre-tax profits at 6 percent of sales, whereas Bioto had forecasted 11 percent! Somehow, he would explain this to his bosses at TAG and make them understand that it was market conditions causing the problem, not his management ability.

Year Two

By the middle of the second year, John was beginning to show the strains of working for a giant corporation. Not in his wildest dreams did he imagine working for a big company would be so much different from his own entrepreneur style of doing business. It seemed that all he ever had time for anymore were meetings and reports, meetings and reports, and more meetings and reports. He had no idea what they did with all that paper, but somebody in the waste paper business must be getting rich.

Nevertheless, with his $500,000 of stock in escrow and another $500,000 on the way in another year, he had no choice but to hang on. He was becoming a little concerned, however. He had missed the first year's sales and profits, and the second year didn't seem to be shaping up any better in profits, although sales continued to climb. The TAG office now insisted on approving all product designs before they went to prototype and his ideas and their ideas were clashing more and more. He was under the impression that when they bought Pla-Day, the TAG management wanted his expertise more than the company and yet he was meeting increasing resistance whenever he suggested an operating change or a new product design.

The most bothersome part of all was that the TAG home office personnel couldn't make a decision. It was always "tomorrow" whenever he called to get approval on anything. The weekly meetings had finally been abandoned, but the monthly meetings took three times as long as before. Whenever John needed to draw additional funds on the operating line he had to get permission from the home office and approval was becoming more and more difficult to obtain, or so it seemed to him.

In addition, there was almost always somebody from the TAG office trying to interfere with his operating decisions. The division office assigned one of their own people to be the on-site controller, and John's financial manager became a bookkeeper and clerk. The new controller determined what bills to pay and when, performed the collections activities, developed the new cost center budget program, implemented a new cost system, and, in general, did everything a controller should do to control the operation. Moreover, he reported directly to the TAG office, bypassing the authority of Bioto completely.

The division office also assigned one of their personnel as vice president of marketing for Pla-Day. This marketing manager, Fred Johnson, became the final authority at Pla-Day for advertising programs, sales literature, and pricing. He even began the development of a new logo for the company. When he suggested to John that he accompany him on sales calls, John's concern mounted. Was something happening with his relationship with the TAG office of which he was not aware? Was Craig or Lescomb or one of the other managers unhappy with his performance at Pla-Day and trying to boost the company's image at the GAME corporate level by putting in their own people to assist John? Or was there something more sinister afoot?

What began to irritate John more than anything else was that Fred Johnson, and a couple of design engineers from division, insisted on having a hand in the design of the new line of toys for the New York show that year. This had always been John's special domain. It was his expertise. Designing toys to fit the educational preschool market was how he had built his company. His reputation in the industry as a creative designer with uncanny market foresight was his strength. And now, Roger Craig threatened that reputation and market image by introducing his own people to the design function. By the time the annual toy show came around, with Bioto and Johnson in daily quarrels, the shadows began to fall on the career of John Bioto.

Financially, Pla-Day was having a good year, but not as spectacular as John planned in his two–year–old strategic plan. Last year's product introductions were doing well, but because he was unable to get a full new line developed, sales were lagging behind the plan. Competition was stronger than anticipated, and the economy was just beginning to show signs of recovery. Consequently, pricing over the two–year period was much more competitive than in prior years. A combination of these factors, lower sales and competitive pricing, together with significantly higher wage rates and an enormous advertising program dictated by the division office, caused profits to lag far behind John's original plan. Table 10–1 matches sales and pre-tax profits of his strategic plan, against which Bioto was measured, and the actual results for the first two years.

Year Three

One day early in the year, Roger Craig called Bioto to his office for a meeting with himself and R.T. Lescomb. John could sense that this was not a friendly gathering. The tension in the air was so thick you could cut it with a knife.

Craig opened the meeting. "John, when we purchased Pla-Day from you over two years ago, we made the decision to go ahead with the deal based on the strategic plan you submitted to us. Even though Pla-Day was floundering and about to go under, we believed you had the capability to turn it around, with financial help from us. We have been very patient with you, but in two years, sales are off almost 10 percent and profits are nearly 50 percent below your own plan. That is not a stellar performance!"

"I know what the financials say, Roger," replied Bioto, "but you need to remember the problems of getting the new line out and the union problems the

TABLE 10-1
Two-Year Comparison of Sales and Pretax Profits

	Sales	Profit
Year 1		
Plan	$3,000,000	$330,000
Actual	2,750,000	165,000
Shortfall	250,000	165,000
Year 2		
Plan	5,000,000	600,000
Actual	4,500,000	360,000
Shortfall	500,000	240,000
Cumulative 2 years		
Plan	8,000,000	930,000
Actual	7,250,000	525,000
Shortfall	$750,000	$405,000

first year. This last year would have been better except that all of the people from the division took so much of my time I couldn't get out with the customers as much as I should."

"Nevertheless," said Craig, "we must do something, and in our judgment, you have not performed the way you should as general manager. Pla-Day has become a drag on our division profits. It's an illness we must cure. Therefore, we have decided that two things must happen:

1. A small lumber company has offered to buy Pla-Day, and we have agreed to sell it to them. They have their own general manager to run the company, so I don't know if they'll need you.

2. Effective immediately, we must terminate your employment as general manager of Pla-Day, for cause. The cause is your non-performance in meeting your own plan.

I'm sorry John, we have no alternative. Pla-Day just hasn't worked out."

"But what about the balance of the purchase price you owe me from the acquisition? I still have $500,000 in GAME stock coming plus the $500,000 in escrow."

"Sorry, John," Craig replied, "but our agreement specifically called for you to remain as general manager for three years and to meet your own strategic plan sales and profit projections over this period. You have not performed satisfactorily and have just been terminated. Obviously, you have not remained as general manager for three years. Also, your financial results to–date make your three–year plan highly suspect. Sorry we have to do this, but that's the way it is."

John had no alternative but to clean out his desk and get out. Of course, he could not collect his stock from escrow nor would he get the $500,000 due after three years. He obviously didn't get the additional $300,000 incentive. John Bioto left a disillusioned man, bitter toward the corporation for cheating him out of his rightful payments, and fully believing that it was the TAG management people who had caused the Pla-Day problems, not himself. John finally retired from active business without ever reaping the financial benefits of building and running his own company.

Within 60 days, Pla-Day was sold to the lumber company who put their own man in as general manager. As a footnote, by the end of year three, the new owner moved the company to a different state and merged it with another of its holdings. Pla-Day was no more.

WHAT WENT WRONG?

This was a classic case of an entrepreneur who marries in haste and repents at leisure. John Bioto was so anxious to get out of his business, he would have taken almost any offer. It's also a prime illustration of what can happen, and very often does, when an entrepreneur sells his company to a large, public corporation on an earn–out contract. Psychologically, an entrepreneur does not have the same mental and emotional traits as a corporate manager. That's why he is an entrepreneur. He wants to get things done now, he wants to do things his way, he wants to be his own boss, he wants to take risks, and he expects to reap the benefits for taking those risks. He has unbounded optimism about his company and his ability to manage it successfully. This same optimism—essential in going it alone—creates disaster in dealing with a corporate empire. On your own, if things don't turn out the way you planned, you make adjustments quickly and move forward. When the same thing happens in a corporate environment, somebody must take the blame and pay the penalty, and this is usually the person who said something would happen when it didn't. The corporate hierarchy doesn't like to take responsibility unless something turns out right, and then corporate managers all claim credit. In a private company, you take both the blame and the credit for all events, good or bad, and never think twice about it.

Occasionally, marriages between an entrepreneur and a large corporation work out. But these situations are rare, and it generally takes about 12 to 18 months for each to be disillusioned with the other and part company.

This doesn't mean that you shouldn't sell to, or merge with, a large corporation. In many cases, it can be the most profitable way to get out. It does mean, however, that if part of the deal is an earn–out or incentive payment, be absolutely certain that you get an ironclad contract stipulating that you get paid a significant portion, or all, of your sell price if, and when, your employment with the Buyer is terminated. It makes no difference whether this termination is voluntary, involuntary, for health reasons, or for lack of performance. Whatever the reason for severing connections, your contract should ensure that you get paid. The odds are very high that you won't last long with the big company, so you better protect yourself going in.

In the case of Pla-Day, Bioto made several serious mistakes in the closing documents:

1. His only protection against being terminated was for just cause, but the just cause was to be determined solely by the Buyer.

2. The escrow of the GAME shares should not have been longer than one year, much less three years.

3. He should have been entitled to at least a portion of the escrowed stock upon termination.

4. The plan against which he was measured should have had annual update provisions. No one can forecast three–years out with any accuracy.

5. He should have negotiated plus and minus ranges to his strategic plan. A strategic plan is a selling tool and not meant to be an operating budget or plan.

6. The incentive provision should not have been made part of the purchase price, and it should have been annual. Although, the way things turned out, he would not have made anything even if it was annual.

7. Finally, clearly defined lines of responsibility and authority for his job as general manager should have been included in the employment contract. Then, if TAG usurped this authority with their own people, Bioto would have a case for breach of contract.

Some might say that John Bioto did well on his sale. He was close to bankruptcy with no visible means of turning the company around. The $500,000 cash payment was sufficient to pay off most of his debts, and he still ended up with a $75,000 job. The deal also provided employment for all of those people who were laid off earlier.

It's hard to argue against this philosophy except to say that John was entitled to some compensation for the skills and effort he put into developing the company over seven years. How much this should have been is open to debate, but it should have been something!

Most earn–out arrangements do not work out well for the Seller. On the other hand, all Buyers love to pay for a company this way, because they control how much they ultimately pay. But a Seller can end up with nothing. Even though Buyer paper is difficult to collect in the event of default, it does give the Seller a measure of certainty that he does not have with an earn–out contract.

11

Lawyers Take Over

Closing the Deal

THE FINAL STEP IN SELLING YOUR BUSINESS IS TO DRAFT AND NEGOTIATE THE language in the Buy/Sell Agreement and other closing documents. Trying to do this on your own without using a qualified lawyer will always be disastrous. This doesn't mean that you can abrogate your responsibility, however, because even lawyers can screw things up. At the tail end of a sale, you sure don't want to lose the Buyer because of inept legal counsel, as almost happened to Marty.

Bob and Marty were confident they had a deal. After seven months of searching, they finally located a Buyer for their pleasure boat manufacturing business. Negotiations were hot and heavy, but at last they reached an accord. Financing turned out to be a real bearcat and, although the Buyer had good banking connections, the lack of hard assets caused difficulty in attracting a loan. His investment banker helped, but they were still $1.5 million short, and Bob and Marty did not want to carry any Buyer paper. Marty went to work on his own friendly bank and, at last, a financing package seemed assured. The only thing left to resolve was the Buy/Sell Agreement and a few other closing documents. Neither Bob nor Marty saw any problems at this juncture and began to plan their respective long–term vacations. Of the two partners, Marty handled most of the administrative work including liaisons with legal counsel. After using the same law firm for over 10 years, he was confident that the company attorney, Robert McK., could easily review the contracts with the Buyer's counsel and reach an amicable conclusion. Marty spent little time worrying about such mundane matters.

Ten days before the scheduled closing date, Marty took his first look at the draft of the Buy/Sell Agreement. Robert McK. had been on the phone with him from time to time to clear certain language difficulties, but nothing arose of any significance. Now, when Marty read through the draft, he hit the roof.

"What in the hell are you talking about Robert. These warranties are impossible. There's no way Bob and I are going to warrant these items," stormed Marty. I should mention that, although their counsel was expert at corporate law, this was his first Buy/Sell Agreement, whereas the Buyer's attorney specialized in this segment of contract law.

"Well, it looks reasonable to me, Marty," replied Robert. "What do you find so onerous?"

"The entire three–page listing of contracts and agreements that we are supposed to warrant and provide as a precedent to closing!" retorted Marty. "I'm not about to list and provide documentation of all sales orders, open purchase orders, agent rep agreements, customer change orders, and open employee grievances. Let them dig those things out themselves. That's part of their due diligence. Not to mention that the Buyer has already spent two weeks at our shop digging around in these same items."

A partial listing of the items Bob and Marty were to provide as exhibits to the Buy/Sell Agreement, under the captions of "Contracts—any and all agreements, written or oral," are as follow:

Contracts or Agreements

1. with any officer, consultant, director, or employee,
2. with any labor union,
3. for the purchase of any materials, supplies, or equipment,
4. for the sale of products or performance of services,
5. relating to licenses or franchises, either as licenser or licensee or franchisee, or relating to distributorships, manufacturers reps, dealerships, or sales agencies,
6. for the lease (as lessor or lessee) of real or personal property, or for the purchase or sale of real property, or for a material amount of personal property,
7. relating to any pension, profit-sharing, bonus, deferred compensation, retirement, stock option, or stock–purchase plan,
8. granting anyone the right to use any property or property right, including intellectual property,
9. for insurance of any officer, director, or employee,
10. for construction or material repairs of any building,
11. any covenants not to compete,

12. any joint venture or agreement for sharing of profits,

13. any borrowing or lending of money,

14. anything else not mentioned above which is material.

To say that Marty was upset put it mildly. "Robert, you're supposed to be the legal-beagle around here, not me! Cut this document down to size and I might be able to understand what they're talking about." "I'll do my best, Marty," was all the lawyer could muster.

Two weeks lapsed and, by this time, the scheduled closing date had been pushed back a month. Finally, Marty decided there was no choice. He needed to personally sit with the Buyer's lawyer and hammer out language that made sense—and that took another two weeks.

By now, the banks were getting nervous and it looked like the deal might fall through. Only a last minute conference between Marty and the Buyer changing the wording in the Agreement so that they could understand it—and the devil with the lawyers—saved the day. The deal finally closed, but it had been very "iffy" right up to the last minute, and all because Bob and Marty tried to delegate a critical step in the selling process—the language that could make or break them after the deal closed.

CHOOSING THE RIGHT LAWYER

How do you avoid making the same mistake Marty did? Try adhering to the following techniques when choosing your lawyer:

1. **Use a large law firm.** I have nothing against sole practitioners or small, local law firms. Most often, they give far better service than a larger firm. A business closing is a complex procedure, however, and usually involves several legal specialties—real estate law, pension law, labor law, creditor's rights and banking law, possible litigation, tax law, government regulations, EPA regulations, SEC law, as well as business contract law. Generally, only a large firm with specialists available to cover all of the bases can do the job.

2. **Get references from local banks and CPA firms.** Don't rely on your own contacts. Ask around for names of contract lawyers used by Big 8 accounting firms and your local bank. Try to get at least three different references.

3. **Interview.** It is a good idea to interview each of the contract law specialists who will actually write the closing documents.

4. **Prior experience is most important.** Find out if the lawyer has ever handled the sale of a company of your size and in your industry. If not,

go elsewhere. If he has, get the name of the client's CEO and interview him about the lawyer. Find out if he knows what he's doing.

5. **Negotiate a fee structure for the entire closing.** Most lawyers will charge by the hour, but try to get at least a maximum, not–to–exceed amount for the engagement.

During the interview process use the following checklist to be certain to ask the right questions:

1. Is there a conflict of interest with the Buyer or the proposed financial institutions?
2. What are your hourly rates?
3. Will you do the work yourself or delegate to assistants?
4. What experience do your assistants have?
5. What are the hourly rates of your assistants?
6. Are you available at home, in the evening, on weekends?
7. What is the professional profile of specialists in your firm whom you will draw upon?
8. What personal contacts do you have in local banking circles?
9. What other sale deals have you handled?
10. Can I contact these clients for references?
11. During the writing of the Buy/Sell Agreement, will you be dedicated to my engagement or will you also be handling other deals?
12. How well do you know the Buyer's attorney?

How these questions are answered will determine whether to go forward or to keep shopping.

CLOSING DOCUMENTS

Closing documents can best be categorized as a set of contractual documents spelling out the rights of all interested parties in a sale transaction. When you sell your house, the closing documents are relatively simple: an offer to purchase, an earnest money agreement, a mortgage note agreement, probably tax clearances, termite inspection certificates, and a closing statement showing the transfer of funds. With the sale of a business, however, the complexities multiply geometrically. Contracts must spell out the rights, obligations, and remedies of each of the parties to a complex set of conditions. You might be able to sell your house on your own, but I caution you to not try to sell your business without the integral participation of an experienced acquisition contract attorney.

Some, or all, of the following contracts and agreements are required for all business closings:

1. A Buy/Sell Agreement between the Buyer and the Seller.
2. A Promissory Note Terms and Conditions Agreement.
3. A Collateral Agreement for Note.
4. Real estate closing papers including title search and title insurance.
5. Lease Assignments.
6. Employment contracts for the Seller or key managers.
7. An Earn–Out Agreement.

The Buyer must provide an additional set of closing documents from his lender, but as a Seller, you won't need to worry about that.

Buy/Sell Agreement

If you sell assets rather than stock, the Buy/Sell Agreement becomes even more complex, because you'll be required to warrant the accuracy of all Balance Sheet account balances as of the closing date. This gets very difficult, and in most cases, the Buyer requires a percentage of the sell price be held back to give his auditors a chance to verify these balances immediately after the closing. Also in an asset sale, you must comply with the Bulk Sales laws of the state in which your business resides, which can be sticky. Bulk Sales laws are applicable when personal property such as equipment, inventory, or vehicles is sold as a single unit. Most states require notification that all creditors be notified of your intent to sell. They can then place liens on the property to satisfy any amounts owed to them. These claims must then be settled before the Buyer takes over.

Fortunately, if you sell stock, you don't need to worry about Bulk Sales laws. All liabilities automatically pass to the new owner, and the Buy/Sell Agreement is much less complex. There are only four parts to it:

1. Price, terms, and conditions of sale.
2. Representations and warranties of Seller and Buyer.
3. Conditions precedent to closing for both Seller and Buyer.
4. The General statements of law.

Price, Terms, and Conditions of Sale

Unless the deal involves complicated deferred payment provisions, the price and terms section is straightforward and merely restates what you and the Buyer have already agreed to in previous negotiations. There will be paragraphs covering:

- What is being purchased.
- The total price.
- How the price will be paid.

Just be sure that your attorney understands the deal you negotiated and this section will be easy. On the other hand, a partial sale, complex payment terms, or performance contingencies can create problems even in something as simple as this section. It's truly amazing how two opposing attorneys can agree on language covering price and terms that has no bearing on what the two principals have already negotiated! Beware that the lawyers don't try to be too clever and muddy up the whole deal.

Representations and Warranties

The Buyer doesn't worry about representations and warranties. About the only things he warrants is that he has the legal right to make the deal. But for you it's entirely different. You need to be especially careful. Representations and warranties can haunt you long after the deal is closed. A constant reminder of the error in trying to cut corners with the closing documents. The Buyer will want you to guarantee everything he has been told about the company. He will insist that any data given him during the due diligence phase, either by you or your employees,

- is unconditionally true,
- that there is no possibility that any fact or contingency has not been revealed, and
- that he knows everything there is to know about the business.

Some Buyers even want you to guarantee the results of your financial forecasts, which of course is impossible. It makes no difference that you've tried to be helpful. The Buyer will want an ironclad guarantee that he knows every fact and condition about the business. If, at a later date, anything should go wrong, and something always does, he will claim either that he forgot to ask some pertinent questions during the investigation phase, that he misunderstood what he was told, or that you lied to him. He will then have grounds for a breach of contract suit. Clearly, it's imperative that your attorney not allow this kind of language to enter the Agreement. Conversely, he should include language protecting you in the event of default by the Buyer. This is where the negotiation process really gets sticky.

Another favorite ploy involves language covering deferred payments. The Buyer will want the Buy/Sell Agreement to allow him to offset any claims resulting from breach of contract against future payments due you on Buyer paper or earn outs. Although entirely logical for the Buyer to want this, it should be totally unacceptable to you as a Seller. Settlement of a breach of contract by either side should be settled at the negotiating table or in court, not automatically through the Buy/Sell Agreement. Contract language to handle the settlement cannot be administered. If the Buyer merely believes there has been a breach, he will automatically withhold payment even though the dispute has not be adjudicated or negotiated. An unscrupulous Buyer can avoid paying on his note simply by picking some small deficiency in the warranties, claiming this as a breach, and you won't get your legitimate payments! Strictly speaking, there might be a breach, but until all of the facts are known and the matter is reviewed by both counsels, you are out the money due you.

Conditions Precedent to Closing

The conditions precedent to closing section lists all of the items to be completed by both parties prior to the close. For example, some of the items pertaining to you as a Seller might include:

1. *Representations and Warranties True at Closing.* You affirm that all representations and warranties made in the contract document are true as of the closing date.

2. *Compliance with the Agreement.* You shall have complied with all conditions required by this Agreement prior to or at closing date.

3. *Seller's Certificate.* You will deliver to Buyer at closing date a certificate stating that items (1) and (2) have been complied with.

4. *Opinion of Company's Counsel.* Your counsel shall deliver to Buyer at closing, his opinion as to the authenticity and authority vested in you and your company.

5. *Injunction.* At closing date there shall be no injunction or other court order restraining the transaction from closing.

6. *Casualty.* There shall have been no fire, flood or other casualty to the business property prior to closing.

7. *Adverse Developments.* There have been no developments in the business which would have a materially adverse effect on the business.

8. *Deliveries.* You shall make delivery of those documents required in the Agreement prior to or at closing.

As you can see, the only potentially difficult item is Adverse Developments. Here, the Buyer tries to guard against any unfavorable conditions that might have occurred since he last saw the last financial statement that could have a detrimental effect on the status of the company such as the loss of a major customer, a write-down in inventory, or changes in pricing strategy. Because of the dynamics and continuous changes that occur in a business, the problem is to determine the meaning of the word material. What is material to the Buyer might be insignificant to you, and it's time for negotiations again.

Another example of deliveries you might have to make before closing is your insurance policies for the business, assuming the Buyer wants to continue the same policies in–force. You might also have to include assignment of leases, a listing of all customers or open purchase orders, or an updated version of the union contract or the pension plan. Clearance from government agencies, creditors, or banks might also be included in this section.

Usually, there's not much disagreement between the parties on the language except for the definition of material, unless one or the other makes an unreasonable demand. In this case, it's customary to reach a resolution through the representations and warranties section rather than including changes here. Very few deals fall apart because of a disagreement on conditions precedent to close.

General Statements of Law

The general statements of law is the lawyer's section, and includes: which state laws will govern in the event of a dispute, arbitration procedures, and, notification of parties. There's not much you can contribute here, unless, of course, you have a legal background. Your legal advisor should be fully capable of agreeing with opposing attorneys on these matters. Therefore, don't spend time worrying about it.

HOW BUYER PAPER IS COLLECTED

As mentioned in Chapter 9, one of the major hurdles in accepting deferred payments secured by a Buyer's Promissory Note is to establish collectible security in the event of default. If the Buyer runs into financial difficulties before your Note is paid in full, his first inclination will be to withhold your payments, not the bank's. Richard J. ran into this problem but came up with an ingenious solution.

Richard sold his company two years earlier to a small group of individual investors who formed a new corporation, PTLE, Inc., to use as a vehicle for acquiring several highly leveraged, small manufacturing and assembly companies servicing the telecommunications industry. Their theory was to build a mini conglomerate of specialized electronics companies nationwide, acquired through high–leverage deals, to serve regional markets. Each of the four investors put little equity into PTLE, and therefore, had little to lose if the parent or any of its subsidiaries failed. One small acquisition had been made prior to acquiring Richard's company, and since then, three more were added to the fold. Richard's company was the largest of the group, and its acquisition was financed almost entirely with debt. To close the deal, however, the Buyers insisted that Richard take back a promissory note for $1.5 million.

The various financial institutions involved in the deal insisted on having a first position in all of the assets of the acquired company, as well as personal guarantees of all the investors. This left nothing for Richard except a second position, which was all but worthless in such a highly leveraged deal. His lawyer did, however, get language into the Buy/Sell Agreement stating that a default against any of the bank loans would constitute default on Richard's note, and vice versa. Default on Richard's note would be a default against the banks. No one objected too strenuously because such a cross-default clause seemed to be meaningless.

His lawyer, who was an experienced acquisition contract lawyer, also advised Richard to take all of the common shares of the parent company PTLE as collateral to the note. The banks were not interested in these shares because the only assets PTLE held were the shares of the acquired companies and the banks had first position on their assets already.

Two years after the sale, Richard had collected only 11 months of interest and no principal payments. PTLE acquired additional companies during this period and was now one of the largest, privately owned companies in the industry. Their debt payment record, however, was abysmal. Richard and I attended the same church, and although I had never done any consulting work for him, because of our friendship, he kept me posted on many of his business dealings.

"What should I do, Larry?," he asked one Sunday morning. "I can't seem to get their attention with letters or phone calls. I've even asked my lawyer to get into the act but nothing seems to move them."

"How are they doing with your old company? Making any profits?" Richard looked gloomier by the minute. "From what I can tell, they're running it into the ground. Most of my management team has left, and I understand that PTLE has sold off some of the equipment to try to raise cash."

"Well, it doesn't sound like your second position on the company's assets is going to do you much good. If they continue to flounder, sooner or later the banks will step in. Of course, the last resort is always liquidation, but that's a drastic step and banks usually don't like to force that. Unfortunately, as long as they're behind in debt service to the banks, you aren't going to get much of anything." It then occurred to me that Richard also held the stock of PTLE as collateral. "How are the other acquisitions doing? Any better?"

"Of course, I have no figures, but rumors in the industry are that at least two of them are doing quite well, and if it wasn't for the cash drain from the highly leveraged one—my old company—PTLE would be profitable overall," he answered.

"Let me make a suggestion, Richard. Why don't you have your lawyer write the parent company, PTLE, a letter threatening to foreclose on the stock of PTLE, and that you then intend to exercise your voting rights as the majority shareholder at their annual meeting to elect a new Board, unless of course, they come up with the delinquent payments?"

"Terrific idea! I'll talk to my lawyer tomorrow."

Without getting into the legal ramifications of conflicts of interest, creditor's and debtor's rights, and bank interference, the lawyer did just that, and within 60 days, Richard had his back payments. I'm not a lawyer, so I don't know if what I suggested was even completely within the law, but it worked. Collateral of common stock in the acquiring company might be a valuable club in the event of default, and even though it might not always be effective, this type of collateral is usually available, and you should take advantage of it.

Another possibility is to try to get a lien on the Buyer's house or other personal assets the banks might not have. There might not be any, but if his spouse hasn't cosigned for personal guarantees, it's conceivable that his residence could still be unencumbered. Foreclosure laws on personal residences vary by state, however, so be sure to check on local conditions before pressing for this type of security.

If you must take back a note in order to close the deal, a first position in almost any assets you can get is preferable to being behind the banks. Even if there are cross-default clauses in the Agreement, a bank is under no obligation to help you collect, and many times, a bank's interests and yours will be diametrically opposed. Don't count on any help from them in collecting your notes!

LAWYERS ARE HUMAN?

This is probably a good place to take a breather and consider some of the human relations aspects of dealing with lawyers, as well as other business advisors. You are correct to assume that lawyers, consultants, accountants, and other business advisors are the same as employees subject to your control and direction. After all, you hired them and you pay their salaries—or fees if they prefer—and therefore, you have the right to terminate services if you are not satisfied with their performance. These professional advisors, because they are professionals, will try to perform their engagements as well as they can. The real trick, however, is to get that extra inch of help that can often make the difference between success and failure in any given deal. It's that extra effort that a lawyer expends, after hours, trying to figure out how to write a specific clause for your benefit, or the extra measure of concern by your consultant in qualifying a Buyer, that can make the difference between a good deal and a bad one. How do you obtain this level of caring and concern from your professional advisors? By giving it to them first.

Everyone wants to feel needed. Everyone wants to feel appreciated. And everyone has his own problems and concerns that rank higher on his list of priorities than your project. Professional advisors are no different than other people. A lawyer, consultant, or accountant might not admit to being influenced by personal cares and problems, but they are. At any given time, family troubles, health problems, or job security worries are far more important than writing the best Buy/Sell Agreement, finding the right Buyer for your business, or helping you with your tax planning.

The most misunderstood facet of doing business is the human element. I find that if I take the time and make the effort to listen to other people instead of becoming wrapped up in my own priorities, strange and wonderful things usually happen. Kindness and understanding go a long way in business activities, as they do in any walk of life. If you really care about other people, and if you make a genuine effort to help others with their own problems and concerns, you'll find greater success in your own endeavors, including selling your company.

Sam had been with the firm for six years and specialized in contract law of all types. A family man, he was constantly reminded of the debt he continued to owe for his college and law school education, even six years after graduation, although he tried not to allow his personal financial problems to influence his work in the firm. Sam's peers and superiors in the firm thought highly of him and continued to assign him more difficult cases. One day, we met for lunch and Sam looked worried. "What's the problem?," I asked.

"Well, I was just assigned a new case last week that involves selling a privately held company. The senior partner, who has been working with this client for years, wants me to draft a Buy/Sell Agreement. The deal is pretty tricky and the standard boiler plate just won't fit."

"So, that doesn't sound too difficult. You've drawn complicated Buy/Sell Agreements before. Why not this one?"

"The problem is," Sam started, his blood beginning to boil, "I really don't like the Seller very much. He's obnoxious and demanding and thinks that just because he's paying us a fee, he can treat us like dirt! I'm sure that's why I got the case. The senior partner can't put up with him. Consequently, I'm having a very difficult time being creative for this guy, and yet I know that's what it's going to take to get a satisfactory Agreement."

"You've been able to put your personal preferences aside before, why not this time?," I kept probing, not believing that he was telling me the whole story.

"This is different. The guy is a real jerk. He's pushy and arrogant." Then Sam began to really open up. "The real problem, Larry, is that my wife wants to send our oldest to boarding school in the fall, and I just don't have the money. Everything extra I make goes to pay the old college debts. I've reached the point where I can't bring any work home at night because my wife just nags and nags.

And I'm not about to put myself out for this client anyway—for the reasons I've already explained. I'll do my job, but that's all."

I decided to take the bull by the horns. "How about letting me come over to the house this weekend and have a cocktail with you and your wife. Maybe I can help in some way. Sometimes it helps just to talk."

That weekend, Sam and his wife had both reached the point where reason was no longer valid. I listened carefully to both of them all evening and it became apparent that I had bitten off more than I could chew. I could not come up with any suggestion for alleviating their problem.

As I prepared to leave, Sam cornered me by the front door. "Larry," he said, "I want to thank you so very much for caring enough about my problems to waste a whole evening with us. You might not believe it, but just having an outsider available to listen has cleared the air. I'm certain now, that we can work out our problems. Thanks again for caring."

A month later, I ran into the young attorney and asked him how his Buy/Sell Agreement came out. He told me that the next weekend after our get-together, he had brought the entire job home with him, and with his wife's support, finished the draft with several creative clauses in it. The client liked it so much he actually wrote a thank you letter to the senior partner.

Caring does make a difference. If everyone in business practiced caring just a little bit more, this world would be a much healthier and better place to live. Give it a try; it really works.

CHECKING ON TAXES

Even though you took a hard look at the tax laws when you began the selling process, and probably developed a good plan to minimize your tax bill, don't forget to review last–minute tax issues. More than likely, Congress has cooked up some variations since then that could have a major impact on your deal. Don't rely on someone else to watch out for tax changes for you. It just doesn't work that way.

"Something just dawned on me, Jim," Earl J., an entrepreneur in the process of selling his company, mentioned to his attorney. "Well, we've all been so preoccupied with finding a Buyer, negotiating the deal, and drafting the closing documents, that no one has actually taken the time to examine the tax consequences of the deal."

Jim was stunned. "I thought you turned that problem over to your consultant or accountant way back when you started this whole process. You know that's not my specialty."

"It's still not too late. I better get my tax accountant on the phone and have him take a quick look at the deal. If there's anything seriously wrong from a tax standpoint, we'll just have to reopen negotiations."

You might be ready to sign the papers to close the sale, but if you haven't already run a last–minute check on tax changes, you better get going. There's still time to back out of the deal or to reopen negotiations, but not much. You are really down to the wire now and its best to be sure this is what you want to do. The following brief checklist can be used as a last–minute reminder of potential changes to be cleared with your tax advisor:

Final Tax Reminders

Since the initial tax planning, have there been any changes in the tax laws affecting:

1. Tax rates—corporate and personal
2. Capital gains or ordinary income definitions or treatment
3. Selling price allocation rules
4. Installment sale provisions
5. Corporate, tax-free liquidations
6. Benefits of an S corporation
7. Employee benefit programs
8. Depreciation or investment tax credit recapture provisions
9. Settlement of personal loans to/from the corporation
10. Real estate transactions
11. Employment of spouse or children
12. Allocation of distributions to shareholders
13. Treatment of dividends
14. Reporting salary compensation
15. Use of autos or other personal/business assets
16. Treatment of non-competing covenants or goodwill
17. State or city tax laws
18. Property taxes, sales or use tax, or other taxes

It always surprises me how many Sellers, with their cadres of busy lawyers, accountants, and consultants, forget about checking tax changes. Even if you did a meticulous job of tax planning in the beginning, don't forget to take the time to review your plan again. By the time you finally get to drafting the Buy/Sell Agreement, several years might have passed and new tax laws might have been enacted. You can't afford to ignore last–minute tax implications now. Fortunately, it's not too late to make appropriate changes in the closing documents, and small changes in contract language could save you a bundle in tax payments.

THE FINAL DAY

The room is crowded and hot. The air conditioning doesn't seem to function too well, and your attorney acts as if doomsday is approaching. Bankers, lawyers, accountants, consultants, two secretaries, the Buyer, and yourself are all gathered together for the first time. Twenty people in a conference room designed for six! This is closing day. About this time you are probably having second thoughts about whether or not you *really* want to get out. All of the good times as well as the bad ones flash across your mind, including the stress and strain of making the acquisition or starting the business in the first place. The uncertainty about success and the nagging worries about where your next meal will come from if you fail. If you purchased the business, the unmitigated fear of the first day you entered the company's offices. The thrill of making your first command decision. The joy of watching your employees grow in stature and capability over the years. All of the little pleasures and some disappointments when your people succeeded or failed in their tasks. And last, but certainly not least, the substantial money you have earned over the years. Maybe not substantial in comparison to the fortunes made on Wall Street, but more than enough for your style of living.

And now you are about to give it all up. A sense of loss creeps in. Will the new owner take care of your business as well as you did? Can he raise your baby with the same loving care and compassion you had? Or will he abort and destroy what you have lovingly developed over the years? Fear begins to grip your heart. What if he screws up? What if he doesn't care?

Even if your baby does receive careful nurturing, what are you going to do now? The money you're making on the sale won't last forever. How are you going to support yourself and your family? Fear, panic, sadness, even mild depression, enter your mind. Do you really want to go through with this?

This is normal "entrepreneur's depression." It happens to every business owner when he leaves. It feels like a very important page in your life has ended and you don't know what to do from here on. There are ways to cope, however, and the next two chapters will give you some ideas.

You've made the decision to get out, however, and the time is at hand. Within a matter of hours you will turn the keys of your company over to a new owner, and you can begin your well-earned vacation. There are just a few more matters that need to be handled, however.

The Signing

Negotiations are over, language differences have been resolved, and the Buyer's financing is in place. He has brought an army of people to the close—lawyers, bankers, more lawyers, consultants, an accountant, more lawyers, even his wife. You and your lawyer have gone over the closing documents many times to ensure that nothing was missed. Although not entirely satisfied with some of the representations and warranties the Buyer has insisted on, they aren't too onerous, and your lawyer assures you they are all manageable. The papers are passed around the table for everyone's signature, and the process begins. The longer it takes, the more morose you become about leaving. But its too late now to back out, and the signing goes on.

Finally, it's time to make the money transfer. You call your banker to tell him to expect the wire, and then you wait. This is the hardest part because "it's never over til it's over." The money must change hands. Eventually, a call comes from the banker, the wire transfer was received. The deal is over, and you can begin your well earned–vacation.

PROTECTING YOUR ASSETS

It's surprising how many business owners ignore this most important aspect of personal financial planning. They assume they can't do anything about safeguarding their assets and promptly dismiss any further consideration. There are steps you can take, however. There are ways to prevent losing everything in a lawsuit. Your hard–earned cash, investments, and retirement funds can be protected from unscrupulous lawyers and inequitable courts. It's especially important to do so when you have sold your business because representations and warranties add a new dimension to potential massive lawsuits. If, in the future, the Buyer chooses to sue you for breach of contract (he has the right to do so—spurious or not), the time to protect your assets is now—tomorrow might be too late.

Although lawyers can conjure up any number of creative, and costly, schemes, I have found either or all of the following options provide adequate protection for most business owners. Unfortunately, each has its drawbacks.

Form a corporation to hold all of your assets. Your house, car, investments, company stock, bank accounts, and so on can be held in your own personal holding company. Your wife, children, lawyer, accountant, or anyone else you trust can hold the stock in this corporation. Of course, you must also then have side agreements governing these shareholder's actions. This corporate shield can be pierced by the plaintiff in a lawsuit, but it becomes increasingly costly and time consuming to do so. There are also federal tax considerations relating to personal holding companies that must be weighed.

Establish an Irrevocable Trust.   You can establish an irrevocable trust with your children or spouse as beneficiary to hold all of your assets. Your attorney or bank officer are usually good trustees. Similar tax considerations, and the ultimate ability to pierce the trust also exist for this strategy.

Transfer everything to your spouse.   This is probably the easiest and cleanest way to safeguard your assets. It is also the most difficult for the plaintiff to recover from. You can put all of your bank accounts, your share of the house, the car, even your company's stock in the hands of your spouse so that you have nothing of your own. The big risk, of course, is if you and your spouse break up. Then the results can be disastrous.

These are just three possibilities. I strongly urge you to consult a qualified attorney and work out a plan to protect all of your assets before it is too late. Personal lawsuits are escalating, and the odds are very high that as a business owner (or an ex-business owner) you will be sued for something during your lifetime. If you have no assets, you can't lose anything.

12

The Tough Way Out

Bankruptcy and Liquidation

"THE BANKRUPTCY CODE IS THE BANE OF THE ENTREPRENEUR," A FAMOUS bankruptcy lawyer once told me. I was not going to include this Chapter because the subjects of bankruptcy and liquidation connote failure and despair, and this is an upbeat book. To ignore these two increasingly common methods for getting out of a business, however, would be tantamount to exploring cures for cancer without mentioning the agonies of treatments that fail.

There are two ways to liquidate your business: through the Bankruptcy Court or voluntarily on your own. The latter will be examined toward the end of this chapter, but first let's cover bankruptcy.

Even though liquidation through a bankruptcy proceeding is not considered a very tasteful or moral way of getting out, there are times when there is no alternative. Conditions have become so severe and creditors so insistent, that the only solution is to declare bankruptcy under Chapter 7 of the Bankruptcy Code, let the creditors take the business, and walk away from it. Chapter 7 is certainly becoming more prominent, and in some circles even socially acceptable! With even a glimmer of hope for recovery, however, filing under Chapter 11, which allows the company to reorganize, keep going, and eventually negotiate a settlement with its creditors, is certainly preferable to a liquidation under Chapter 7.

Both types of bankruptcy filings are additional ways of getting out. Bankruptcy is such a drastic step and has such far reaching consequences, however, that it should be used only in the most dire circumstances. Bankruptcy is no fun. It's a demeaning experience for everyone involved—employees, customers, vendors, banks, and of course, you, the business owner. The decision to file bankruptcy should never be made lightly. In the long–run everyone will be hurt, even though it can offer you a means to get out. Let's take a look at how bankruptcy works.

WHAT IS BANKRUPTCY?

Right up front, I issue this disclaimer: I am not a bankruptcy lawyer nor am I a specialist in the intricacies of the Bankruptcy Code. My experience has come as a consultant, working with financially troubled clients, both before they have filed for protection under the Bankruptcy Code, and after they are in bankruptcy. If you are contemplating bankruptcy, don't rely solely on this book for guidance, but seek advice from a qualified bankruptcy lawyer.

For decades, the Federal Bankruptcy Code has helped assist financially troubled companies get back on their feet again by holding creditors at bay—commonly referred to as a Chapter 11 filing—or to effect an orderly liquidation of a company's assets and an equitable distribution of the proceeds to the creditors under Chapter 7. There are other types of bankruptcy filings designed to serve specific purposes but, because we are concerned only with methods of getting out of a business, we'll deal primarily with Chapter 11 and briefly with Chapter 7 filings. In fact, let's dispose of Chapter 7 right away.

Chapter 7 Filing

A filing under Chapter 7 of the Bankruptcy Code means that you have really given up, with no hope for the continuation of your company. Usually, a Chapter 7 is initiated by creditors of the business, either secured bank creditors or unsecured trade creditors. Under unusual circumstances, however, the business owner can also initiate such a filing. The results are the same whoever brings the action.

The Bankruptcy Court immediately appoints a trustee to administer the liquidation of assets and the distribution of the proceeds. This trustee has complete jurisdiction over all aspects of the company from administering it's business up to the liquidation to the liquidation auction itself, including the distribution of proceeds. You, as the owner of the company, are no longer in charge. You cannot make any decision regarding the company without the approval of this trustee. In effect, by filing under Chapter 7, you have said to the world, "I can't run the business anymore. I give up and turn the business over to the courts." Don't expect any sympathy from anyone. You will be regarded as a leper by your closest friends and associates. You're a failure. Does this sound grim? It's worse than it sounds, so don't make the decision lightly.

Most companies filing under Chapter 7 are insolvent (total liabilities exceed total assets) and illiquid (current liabilities exceed current assets) with no foreseeable way to pay off debts. From a creditor's perspective, it's better to get something than nothing, and through a liquidation, he hopes to get at least part of what is due him, although it is seldom dollar for dollar. Because of the lasting stigma of failure attached to a Chapter 7 filing, it's hard to imagine why any businessman would voluntarily choose this as a method of getting out. If the condition of the company is so bad that there is no possibility of disposing of it as a going concern, and closing the doors is the only way out, then it is far better to voluntarily liquidate (as discussed later in this chapter) rather than file bankruptcy under Chapter 7. A voluntary liquidation is always preferable to Chapter 7. The possibility does exist, however, that creditors might force a Chapter 7 filing right up to the day of the auction, so if you are planning to liquidate voluntarily, don't broadcast your decision.

Chapter 11 Filing

If you must file under the Bankruptcy Code as the last means of getting out, then Chapter 11 is the way to do it. This is a voluntary filing and, under the protection of the court, allows you to either straighten out the affairs of the company or sell your ownership. Of course, the sale must be court–approved, and you can't expect to make any money on the deal, but at least you can get out. The remainder of this chapter will be devoted to explaining the how, what, and when of getting out under a Chapter 11.

WHY CHOOSE BANKRUPTCY?

I say it again: taking a company into bankruptcy is not fun. It creates potentially severe personal financial risk for officers and directors of the company, has devastating psychological ramifications, and can tarnish your reputation for further activities in the business world. Sometimes, however, it's the only way out. The following questionnaire will help you determine if bankruptcy is for you:

Questionnaire for Declaring Bankruptcy Under Chapter 11

1. Is my business incorporated? (If not, forget about bankruptcy and proceed directly to the section on liquidation.)
2. Have I tried all other feasible means for selling my company including the open market, partnerships, hiring a successor, merger, and sale to employees?
3. If I do take the company into bankruptcy, is there a Buyer standing by to take over my ownership? (If not, then don't start.)
4. Is the court likely to approve such a take over?
5. Are the banks likely to approve of such a take over?
6. Do I have a legally sound plan in place to protect my personal assets?

7. Are the company's liabilities equal to, or more than its assets?

8. Are the vendors, secured creditors, government, or the IRS threatening to force the company into Chapter 7 or to close the doors?

9. Have I done sufficient research and consulted with a qualified bankruptcy attorney so that I fully recognize all the implications of filing a Chapter 11?

10. Have I firmly decided that I must get out of the business at this time and there is no other way?

Because of the complexities, not only of the Bankruptcy Code itself, but also in the implementation of a filing, the clearest way to understand how to do it is probably by looking at the experience of someone who already took the plunge. The following true case illustrates how to use the Bankruptcy Code to get out of your business, albeit not at a profit.

Two Brothers Take the Plunge

David and his brother Jimmy came to me for assistance in structuring a spin off company they wanted to form. David was a salesman with a flair for selling anything. Jimmy had a background in design engineering and could usually be found bent over his drafting table creating a new design for some machine. The brothers had inherited a small machine shop from their father. They ran it with modest success for three years but were now eager to branch out with a new product designed by Jimmy: a machine to automatically cap bottles faster and with greater precision than any competitive model.

We formed a new corporation and set up the equipment to produce the new machine in a corner of their plant. I helped them to obtain additional bank financing for working capital to get the business going, helped them recruit appropriate management personnel, and implemented a computer system. They seemed to be off and running and I didn't hear from them for several years.

One day, Jimmy called and was very distraught. "We need your help again, Larry. RapidCap is in deep financial trouble and we want to get out of that business. Our dilemma is that we now have 10 employees in RapidCap who had been with our father for years, and we feel obligated to try to keep them employed. Also, we have several machines in the field under warranty, and if we just close the doors, our lawyer has advised us that our other business might be held liable for performance under these warranties. Can you help?"

After an investigation, I learned that the machine shop business was also in financial difficulty, and their friendly banker was ready to call their loans. The question was, could I find a Buyer quick enough to stave off the bank and other creditors?

None of the more conventional getting out alternatives seemed viable. Neither of the brothers had turned out to be a very good manager nor did they have any real interest in running a company. David wanted to sail his boat and Jimmy wanted to invent. Both had sufficient funds invested outside of the business to do whatever they wanted, so I recommended that they get out of both businesses and go do something with their lives they would enjoy. Both David and Jimmy were enamored with the idea, so now all I had to do was find a Buyer for two distressed companies instead of one!

I combed my files, went through the consulting network, ran ads in the Journal and did everything I could think of to find a Buyer, but to no avail. The balance sheets of the two companies killed any interest by viable Buyers. Both were solvent, but both were also very illiquid. Trade liabilities and short–term bank debt far exceeded receivables and inventory, and of course, there was no cash. I was at wits end when David came up with an idea. "I've been talking to Bill, our director of operations. He and a couple of other guys would like to buy the company if there was some way to reduce the liabilities. I spoke to our lawyer and he suggested making a deal with Bill where we would put the companies into Chapter 11, Bill and his friends would buy the stock for $1, and then negotiate a long–term settlement with the creditors at 10 cents on the dollar. Jimmy and I don't need the money anyway, and if we could get out from under this mess, free and clear, we'd be happy. Now, what do you think of that idea?"

I told him I didn't think much of it, but the decision was up to them. I asked them to come to my office and allow me to explain, in detail, what it really meant to file bankruptcy.

WHAT ARE THE RISKS?

There are three major personal risks when you file under Chapter 11:

1. Personal guarantees against bank loans and leases.
2. Damage to personal reputation.
3. Lawsuits against yourself after you are out.

Personal Guarantees

If you have personal guarantees outstanding against bank loans, leases, pension trusts, and so on, they will not go away simply because the company files bankruptcy. In fact, most loan agreements and long–term leases specifically state that in the event of a corporate bankruptcy, the obligation is automatically in default and subject to call. This means that a bank or lessor might come against you on your guarantee, independent of the company, and the company's bankruptcy protection will not apply to you.

If you have any guarantees outstanding, then the Buy/Sell Agreement you negotiate with the Buyer should deal with the problem. There are a number of ways of doing this, which your lawyer can help you with, but whatever language is used, be certain that it removes, unequivocally, any further liability on your part for company debts or performance. The really difficult part in accomplishing this, however, is that even if the Buyer agrees to hold you harmless forever, if the bank or lessor doesn't agree, you're out of luck. You must negotiate separate agreements with any bank or lessor holding your Personal Guarantee and such third parties are very reluctant to let you off the hook.

Damage to Personal Reputation

Damage to your reputation is not to be scoffed at! Most entrepreneurs, having once tasted the independence and power of owning a business, find it difficult to retire completely and nearly impossible to become an employee again. Except in cases of poor health, having disposed of his business, eventually an entrepreneur will probably be tempted to look for another business to start or to acquire. As an ex-pilot can't stay away from planes and an ex-sailor can't forget boats, so the ex-entrepreneur will have a hard time staying away from new business challenges.

Once you take a company into bankruptcy, however, regardless of the reason, bankers will be afraid to ever loan you money again, regardless of the collateral. It's unfortunate that bankers regard bankruptcy with so much distaste and scorn. It's a sad commentary on our banking system when a bank will not give a businessman who has taken a company into bankruptcy a second chance—even when secured creditors lose nothing.

A client of mine learned how unreasonable that friendly banker can be. Bob owned a steel–wire drawing manufacturer and had experienced several years of labor unrest. The union leadership was constantly antagonistic and, over the past decade, had called two strikes, one six weeks long, that had a profound effect on the company. Contract negotiations were currently under way and Bob wasn't making any progress. He finally told the union rep that if they couldn't reach an agreement in two weeks, he would take the company into Chapter 11 to either force a settlement or get the court to throw out the contract completely, and if that didn't solve the problem, he would liquidate the company. The union rep scoffed at him, not believing he would do it, and two weeks passed with no progress. Bob filed under Chapter 11 as promised, and the contract was broken.

It seemed as if Bob had won the war. Two years later, however, after the Court approved his reorganization plan and the company came out of bankruptcy, Bob needed an additional working capital loan. He approached the same bank he had dealt with for years, which, by the way, didn't lose a penny during the bankruptcy proceedings, and was turned down flat. In fact, he was told that the bank would not even give him a good reference should he choose to go elsewhere!

The bankruptcy stigma in the financial community is deadly, and once you have lead a company into such a filing, even though it had nothing to do with insolvency, your personal reputation as a reliable debtor is blackened. Right or wrong, financial institutions will look askance at such a tarnished reputation.

LAWSUITS AGAINST THE EX-OWNER

The biggest risk of all, is losing your personal assets—bank accounts, investments, car, even your house. If you file Chapter 11 and continue to own and manage the company under the supervision of a trustee, of course, you will at least retain some measure of control. By selling your interest in the business, however, you lose this control, and the new owner will be in a strong position to bring suit against you for taking what are called preference payments.

The Bankruptcy Code is a world of its own. A completely separate set of laws come into play under which a business or an individual must perform. State and federal laws that we all live by from day–to–day are not applicable. New laws, mysterious to all except the bankruptcy lawyers, concerning contracts, wages, debtor/creditor relations, individual rights, and so on, go into effect. No one has the right to bring suit against a company once it is in bankruptcy, but the company has a right to sue others! Chapter 11 laws exist to protect the company, pure and simple. The individual has no rights, the unsecured creditors have few rights, and the secured bank creditors have substantial rights. The court places the company's interests first, secured creditors second, and leaves the rest to fend for themselves, including the owner.

This is probably a good place to explain the pecking order of payments under the Bankruptcy Code. When settlements are negotiated, the following creditors get paid in the following order. If the money runs out part way down the list, then the remaining parties get nothing.

1. Administrative costs of operating the company while in Chapter 11 or 7. These are the normal, current costs of operating the business, such as wages, purchases, utilities, taxes, and rent, as determined by the court.
2. Secured creditors such as banks and lessors.
3. Employee wages unpaid prior to filing.
4. Federal and state income taxes.
5. Unsecured creditors, such as vendors.
6. Preferred shareholders.
7. Common shareholders.

But getting back to the potential lawsuit against you as the previous owner of the business, under the Bankruptcy Code, preference payments, are any payments made by the company to an insider, such as an officer or a director, within 12 months preceding the filing. Before the company can get approval from the court for its reorganization plan, it must negotiate a settlement with everybody in the above pecking order except common shareholders. Usually, the settlements will be substantially less than the debts owed, such as 10 cents on the dollar, and will be paid off over a number of years. Whatever the company can recover from you in preference payments can be used to pay these settlements. So the company is practically obligated to bring suit to try to collect whatever it can from you.

Without getting into a lot of detailed bankruptcy law, and in very general terms, any payments of salary, bonus, profit sharing, fringe benefits, or travel and entertainment expenses paid to you, an insider, by the company in the 12 months preceding the bankruptcy filing, are subject to reclaim by the company, assuming the company was insolvent during this period. This is true whether you continue to own and manage the company while in Chapter 11, or you sell your stock holdings and get out. The court will decide whether you win or lose. By the way, this is not a jury case. The judge alone decides your fate, and be advised, he is always on the side of the bankrupt company.

Even if by some miracle you win, it will still cost you substantial legal fees. I should add here, that the law is strongly biased in favor of the company, and you will probably lose the case. As I mentioned earlier, bankruptcy laws protect the company, not the individual, who is presumed guilty until proven innocent. Now isn't that a great legal system for a democracy!

What Happens When You Lose?

Let's assume for a moment, that in spite of all the risks, you elect to get out of your business via the Chapter 11 route. The court approves your transfer of ownership for $1, and you walk away from your company forever. But not really forever, because within a year, your old company, which you had nurtured and struggled with all those years, turns around and sues you for $250,000 of preference payments.

You hire a qualified bankruptcy lawyer. Unfortunately, even the worst are very expensive, and the good ones charge outrageous fees. You build your defense and a year after the case began, it finally comes to trial. Remember, this is not a jury trial, and remember, you are guilty going in, unless you can prove your innocence. The Bankruptcy Court judge will assume you are guilty before he even hears your side of the case. You took the money, therefore under bankruptcy law, you are guilty. These laws do nothing to protect the rights of the individual. Your lawyer pleads your case, but obviously loses and the judge tells you to pay the company $250,000! Now What do you do? Well, you have four choices:

1. Pay the amount ordered.
2. Negotiate a deferred payment schedule with the company (with the judge's approval).
3. Appeal the ruling and spend more legal fees.
4. File personal bankruptcy under Chapter 7 or Chapter 13 of the Code.

Clearly, none of these solutions are very palatable. If you pay up, it means that you worked the entire last year in your company for nothing. You will also have legal fees for your defense, probably running between $25,000 and $50,000. There are not many small businessmen who have $300,000 available, especially if they have sunk their life savings into the company, which is now all gone. At this point, many elect personal bankruptcy, simply because there is no other choice. If they don't have the money, they can't pay the judgment.

The Final Straw

The subject of personal bankruptcy is another one of those subjects people don't like to talk about. If there is a failure stigma attached to bringing a company into bankruptcy, imagine what it must be like when you file personal bankruptcy! Your friends shun you, your wife won't talk to you, your credit rating is gone, so you can't borrow money, you can't get a decent job, you have no cash, and you certainly cannot acquire another company. It's a pretty dismal picture, but individuals declare personal bankruptcy with increasing frequency.

In 1988, nearly 600,000 people filed for personal bankruptcy, up from under 200,000 cases in 1984. That's an increase of over 200 percent in four years! Filing under Chapter 13, which allows you to reorganize your personal finances and pay off your debts well into the future much the same way as Chapter 11 does for corporations, is generally more popular than Chapter 7. If your situation becomes so severe that you need to seriously consider personal bankruptcy, a good starting point for information is your local consumer credit counseling service.

No one can foretell the future, so while you still own your company and have some flexibility, develop a plan to protect your personal assets, just in case you need to use the bankruptcy laws. Most entrepreneurs believe they are invincible. The overriding confidence that got them where there are is often the cause of a disastrous personal financial loss further down the road. Why lawyers don't put the protection of personal assets high on their list of priorities in counseling entrepreneurs is a mystery. They certainly should if they are really serious about serving the client.

There are many ways of protecting personal assets as explored in the previous chapter, and the methods employed will vary with each individual. Estate planning, IRS tax laws, and family considerations all play a major role in determining how to structure such a program. But whatever methods are used, it cannot happen overnight. It might take several years to rearrange your personal assets in such a way that they are thoroughly protected. State laws also come into play, because each state has its own set of laws governing rights of spouse and children, transference of property, estate taxes, survivor rights, and debtor/creditor rights. Whereas, corporate bankruptcy laws fall under the jurisdiction of the federal court system, personal bankruptcy is governed by state laws. That is, by the state in which you have your residence.

In some states, joint ownership of assets such as a residence or bank accounts is sufficient protection, but consult an attorney for the final word. A qualified lawyer well versed in creditor/debtor rights can give you a broad spectrum of ways to protect your assets far beyond the scope of this book.

Regardless of the method you choose, and even if you cannot visualize the need for it, begin immediately to develop and implement a legally sound program to protect your personal assets.

HOW CHAPTER 11 AFFECTS PEOPLE

So far, we've concentrated on describing what the law is, how it works, and some of the pitfalls to avoid, if possible. These are all matters directly affecting you, the business owner. But what about the effects on your employees, customers, and vendors?

Employees

By getting out through Chapter 11, you will hurt your employees more than anyone else. Assuming you have been a reasonably good owner/manager and practiced the principles of merciful management, your employees should now have the same caring and compassion for you that you had for them over the years. Obviously, you would never use Chapter 11 if your company wasn't in poor financial shape. If everything was rosy, you'd sell the company, bring in a partner, or use one of the several other methods at your disposal to get out. When in a financial crisis, however, the options narrow. The fact that you choose to use Chapter 11 rather than liquidation, even though your personal loss will be far greater, should count for a lot with your employees. The company might be in trouble, but at least they still have their jobs, which they wouldn't if you liquidated.

This is the time when employees who have been treated kindly over the years normally begin to pull together to help you. They know this is the last ditch effort to save their jobs and that you'll need all of the help they can muster. Yes, you'll be gone soon, but until then, they can be very helpful in getting you through the first 45 days of the bankruptcy. This, by the way, is the toughest period of the entire bankruptcy proceeding, and you should be there to manage the company during this difficult stage. The shift in command from you to a court–appointed trustee will be bad enough, but the myriad of forms to fill out for the court and regulations to follow for the banks should encourage you to be fair with the new owner and take responsibility for this effort.

Unfortunately, even though your employees should be pulling for you and doing their utmost to keep the company afloat, the mere fact that you put them in this position will cause a substantial amount of pain. Some will be mad, some will just be hurt. But there is really very little you can do now to ease the agony. The faster you get out after the first 45 days and let the new owner get on with the reorganization plan, the better for everyone.

Customers

Customers are a real problem! No matter how good your relationships might be with customer purchasing agents or CEOs, once they hear the word bankruptcy, they will probably panic. A customer's biggest concern, obviously, is that his supply line will be interrupted. Unless you happen to be in an industry with little customer loyalty or non-differentiation in products, your customers depend on you as a principal source of supply.

Because the term bankrupt automatically implies that you can't pay your bills, and therefore, might be unable to purchase required materials, many customers will have no choice but to either go elsewhere for their supplies or at least use a second source for part of their needs. It's crucial to get the message out to the field as soon as possible that you filed Chapter 11 to transfer ownership, you were not forced by creditors. It will be hard to sell this concept, but you must try. Those people with whom you have been honest with over the years will believe you and will probably help all they can, but be prepared to lose some business—it's inevitable.

Vendors

About the same reaction you received from customers will be forthcoming from vendors—only in spades! Once a Chapter 11 is filed, these unsecured creditors automatically know they will receive less than full payment on their old bills. Some will panic; some will threaten; but most will stay with the company and continue to supply its purchasing needs, at least for a while—albeit, probably with C.O.D. terms.

Vendors will eventually form a Creditor's Committee to negotiate a settlement with the company, so they are usually not quite as hesitant as customers to continue to do business with the bankrupt company. They feel they have some measure of control and as long as they can get C.O.D. terms, or at the worst thirty day terms, most vendors will continue to support you. They may not be happy, but they will continue to be your suppliers.

Back to the Intransigent Brothers

David and Jimmy listened patiently to this lengthy description of what bankruptcy was all about. They asked some questions along the way and I had the feeling they understood nearly all of what I explained.

"Well, that's it boys. Don't you agree that bankruptcy is a tough way to get out? Everybody loses in a bankruptcy except the lawyers. You don't really want to go ahead with this do you?"

David piped up, "Yeah, I can see it's a pretty drastic step. Nevertheless, it is a way to get out. We could probably do it very quickly with as small a business as we have. We're not exactly a Johns Manville you know."

"But David, look at it this way. Even if it can be done quickly, which I doubt, and even if Bill and his group will pick it up and keep the company going, there's still the problem of negotiating with the unsecured creditors and dealing with the bank. Are you sure you want to go through all of that?" I tried my best to talk David out of it but wasn't getting very far.

"Bill and I know most of the vendors on a first name basis. We'll play a few rounds of golf or go sailing with them, and they'll come around. That doesn't bother me", replied David.

Jimmy had been quiet all this time soaking up my explanations and listening to the two of us go at it. "I have something to say on the subject, gentlemen. I think the biggest problem of all is the potential of a lawsuit for preferential payments. We've taken a fair amount of money out of the company in the past year and I don't want to start a legal battle with Bill and the other guys. As far as I'm concerned, if we can't solve that problem, I don't want to get out. We'll just hang on and wait."

"Well, to be honest with you," I added, "there are contractual clauses you could put in the Buy/Sell Agreement to prevent a suit being brought by the company. It sounds as if your relationship with Bill and the guys could make that possible. There might even be a backhanded way of discouraging a suit by the unsecured creditors. You could write the Buy/Sell Agreement in such a manner that Bill and the other new owners would warrant that if any suits were brought against you for preference payments, the new shareholders would personally hold you harmless from any liability. It won't help you much in court, but if the vendors want to maintain good relations with the new owners, it might be enough to preclude a lawsuit. On the other hand, I certainly won't guarantee this will work. The whole bankruptcy thing is still very, very risky."

Eventually, after considerable discussions with their lawyer, the brothers decided to go ahead and file Chapter 11, providing they could first negotiate the proper Buy/Sell Agreement with the MBO group.

Chapter 11 was not conceived as a method to sell a business. It was designed to offer protection from creditors until the company can become healthy again. Yet, with increasing frequency, small and large businesses alike are using the Bankruptcy Code to their own advantage for reasons completely independent of insolvency. Getting out of a business is one such use.

But, it is expensive, risky, and time consuming. It is truly the **tough way out** and should only be considered if all other means fail.

THE PSYCHOLOGY OF FAILURE

Nobody willingly fails, whether it is in business or in any other walk of life. In a capitalist society such as ours, we are taught that winning is good and failing is bad. In our free enterprise system, a corporate bankruptcy is considered about as bad as you can get. It is regarded as a failure by management and, for a privately owned business, the owner as well. For an entrepreneur who invests a good portion of his savings and his life in striving to succeed in his own company and then files bankruptcy, for any reason, the impact on his emotions and dreams can be shattering. He feels sick, disillusioned, and emotionally drained. What's worse, he usually believes that he has let his employees and business friends down. Where they had trusted him and believed in his ability to continue functioning in the business environment, they now consider him a failure, a traitor. Or so it seems. Many business owners actually suffer nervous breakdowns as a result of filing a corporate bankruptcy.

The Case of the Failing Foundry

What can be done to alleviate such personal pain and anguish? The trauma of failure can probably never be eliminated completely, but there are certainly things you can do to reduce the upheavals as much as possible. The following story illustrates how one business owner recognized what was coming and the steps he took to reduce his own feelings of guilt and remorse.

John M. inherited an iron foundry in the Midwest from his father many years earlier when gray iron foundries were one of the mainstays of American industry. For many years, the company prospered. John was a reasonably good manager of people. He made a sincere effort to help his employees when they had problems and knew most of their families. A union represented hourly employees, but labor relations had been peaceful for years.

As the gray–iron foundry industry began to feel the impact of foreign imports and changes in metallurgical technology, John's business suffered along with the rest of the industry. He tried to hold on as long as possible but eventually cash flow became so bad he could not pay his bills. Customers kept demanding reduced prices and the cost of raw materials continued increasing. Creditors and banks began to close in. Faced with either liquidating, and throwing all of his employees out of work, or filing for protection under Chapter 11 while he tried to find a new owner with strong financial resources, John chose the latter.

The decision was not precipitous, however. John could see the end coming and began planning for it well in advance. He knew that if he could do four things before being forced to file Chapter 11, his conscience would be as clear as possible and the emotional impact on he and his family would be as minimal as possible:

1. Provide new jobs for his employees in the event he was forced to file a Chapter 7.
2. Take care of all his personal obligations, including all outstanding personal debts.
3. Plan a new career for himself so that he would have a source of income after filing.
4. Alert his family and personal friends well in advance of filing what was coming and explain the reasons for it.

John allowed himself a year to get these matters in order before filing Chapter 11. He discreetly contacted several friends in the industry about possible job openings next year and was able to line up jobs for over three-fourths of his employees—if they needed them. He then began setting aside a personal reserve fund to help pay for their relocation costs. Over the next twelve months, he began explaining the demise of the gray–iron foundry business to his friends and family and kept them all alert of the progress of the industry, and to a lesser extent, of his company. He also paid as much as he could on his mortgage, paid off his car loan, and liquidated all of his charge cards.

The last step was for John to decide what he would do with his life after the filing, assuming he could find the right Buyer for his company. Choosing a second career at 53 was the biggest challenge, but he had always wanted to study law and after inheriting the business, never had a chance to do so. John contacted some law schools in the area and enrolled in night school classes for the fall semester.

John had done everything he could think of to minimize his own emotional upheaval. Now he just had to remain cool and try to do the best he could for the creditors. When John finally filed Chapter 11 13 months after he began his planning, he felt bad about failing, but was not decimated. His preparations had paid off, and John was able to concentrate his full efforts toward solving the company's cash problems and finding a Buyer. There was no way he could avoid the sick feeling of failure, but at least he knew he had done his best to fulfill his obligations to other people. This knowledge kept him going for two years in the Bankruptcy Court, until a large conglomerate finally stepped forward and took over the company. He couldn't avoid all of the hurt to his employees or himself, but his planning for the worst enabled him to come through the trauma in one piece mentally and emotionally and eventually go on to earn his law degree.

LIQUIDATION—AN ALTERNATIVE TO BANKRUPTCY

When I speak of liquidation of business assets as a viable alternative for getting out, I do not mean to suggest this in the same manner as selling on the open market, bringing in a partner, merging, or issuing public stock. Liquidation is a very serious matter that can later have dire consequences. The implications of a voluntary liquidation on your future opportunities are slightly different than with a bankruptcy, however. In most cases, with a reasonable explanation, banks might be willing to forgive an entrepreneur for liquidating his company, assuming any bank debt was paid in full. But not always. It is a risk you will have to take and hope you can find an understanding banker in the future. This is not easy, however, as can be seen in the following case. Some bankers view voluntary liquidation with as much disdain as bankruptcy.

Vern owned a midsized manufacturing company that produced electrical wire for the construction industry and cable for water and oil drilling industries. Historically, sales and profits fluctuated with the price of copper. The copper wire business is, at best, risky, and at worst, can be disastrous because the product pricing is almost exclusively controlled by the economic cycle of the copper industry. As copper prices increase, prices of copper wire go up even faster. As copper prices decrease, wire prices decrease below the cost of the raw material.

Vern rode this copper curve for a number of years and had never been able to keep the business consistently profitable. The water and oil cable products did better, however, and during the oil industry boom of the seventies, Vern did very well with these product lines. Although when the bottom fell out of the oil drilling market, even cable products began to lose money.

First, he tried to sell the company. When that failed, he tried to interest several larger companies in a merger, but there were no takers. Finally, desperate for cash, he realized he better get out before the wolves forced him into bankruptcy. The company owned a sizable amount of machinery and equipment and some very old manufacturing buildings, so Vern hit upon the idea of an auction to liquidate all of the business assets and to try to raise enough cash to settle his debts. Of course, this meant the end of the business, but it couldn't be helped.

Actually, he held two auctions, one for the inventory (which went for approximately 20 cents on the dollar) and one for the hard assets. Net proceeds were just enough to pay off the banks and the other creditors. Vern was left with nothing.

After a year or so, Vern began to recover emotionally and started looking for another acquisition. He found a viable target, but because most of his funds were lost in the wire and cable business, he needed to borrow a significant amount of acquisition debt. But this time he could find no takers. His reputation as a loser kept getting in the way. The response was unanimous from every financing source he contacted. If he liquidated one business, what comfort would a bank have that he wouldn't do it again, perhaps not raising enough to pay off his debt this time? The fact that the industry had killed the business, not his management skills, had no bearing on the matter. The typical blind side approach from financial institutions prevailed, and Vern never did make another acquisition. He later felt he had gained nothing by trying to maximize the return to the creditors through a liquidation. He might just as well have filed a Chapter 11 bankruptcy and let the creditors suffer. At least he could have kept his employees working a while longer.

Although Vern was very bitter toward the banking community for many years, he did survive. After much soul searching, he finally decided to change his career direction, went back to school and eventually ended up with an international social services organization to help people in underdeveloped countries. The stigma of failing in the business world did not carry over to his new career. In the end, it became clear that by liquidating when he did, his reputation suffered far less than it would have with the destructive chaos of bankruptcy. If you must liquidate, do it voluntarily. Don't wait for your creditors to force a Chapter 7.

There is one more advantage of a liquidation over a bankruptcy filing. If you liquidate your company, there is virtually no way for a creditor to come after you personally unless you have personally guaranteed the debt. In a bankruptcy, it is almost certain that the new owners will sue you in Bankruptcy Court, and we've already seen what that can mean. Except in very rare instances, by liquidating and using the proceeds to pay creditors, even at a substantial discount, you are safe from further legal action. Check with your attorney, however, because creditor/debtor rights is a tricky part of the law and not a game for amateurs!

How do you actually go about liquidating a business? Of course, any business owner knows how to sell his assets to competitors, customers, or even business acquaintances. Most liquidations, however, are done through an auction. Because an auction is something a person will only do once in a life time, you probably are not familiar with the mechanics. Let's take a look at how to arrange a liquidation auction. An auction requires three things:

1. A drop–dead value on each of the business assets.
2. An auctioneer to perform the auction.
3. A announced date and place to hold the auction.

There are many reputable auctioneers around the country, but even more disreputable ones. Your best bet for locating the right auctioneer is to contact one of the asset–based lenders in your area and find out which firm they use. Asset–based lenders are major customers of auctioneers because of business foreclosures and forced liquidations, so they usually have the most experience. Two reputable auction firms you might consider are Plant & Machinery, Inc., Houston, Texas (for machinery and equipment) and Traimon Company, Philadelphia, Pennsylvania (for real estate). Most auctioneers charge fees of 7 to 12 percent of the actual proceeds of the auction, plus out-of-pocket expenses, and deduct these charges from the proceeds before delivering the final check.

Out-of-pocket expenses can be substantial, and as part of the negotiating process with the auctioneer, be certain to cap the travel and advertising expenses. These are the two highest expenses and, if not controlled by you, can easily be more than the auctioneer's commission.

Once an auctioneer has been selected and a fee and expense contract executed, he will give you his best estimate of what each of the business assets will bring. The auctioneer will base this estimate on current market conditions for the type of assets you have for sale. It will bear no relationship to any appraisal you have had for financing or insurance purposes. Ninety–nine out of one hundred cases, the auction value will be substantially less than any previous appraisal.

There are many ways to conduct an auction. The auctioneer might buy all of the assets from you directly (at distressed prices, of course) and then turn around and sell them himself. Or, you might tell him the minimum price you will accept on certain assets and if the auction doesn't bring this amount, the asset isn't sold. You can also let the auctioneer make arrangements with his contacts to artificially bid up the prices of certain assets and, if there are no takers, his crone will negotiate a separate price after the auction. (Not strictly legal, but frequently employed.) Whatever arrangements you make, be sure to get the agreement in writing. If it can't be reduced to contractual language, it should not be agreed to.

Normally, an equipment auction can take place within 90 days of the execution of an auction contract. The auctioneer will want to visit your facility, supervise the clean up of the buildings and the equipment, organize the equipment to show it in its best light, arrange for any cranes or other heavy equipment to be rented, and in general, take over the entire disposition of your assets.

The auctioneer collects all of the proceeds and, after deducting his commission and expenses, gives you a written accounting and the net proceeds check. You are then free of your business—forever.

I should mention in conclusion that there are some states where Bulk Sales laws covering the disposal of business assets at an auction are very sticky. Creditors must be notified, public announcements must be made, and a waiting period before holding the auction must be observed. California is especially difficult, and you should work closely with your legal counsel prior to, during, and after the auction process.

Don't view the liquidation alternative lightly. Although less severe than filing under the Bankruptcy Code, it is truly a step of last resort, and should never be used unless there is no other possible way of selling your business.

13

The Perplexed Professional

Selling a Professional Practice

DR. ROBERT CLOSEEN WAS OF THE OLD SCHOOL. NEAR 70, HE HAD BUILT HIS family practice from scratch after the war and had seen it grow far beyond his capacity to provide the type of personal care to all his patients he would have liked. As the neighborhood began maturing and more people moved out than in however, the practice began to shrink to a manageable level. For several years, he had been thinking about getting out but none of his medical friends seemed to have any concrete suggestions about how to do it. His main concern was to be sure his now predominantly elderly patients would be cared for. Robert knew he must do something. Recent chest pains produced growing concern that the pressure of daily crises was beginning to take its toll.

One Saturday, while having my annual checkup, Dr. Closeen brought up the subject of selling his practice and asked if I had any ideas. My initial reaction was to recommend bringing in a young partner and in about two or three years selling to him. This idea fell on deaf ears. Robert was afraid his health wouldn't last three years. My next suggestion of selling to the local clinic brought a tirade of language I can't repeat here. The good doctor believed clinics were the modern equivalent of socialized medicine and he would have none of it. Finally, I suggested the possibility of selling to a doctor currently employed by a hospital without a practice of his own. This hit his hot button. Working with Robert over the next six months, we closed a deal netting the good doctor half a million dollars and the immediate freedom to move on to a less strenuous life–style.

Selling a professional practice, whether in medicine, law, dentistry, accounting, consulting, or any other personal–service profession can be difficult, time consuming, and confusing. Although the same process must be employed as in selling a business, because of the extreme variety of types and structures of professional practices, the emphasis on specific steps varies. The most obvious—setting a selling price—was discussed in Chapter 4, but there are other dissimilarities.

For example, just locating a Buyer with appropriate qualifications can be a major hurdle. Then there's the problem of encouraging clients or patients to continue with the new owner. Financing the deal, legal contracts, and a myriad of other business details often worry the uninitiated. Psychological trauma upon leaving also hits professionals. Friendships, loyalties, and confidences built up over the years are not easily cast aside for pure business reasons. They must be dealt with, however, just as directly as if it were a manufacturing, distribution, or retail business.

This chapter presents proven guidelines to assist the professional in these troublesome areas. It highlights those differences in the selling process that are unique to the professions. Having sold three of my own accounting practices, I empathize with anyone beginning this trip without some guidelines to follow, both for the sale and in coping with the trauma.

Because of the wide array of professional practices, I should define the word "profession" as its used here. Selling techniques included in this chapter address practices in the purely personal services arena—law, medicine, accounting, management consulting, dentistry, financial planning, investment advisory services, psychology, psychiatry, counseling, and so on. Selling techniques for other vocations commonly called professions such as insurance brokerages, real estate agencies, advertising agencies, and employment bureaus, are the same as those used in the rest of the book.

In addition, a lawyer, doctor, accountant, or dentist who is a partner with several other practitioners in a large firm or clinic will generally find readily established procedures within the partnership documents for selling his share back to the partnership. Therefore, this type of practice will also be excluded even though it matches our definition of profession.

This chapter deals with techniques for selling businesses defined as traditional professional practices. These professional owners offer personal services on their own or with one or two partners. If a partnership, there is no ready-made partnership policy that outlines getting-out procedures.

GETTING STARTED

Just as in selling a business, before a professional even begins to look for a Buyer, he should get his practice ready for sale. This involves cleaning up a host of loose ends such as:

· Renovating the facilities.

· Liquidating outstanding debts or liens against the practice, including tax matters.

· Resolving any outstanding lawsuits, either against the practice or in favor of it.

· Resolving non-current or disputed receivables.

· Getting the full staffing contingent in place.

· Straightening out the accounting records.

· Getting all client records in shape.

· Clarifying the transferability of equipment or facility leases.

· Getting equipment or real estate appraisals.

No one wants to buy a messy looking business. Regardless of whether you lease or own the facility, spruce it up. Give it a new paint job. Clean the carpets. Repair any broken furniture. Throw out worn equipment or fixtures. Get rid of boxes of papers or files laying around. In other words, treat your office facility as if it were your home.

Paying off old bills is also important. Even if the Buyer doesn't assume the liabilities, there's no sense taking a chance that some creditor will get noisy when you're ready to close. Most important, resolve any outstanding tax issues. All payroll, property, sales, use, and federal and state income taxes should all be current, and kept current up to closing. Most professional practices sold are asset sales. An asset sale must meet the legal requirements of state Bulk Sales laws. This usually involves contacting each creditor before the sale and getting a signed affidavit that the creditor will not place a lien against the business or any assets after the sale. If you're not current with taxing authorities, you can be sure they will not consent to such a request.

Some practices have no staff and nothing needs to be done in this area. If employees of any sort are required to operate the practice, however it's imperative that open positions be filled before letting a potential Buyer visit the office. No dentist, lawyer, or other professional wants to step into a new practice and start hiring people right away.

Other than perhaps a few pieces of equipment and furniture, the only asset of value in a professional practice is goodwill. As a means of valuing goodwill during the due diligence investigation, a Buyer will want to ascertain the volume of billings for recent periods and the probability that the existing client/patient base will remain. In terms of getting the practice ready, this means that all billing records must be in one place, current, neatly filed, and easily accessible. It also means that client/patient files must be neat, up–to–date, and available for the Buyer's scrutiny. Most professionals are horrible administrators and, if the shoe fits, maybe it's worthwhile hiring some part–time clerical personnel to get these records in order. It can't hurt, and it might encourage a quick sale or a higher price than otherwise possible.

Along these same lines, nearly all professionals, including CPA's, seem to be atrocious bookkeepers for their own practice. Although it's unlikely a Buyer will insist on financial statements, a smart one knows he will need to estimate his own expenses and draw. The mere fact that accounting records are maintained and available could result in an easy sale. As a minimum, a Buyer will want to see billings and collections records for the past three years. He will also probably want verification of the cost of any recently acquired equipment or furniture. Usually, the fastest and easiest way to get accounting records cleaned up is to hire a part–time bookkeeper about six months before listing the practice for sale. This provides enough time to reconstruct, adjust, or create any necessary accounting records.

Finally, don't forget to get appraisals of major pieces of equipment or real estate included in the sale. This saves time and confusion later on when the prices for hard assets are negotiated. Even if the Buyer gets his own appraisals, you can get a leg up by doing it ahead of time yourself.

Chapter 4 discusses the most common methods for valuing an individual professional practice, so there's no need to reiterate the process here. One warning, however, the price you finally negotiate will be directly dependent on how eager you are to get out. With a little patience and a willingness to defer part of the payment, the price could end up being substantially higher. This leads to one of the key elements in selling a professional practice, the terms of sale.

TERMS OF SALE

This book has explored a variety of ways a Buyer might choose to finance the acquisition of a business, including the use of Buyer paper. In a professional practice, regardless of the type of profession, the Buyer's main concern will be the continuation of the client/patient base. If your clients or patients don't keep coming back after you leave, what would entice a Buyer to acquire your practice? He might just as well go out and buy some equipment, lease some space, and start his own practice from scratch. So a repeat client or patient base is crucial to selling a practice. If a Buyer pays all cash at closing, and the client/

patient base evaporates, he has thrown away a lot of money. Consequently, 99 out of a 100 times, a Buyer will want some type of deferred payment that is tied to the retention of clients or patients over a period of time.

The terms of sale are usually structured on the basis of paying a percentage of the sell price over one, two, or three years based on collections from existing clients/patients. For example, assume an accounting practice with annual gross billings of $200,000. A deferred payment schedule might be structured as follows:

Negotiated selling price—1½ times gross billings	$300,000
Payment as follows:	
Cash down payment at closing - 40%	$120,000
At the end of the first year—30%	$90,000
Calculated at 30% of collections for this year from clients existing at the time of close	
At the end of the second year—30%	$90,000
Calculated at 30% of collections for this year from clients existing at the time of close	
Total	$300,000

At this point, the Seller has recovered his full price but has lost potential interest income during the two years. Also, bookkeeping for the Buyer gets confusing because he must keep track not only of new clients added since the close, but additional work done for old clients that is not part of the calculation base.

A common way around these problems is to either calculate the 30 percent, or whatever other percentage is negotiated, against the total billings each year, regardless of the client or type of work. A cap can then be placed on the amount so that the total annual payment does not exceed the negotiated percentage of sell price plus interest. Although there are as many variations of this concept as the mind can conjure, most professional practices are sold on terms such as this one.

LOCATING A BUYER

Locating Buyers for some types of professional practices is no more difficult than finding one for the sale of a business. Many of the same techniques are used. A CPA or a lawyer practicing in or near a large metropolitan area can usually locate interested prospects through local chapters of professional trade organizations. A consultant located in a desirable resort region within an easy commute of a metropolitan area usually has no difficulty attracting Buyers either through trade organizations, or an ad in the local or nearby metropolitan newspaper. But what about a family physician practicing in a rural community—say a coal–mining town in West Virginia? That's not quite so easy.

Unfortunately, I know of no simple answer to this dilemma. There are ways, however, that work in specific situations, as with Dr. Emily Nelson.

Dr. Nelson had been practicing family medicine in Kenmare, North Dakota, population 1,456, for 30 years. A recurring asthmatic condition finally forced her to retire, only she was stuck with her practice. As the only family physician within a 75-mile radius, she didn't want to just walk away and leave her patients with no medical care. A year later, I met Emily vacationing in the islands and she related the following story.

"I wracked my brain trying to figure out how to get rid of my practice without hurting all those kind people I had known for more than 30 years. I tried advertising in the Fargo and Grand Forks papers, even the Chicago Tribune. Nothing. I contacted the North Dakota Medical Society for help. Nothing. I even let everyone know I would be willing to take in a successor and stay on for a couple of years for training. Nothing. No one had any interest in practicing in such an out of the way place as Kenmare, North Dakota. Finally, I was desperate and contacted the alumni office of my medical school at the University of Pennsylvania. A real long shot. But I'll be dammed if it didn't pay off. One of the recent graduates interning at the University Hospital was from North Dakota. When he heard about my offer to sell, two phone calls and a letter later, and he was on a plane to Minot to negotiate a deal. Six months later, I was out of it free and clear. And here I am soaking up the Caribbean sun. You'll never convince me there isn't someone up there looking out for me."

Although it doesn't always work this smoothly, certainly colleges or graduate schools are excellent sources of young, aggressive professionals eager to try their hand on their own. Large laws firms, accounting firms, hospitals, and clinics are other excellent sources of potential Buyers. Often, a young professional joining a large firm right out of school eventually gets fed up with big bureaucracy and longs for a way to get out on his own. This is especially fertile ground for lawyers and accountants. An inquiry can easily be made by notifying the institution or firm what you have in mind and asking that any interested parties contact you directly. Most large professional establishments are only too willing to help their staff people in an entrepreneurial venture and usually respond favorably to such an inquiry. Of course, there are always exceptions.

Because of the close, almost fraternal attitude in most professions, personal contacts with other professionals can often yield the best results. When I looked for a Buyer for my Midwest accounting practice years ago, my first stop was the state CPA society to get a listing of all the members. I then mailed inquiries to all the firms within a 50–mile radius of the office. Several potential Buyers stepped forward and within three months the deal closed. It was a win-win situation for all parties.

A SUCCESSION PARTNERSHIP

A professional practitioner might not want to get out of his practice right now but would rather phase out gradually over a period of years. Perhaps he has become bored with the daily routine and prefers to concentrate on more esoteric phases of his practice with the eventual goal of getting out completely. Such conditions dictate a successor partnership as the logical solution.

As mentioned earlier, there are two major problems in selling a professional practice:

1. Other than a few pieces of equipment and furniture, the only asset of value is the goodwill the practitioner has built up over the years with his clients or patients. Therefore, the Buyer's main concern will be the retention of this customer base.

2. Goodwill is an intangible assets—you can't touch or see it and it cannot be easily valued—and trying to raise outside financing to purchase this asset can be a nightmare for the Buyer.

There is also a third factor that makes some professional practices especially difficult to sell. A medical, dental or accounting practice maintains a repeat patient/client base, but many legal practices do not. Divorce action, will preparation, personal injury cases, and most litigation work are one-time efforts. The likelihood of servicing the same client again for a similar case is remote. The lawyer builds and maintains his practice not on repeat clients, but by reputation and referral work. Therefore, a Buyer does not acquire a client base and, of course, he cannot purchase someone else's reputation. So how does a lawyer or other professional without a client base attach a value to his practice, and how can a Buyer be assured that making the purchase won't be pouring money down the drain? The answer is usually a succession partnership.

As discussed in Chapter 8, a succession partnership is a structure for selling a business that allows the Buyer to join forces with the Seller in a partnership for a specified period of time, generally two to five years, under a contractual arrangement to buy out the Seller's interest over this period. For a practitioner, such as the lawyer described above, this procedure serves four purposes:

1. It allows the Buyer to use the goodwill of the Seller's reputation to build his own client base.

2. It permits the Buyer to reduce costs by using the Seller's facilities, equipment, library, and other hard assets.

3. It provides a way for the Buyer to finance the purchase out of his own partnership earnings.

4. It enables the Seller to quantify the value of his goodwill, which makes it a valuable asset to be sold.

Even in an accounting, dental, or medical practice where there is a repeat client/patient base, a succession partnership is, by far, the most popular method for selling practices, except in case of death or when a Seller has overriding reasons for getting out immediately.

Chapter 8 details how to structure a succession partnership through the "Eleven Rules of Partnership" and some basic principles for handling the financing. To specifically see how it relates to selling a professional practice, however, let's look at a typical example of how a succession partnership works.

The Case of the Literary Lawyer

Bob Calhoon had built a successful practice near Philadelphia that specialized in bankruptcy law. Although he is a sole practitioner, he shared offices with two other lawyers that handled personal injury and divorce cases. It was a convenient arrangement and, although no referrals had emanated from the other lawyers over the 15 years they had shared quarters, Bob found the arrangement less expensive than staffing his own office. At 54, and with his case load escalating significantly, Bob was getting very tired and a bit bored with fighting the same battles over and over again in the bankruptcy courts. He really wanted to write. The past six months had been especially hectic and Bob found himself dreaming of the time he could reduce his case load and start a monthly newsletter to help other bankruptcy lawyers with new developments in the bankruptcy laws and court precedents.

Through a friend, Bob learned of a young assistant in a Center City bankruptcy firm who had let it be known he would like to start his own practice. A few phone calls and brief negotiations resulted in a succession partnership with the young attorney. They structured the deal as follows:

Bob Calhoon averaged slightly over $200,000 in gross billings for the past three years. He agreed to sell the entire practice to Tim for 1.2 times the annual billings, or $240,000, including his library, furniture, and his share of the office lease with the other two attorneys. At the end of five years, Bob would retire to his dream home in Vermont and agreed to execute a non-compete covenant at that time. Tim agreed to pay for the practice in the following manner:

1. On June 1, when the partnership began, Tim would make a down payment of $24,000.

2. At the end of each year for five years, Tim would pay Bob according to the schedule shown in Table 13–1 plus 9 percent simple interest calculated on a declining balance:
3. Partners' billings would be shared as shown in Table 13–2.
4. The partners would share office expenses fifty/fifty.
5. Tim would receive a monthly draw against his share of earnings on the following schedule:

TABLE 13-1
Payment Schedule
(Plus 9% Simple Interest)

	Principal Payment	Cumulative % of Ownership
On Signing Agreement	$24,000	10%
End of Year 1	$24,000	20%
End of Year 2	$24,000	30%
End of Year 3	$24,000	40%
End of Year 4	$48,000	60%
End of Year 5	$96,000	100%

TABLE 13-2
Partners Shared Billing

	Bob's Billings		Tim's Billings	
	To Bob	To Tim	To Tim	To Bob
			100%	
Year 1	90%	10%		-0-
Year 2	80%	20%	$50,000 + 20% of Balance	80% of Balance
Year 3	70%	30%	$50,000 + 30% of Balance	70% of Balance
Year 4	60%	40%	$50,000 + 40% of Balance	60% of Balance
Year 5	40%	60%	$50,000 + 60% of Balance	40% of Balance

Year 1	$4,000
Year 2	$5,000
Year 3	To Be Negotiated
Year 4	To Be Negotiated
Year 5	To Be Negotiated

As it turned out, both parties were more than satisfied with the arrangement. To illustrate how the agreement actually worked in practice, try to visualize yourself in Bob's shoes by looking at Table 13–3. During the five years, Bob Calhoon earned a total of $731,000 from billings, or an average of $146,200 per year. In addition, he received $240,000 for his practice and $73,440 in interest income. From the Buyer's perspective, it was also a good deal. Tim was able to average over $55,000 per year in earnings after paying interest expense and buying the practice. And of course, beginning in the sixth year, he had the busi-

TABLE 13-3
Overall Financial Plan

Year	Bob's Billings	Bob's Earnings	Tim's Billings	Tim's Earnings
Down Pymt.		$24,000		($24,000)
1	$210,000	$189,000	$50,000	$71,000
Principal		$24,000		($24,000)
Interest		$19,440		($19,440)
2	$200,000	$184,000	$80,000	$96,000
Principal		$24,000		($24,000)
Interest		$17,280		($17,280)
3	$190,000	$154,000	$80,000	$116,000
Principal		$24,000		($24,000)
Interest		$15,120		($15,120)
4	$100,000	$120,000	$150,000	$130,000
Principal		$48,000		($48,000)
Interest		$12,960		($12,960)
5	$120,000	$84,000	$140,000	$176,000
Principal		$96,000		($96,000)
Interest		$8,640		($8,640)
TOTAL		$1,044,440		$275,556

ness all to himself. This was a win-win deal for both parties as is so often the case in a successor partnership. By the way, during the last three years, Bob had enough spare time to get his newsletter started, and by the time Tim took over completely, it was already a thriving success. Thirty days after the deal was completed, Bob sold his house and moved to Vermont where he lives happily today, still writing his newsletter. Tim has become one of the outstanding bankruptcy lawyers in the Philadelphia area.

GETTING OUT OF A PARTNERSHIP

Although large professional practices nearly always have agreements and procedures for buying back a partner's share, many small partnerships do not. Increasingly, either to cut overhead costs, share expertise, or increase the client/patient base, professionals find that small partnerships are more desirable than going it alone. To the extent that the partners have had the foresight to execute definitive partnership agreements in the beginning, complete with getting out provisions, there is no need to go any further. But this is not always the case. Partnerships in law, medicine, dentistry, psychology, counseling, even accounting, are often formed with only the bare essentials covered in a partnership agreement, with no defined method for a partner to get out. Without such a definitive agreement, selling a partnership interest can be a real headache as three dentists in St. Paul learned the hard way.

Bob Swanson, an oral surgeon, Terry O'Sullivan, an orthodontist, and Jerry Jones, a general practitioner, joined forces in the early sixties to share overhead and technician expenses. Ten years later, their practices had become so intertwined that they initiated a formal partnership without bothering with an attorney to draft an appropriate agreement. The three dentists continued to build their practice until 1985 when Jerry suffered a mild heart attack. On the advice of his physician, Jerry told his partners he wanted to sell his share of the practice and retire to northern Minnesota.

The three tried in vain to reach an agreement on the value of Jerry's share. Jerry wanted $300,000, Bob thought it was worth about $100,000, and Terry, not interested in buying him out suggested, Jerry look on the outside for a Buyer. This displeased Bob who didn't want an outsider joining them. Deadlock. Their disagreement continued for several months, patients began to sense the tension in the air and started going elsewhere. Eighteen months later, no agreement had been reached, and the practice was rapidly disintegrating. The partners finally disbanded and Jerry moved to his favorite fishing lake with nothing to show for his efforts except some used dental equipment.

Had the three dentists been willing to listen to reason, there was a way out. Although valuing a professional partnership is difficult, there are ways to do it. One of the most common solutions is to proceed as follows:

1. Get an outside appraisal of the equipment and furniture at liquidation value. This will at least provide a starting point.

2. Determine a value for the partnership as a whole. This can be done in a number of ways, the least desirable being a business appraisal performed by a qualified appraiser. Usually, however, this involves more disagreement than it is worth, and it is certainly more costly than doing it yourself. A more common method looks at gross billings for the partnership for the past two years along with an estimate of the next year's billings. The three are averaged and that becomes the base amount. Next, take an average of the operating expenses for the past two years, being careful to eliminate all draws and direct or personal expenses of the partners. Add to this average any unusual expenses anticipated for the following year. Then subtract the total from the average billings and that's the profitability of the practice.

3. Compare the amount of billings contributed each year by each partner. This can be done in a number of ways, but the easiest is when individual billing records are kept for each partner. In some professions, this can be done by keeping time cards. In others, individual client billings can be used. A third way might be one of the above plus or minus referrals from one partner to the other. This gets pretty complicated, however, and unless intraoffice referrals are a major part of the practice, it should not be attempted.

4. Weigh these factors against the average billings to determine each partner's share of revenues. A profit contribution for each partner can be calculated by applying the average profit percentage to this weighted billing total.

5. Negotiate a multiplier factor. Most often, factors between two and five are used representing the number of years it will take to theoretically diminish the absent partner's goodwill.

6. Multiply a partner's profitability by the negotiated factor and add his share of the hard assets—minus any liabilities, of course. This results in a value for his share of the practice.

The example in Fig. 13–1 illustrates how to make the calculations, assuming that:

- There are three partners in an accounting practice.
- Billing time cards are maintained.

- No unusual expenses anticipated next year.
- The cash in the bank plus receivables, equal liabilities.
- The appraised value of the equipment and furniture is $20,000.

	Billings	Expenses Ex-Partner Draws	Profit
Year 1	$325,000	$232,000	$93,000
Year 2	$405,000	$264,000	$141,000
Next Year	$375,000	$250,000	$125,000
Average	$368,000	$249,000	$119,000

	Average Last Two Years and Next Year's Estimate		
	Hours Billed	Percent	Partner Profitability
Partner A	2,720	35%	$41,650
Partner B	1,956	40%	$47,600
Partner C	1,224	25%	$29,750
Total	4,900	100%	$119,000

Assume that Partner C wishes to sell his share and the negotiated multiplier is three. Then the following calculation yields the value of C's share:

Partner C's Profitability	$29,750
Multiplier	×3
Value of Goodwill	$89,250
Add: ⅓ of hard asset appraisal	6,666
Value of C's share	$95,916

Fig. 13-1. These sample calculations can be used to value a business.

Of course, the type of work each partner does might yield significantly different billing rates per hour. In this case, a weighted adjustment must be made for that variance. There's nothing magical about this procedure. It's straightforward, easily calculated, and only the multiplier needs negotiation. Because of its simplicity, many professional partnerships incorporate this procedure in the partnership agreement as the definition of value for getting out purposes.

Once the sell price has been established, terms of payment must be negotiated. There doesn't seem to be any one method of payment favored over others, and it generally depends on the cash position of the other partners at the time of one's withdrawal. Of course, tax considerations also play a role in determining whether it should be a lump–sum payment or deferred over a period of years. As discussed in Chapter 3, goodwill is a capital asset and subject to capital gains treatment by the Seller.

WRAPPING UP THE LOOSE ENDS

Another unique feature of professional practices is the personal relationship between the practitioner and clients/patients. In a manufacturing, retail, or service business, the customers might know the owner, but there usually isn't a personal relationship. The customer buys from the establishment for price, convenience, service, or quality, not necessarily because he happens to know and like the owner personally. In a personal service professional practice, however, just the opposite occurs. The client/patient buys the service mainly because of the personality and capability of the professional. This not only creates difficulties in transferring the practice to a Buyer, it also necessitates careful planning to ensure clients/patients are not hurt or inconvenienced by the absence of the Seller. Compassionate understanding of others needs is the hallmark of most successful professionals, so little needs to be said about notifying clients or patients well in advance of leaving. The following are a few thoughts that might be some help, however.

When I sold my accounting practice, I made the major mistake of sending notification postcards to all of my clients the week my successor took over. This left virtually no time for face–to–face good-bys, which caused a great deal of grief to many of my clients and to the Buyer. An even worse way of handling the transition occurred with my personal physician of 20 years. When he retired and sold his practice in January, he did not notify anyone of the transition. In June, when I needed a medical diagnosis and called for an appointment, I was informed that it was now Dr. Cooperman's office not Dr. Bolster's. I was dismayed and hurt that our family physician of so many years didn't care enough to even send a postcard.

Once a Buyer has been selected and the deal negotiated, the very least you can do is let your clients/patients know that you are leaving and who your replacement will be. Even better, try to personally contact as many as possible and explain your reason for leaving and the qualifications of your successor. This can be done either through a warmly written letter or a phone call. In a personal service practice with a personal relationship between client/patient and practitioner, anything less than this abdicates responsibility.

This holds true even if a professional sells out to his partners. Fortunately, some of his clients/patients have already met his partners and the transition will be easier. Certainly selling to a partner maintains some degree of continuity in the practice, but common, client/patient caring still dictates some type of personal communication when a practitioner leaves.

Obviously, when you bring in a successor partner, it is not necessary to notify your clients or patients of your plans. You're not leaving now, so there's no need to notify anyone. By the time you do get out, all of your clients or patients should already know your successor and have a good working relationship with him. Also, if you have a practice with little or no repeat clientele—such as the case with the bankruptcy lawyer Bob Calhoon—there is nobody to notify personally.

Unfinished Projects

When a business is sold, it's easy for the owner to leave knowing his customers will continue to receive comparable products or services. With a professional practice, however, because services are personal and there is always a continuing array of unfinished projects (work in process), a Seller must be especially careful to either complete the in-process jobs before he leaves, or make mutually satisfactory arrangements for their completion.

A case in point is the litigation lawyer who has cases pending before the bench. If they cannot be resolved before his departure, arrangements must be made with the court, the client, and the Buyer for a smooth transition of activity. The court and the Buyer normally won't object, but it's entirely possible the client will want his original lawyer to finish his case. Although he is probably under no obligation to do so, a caring approach would certainly dictate that the lawyer comply with the client's wishes, even if it means delaying a complete takeover.

Similarly, a CPA practice might have tax returns in various stages of completion. In this case, the Seller should make every effort to complete the returns before turning over his practice. The client will certainly appreciate such personal concern.

Every professional has an obligation, like it or not, to transact business in the client's interest, even when it comes to selling his practice. Whether formally stated in a profession's code of ethics or not, an underlying assumption in nearly all client/patient relationships demands that the practitioner perform his services in the best interests of the client/patient. If caring and compassion mean nothing in professional ranks, what hope is there for the business arena?

When I've been asked to assist other professionals getting out of their practice, either by selling to an outsider or to a partner or group of partners, I have used the checklist shown in Fig. 13–2 as a means of keeping track of the major items to be resolved before closing the deal. It's not very complex but it does provide a guide to the type of matters you will need to attend to, regardless of what kind of practice is being sold.

Fig. 13-2. Keep this checklist nearby as a reminder of all you must do before closing the deal

---

Checklist for Getting Out of a Professional Practice

Getting Ready

1. Repair and paint the office   _____
2. Repair/replace carpets and curtains   _____
3. Repair/replace worn furniture and fixtures   _____
4. Throw out all boxes, old papers, outdated files, trash   _____
5. Pay down all trade payables to current balances   _____
6. Pay off loans against equipment or furniture   _____
7. Settle all tax disputes—payroll, sales/use, property, state and federal   _____
   income taxes
8. Get all lease payments current   _____
9. Are all leases transferable?   _____
10. Settle outstanding lawsuits or claims against the practice   _____
11. Settle/resolve all lawsuits or outstanding claims by the practice against   _____
    outsiders, including old receivables
12. Fill all required personnel openings   _____
13. Hire a part time bookkeeper to straighten out records   _____
14. Hire part time clerical help to sort out files   _____
15. Update all recurring client files   _____
16. Take a physical inventory of supplies and materials   _____
17. Arrange for equipment appraisal   _____
18. Arrange for real estate appraisal   _____
19. Review tax planning with tax counsel   _____

Set a Selling Price

20. Check with other practitioners or trade association to determine current   _____
    pricing standards
21. Prepare calculation of value (get outside advice if necessary)   _____
22. Determine asking price and drop–dead price   _____
23. Determine acceptable alternate terms of sale   _____

The Buyer Search

24. Contact state and local trade associations   _____
25. Make inquiries of friends and professional acquaintances   _____
26. Get listing of major firms/clinics/hospitals in area   _____

(Fig. 13-2 continued)

27. Mail letters of inquiry to these sources _____
28. Get listing of all firms within a fifty mile radius from state board or trade association _____
29. Mail inquiries to these firms _____
30. Contact local university placement offices and graduate school alumni offices for possibilities _____

Loose Ends
31. Hire an outside lawyer to draft closing documents _____
32. Complete all unfinished projects/cases/jobs _____
33. Instruct buyer about unfinished work _____
34. Compose a farewell letter to clients/patients _____
35. Make farewell phone calls as appropriate _____
36. Introduce buyer via mail or in person _____

AFTER IT'S OVER

Professional practitioners seem somewhat better equipped to deal with the psychological trauma of getting out than business owners. Perhaps because they form close personal relationships with clients/patients and are generally careful to inform these people of a transition in ownership. Perhaps with fewer employees, a practitioner can also bridge the gap of leaving with little hurt to them. Whatever the reason, it seems that in most cases, when professionals finally do leave, they suffer far fewer pangs of guilt, anxiety, fear, and self-recrimination than a business owner.

This doesn't mean it's all smooth sailing, however. A consultant, doctor, dentist, or lawyer is just as human and just as protective of his baby as a business owner. In many cases, a professional might be even more sensitive to personal relationships than a business owner. He faces the same emptiness and fear of the future as anyone else in business does—the same worries about keeping busy and perhaps producing some income after the sale; the same problems of inactive retirement; the same desire to remain productive and challenged; and the same feelings of loss once the sale is culminated.

But don't despair, the following chapters offer recommendations and guidelines for coping with the trauma of leaving. They also offer alternatives for starting a new life in productive, even income–producing, activities.

14

The Human Story

Coping with Psychological Trauma

"SELLING A BUSINESS IS LIKE LOSING A LOVED ONE."

Dr. Jack M. was distraught, disordered, and depressed after selling his pediatric practice to a new partner, and cried like a baby over coffee that morning. He felt lost, alone, and disoriented. As he explained, the worst feeling was losing contact with many of the children he had doctored for several years. He believed they needed him and there was nothing he could do about it now. He was sorry he had ever decided to get out, even though he had looked forward to a new life of retirement for five years now.

Why a chapter about coping with psychological trauma in a book about selling businesses? Because in the more than 65 cases of business sales, bankruptcies, and liquidations I have seen, the business owner or professional practitioner always faces varying degrees of anxiety, fear, anger, self-doubt, and depression. No one has escaped. These feelings occur before, during, and after the sale. With only one exception, and that was a psychologist who recognized ahead of time what he would face, and took steps to alleviate the bad feelings, everyone experienced a radical change in his personal life—some for the better, most for the worse.

This chapter includes some ideas and concrete suggestions that have worked for others in mitigating the psychological trauma of leaving their businesses, and I hope they will be of use to you.

THE PROBLEM

The psychological problems that a business owner faces when he decides to sell his business are threefold:

1. Loss of his "way of life."
2. Feelings of failure.
3. Fear of the future.

Over the years of struggling to be a success, the company, or practice, has become, in its owner's eyes, almost human—like part of the family. Sacrifices of time, money, and energy to build and sustain the business give him the right to feel this way. An employee working a nine–to–five shift has the time and energy to develop hobbies, a family life, and athletic or community pursuits, but the entrepreneur seldom has time for these activities. Even when away from the company, his thoughts remain with the business. The telephone is always nearby to constantly check on one thing or another at his company. He has become addicted to the power, money, and yes, even the fun and excitement of running the business. And just like any addict, when the source of his addiction is taken away, or even threatened to be lost, he panics. Fear, anger, rebellion, and aggressive behavior create feelings of disorientation and anxiety.

The second problem is created by how society views a business owner who "sells out." The free enterprise system, which permeates every walk of American culture, is founded on the premise that to succeed in the continual accumulation of wealth is good, and not to seek ever more money and material possessions is bad. To stop the money–making treadmill is viewed as failure, and society will not accept failure of any kind. There are no allowances made for that very human characteristic—the possibility or even inevitability of failure. Two of the worst feelings created by such perceived failure are worthlessness and social abandonment.

How does a business owner fail? By selling his business. In the business community, selling a business often connotes quitting, and a quitter is judged a failure. If you accept this nonsensical concept promulgated in our society, you will automatically saddle yourself with a feeling of worthlessness, which is quickly followed with a loss of self-esteem. A quitter is also a social outcast so, in one fell swoop, by getting out, you have lost your social status and self-respect. You'll probably end up with more money after the sale than you ever had before, so maybe that will make you feel better. Nevertheless, whether or not you believe you've failed, society will mark you with this label as soon as you broadcast your intentions to get out, just as surely as if you wore the word *Failure* emblazoned across your chest. This perception of failure reinforces the anxiety and disorientation you probably already suffer from losing your baby.

The third problem is the blinding fear of the unknown future. One of the advantages of having your own business is that you are in control of your own destiny. True, customers must be satisfied, employees nurtured, bank requirements met, but you still have the choice of doing or not doing, complying or ignoring, following or rebelling. You can plan your future and be reasonably certain that you can achieve your goals. Once you sell out, however, you are no longer in control. The future is a ghost in the mist—indefinable, unclear.

No amount of planning and preparation can completely eliminate the trauma of losing your baby, and no one person has the wherewithal to change a prevalent attitude of society. That is why, with nearly complete certainty, you will experience some psychological trauma before, during, and after the sale. Fortunately, however, there are steps to be taken and things to be done to reduce this trauma. The following Nine Steps to Sanity listed below might not completely eliminate bad feelings, but it will certainly stop your emotions from getting out of control.

Nine Steps to Sanity

1. Recognize your addiction to the business and what it means in terms of addictive behavior.
2. Learn to deal with anger, fear, and depression in positive ways.
3. Prove to yourself that you are not a failure.
4. Disengage yourself from the father figure you held in your business.
5. Establish financial security independent of the company.
6. Re-establish personal goals to live the rest of your life away from the business.
7. Develop new relationships with family and friends.
8. Research potential new careers and new life–styles.
9. Prove to yourself you are a survivor.

ADDICTED TO THE BUSINESS

Owning your own business gives you power to control the actions of others; and power leads to addiction. It's not at all unusual to become addicted to the feeling of omnipotence that comes with the power to control other people. It's fun to cause other's to do what we tell them to do, when we tell them to do it, and how we tell them to do it. When people obey our orders we feel like a king, exhilarated, commanding, and powerful. In time, we thrive on exercising this power so that we can't do without it. We become addicted to this godlike feeling. It becomes our major source of stimulation, our primary objective. We become obsessed with protecting the source of this power, namely our own business. When the time comes to sell, the mere thought of being deprived of such a wonderful feeling of control can leave us helpless. Without this control, our lives will be meaningless, we can't go on. We have become addicted to power.

Bob S., a well–respected physician in a small midwestern city, was in practice for more than 30 years. Many of his patients depended on his advice, not only for solutions to medical problems, but for general counsel and guidance in everyday family disagreements, career counseling, and social problems in the community. When Bob spoke, his patients listened. The amount of control Bob exercised over people would have been frightening to an outsider, but his patients accepted this powerful man's judgment without question.

Bob reveled in his power. His stature in the community enabled him to park his car where he liked, join the best golf club, be invited to the most ostentatious social events, and even had many of the females in the community at his beck and call. He was truly addicted to power and demonstrated many additive behavior patterns. He was controlling, a perfectionist, very self-centered, had a hard time remembering things, and denied the importance of this power in his life–style.

His wife, who suffered with arthritis, finally convinced Bob it was time to sell his practice and retire to warmer climates for their remaining years. Bob agreed and engaged me to find a successor he could train and then sell his practice to, which I did. Bob liked Marvin, and within 18 months, Bob and his wife were off to Florida.

Three months later, however, suffering from daily headaches, a loss of weight, and altogether miserable, Bob called Marvin and asked to come back as an equal partner. He could not stand losing the source of his addiction, and the acquiescence of his patients to being controlled. Marvin would not hear of it, and Bob is still trying to recover from his years of power addiction.

In my book, *The Battle-Weary Executive*, I describe what I call the "power circle," which refers to how the corporate leader feeds his addiction to power. Although used to describe corporate addiction, the concept is equally applicable to entrepreneurs.

The desire for more money is a natural phenomenon in the business world. This desire for more wealth can quickly reach the level of greed, however. Greed leads to the hunger for more power to obtain more wealth. This hunger generates fear. The fear of losing the power you already possess. Unable to cope with fear, the individual turns to artificial supports, alcohol, drugs, food, or sex, and becomes addicted to one or more of these external stimuli. To support these habits, a person requires more money. Greed then re-enters the scene, leading to the hunger for more power, and away we go in an ever–increasing concentric spiral.

The basic problem of wanting to exercise godlike power over others is that it goes against the natural fiber of human life. Consequently, an entrepreneur suffers stress, anxieties, and becomes obsessive in his behavior in order to protect his power.

Addiction to power can destroy both your business and yourself, and must be dealt with as a preliminary to the selling process. Trying to sell your business while addicted to either power or one of its external supports will surely result in an unsuccessful attempt to sell or, even worse, physical and mental devastation after the sale. But how do you know if you are addicted to your business? The following list of addictive behavior characteristics can help pinpoint any addictive characteristics that are common to entrepreneurs.

I am Addicted to my Business if I am:

1. **Repressive.** Rigid and controlled, I'm afraid to let myself go. I keep my feelings to myself.

2. **Self-deprecating.** I get angry, defensive, and self-righteous when someone criticizes my actions or opinions. I feel guilty and afraid of making mistakes.

3. **Obsessive.** I focus most of my energies on other people's problems, worry a lot, and feel a strong need to influence other people. I'm obsessed with the success of my business.

4. **Controlling.** I need to control other people. I use every means possible including threats, coercion, and domination. I have a strong need to give advice to others and have them follow that advice.

5. **Overcommitted.** I feel pressured and stressed out. I blame others for the situation I'm in and the stresses and anxieties I feel. I manage by crisis because there's never enough time to plan.

6. **Distrustful.** I don't trust other people. Other's decisions are never as sound as mine. I'm always right.

7. **Angry.** I frequently get angry with other people, especially when they don't do things my way. But I repress my anger.

8. **Dependent.** I need other people to approve of me and my actions. I need to be well liked. I use other people as a crutch if things go wrong.

9. **Deny.** I ignore problems and pretend they don't exist. I get confused and depressed at times, and use tranquilizers or alcohol to cover up my feelings. I am a workaholic. I never admit I am wrong about anything.

10. **Misunderstood.** People don't understand what I mean. I talk too much and am cynical or self-deprecating. I think I am a good communicator but I'm really not.

11. **Depressed.** Nothing is going right. I need to escape. Excessive use of drugs, alcohol, food, or sex help me face my problems.

12. **Responsible.** I feel responsible for everyone. When I can't control events, I feel responsible and I get depressed, confused, or frustrated.

You don't need to have all of these traits to be a power addict, although chances are high that if you can honestly admit to having three or more of these behavior patterns, you also have the rest, but to lesser degrees. Don't feel too bad, however. Most entrepreneurs are addicted to their business. This seems to be one of the hazards of being your own boss and running your own show. It's bad enough to be an addict while running your company, but it can be devastating to the psyche when selling your business. So what can you do about curing most, if not all, of this addictive behavior before the sale?

The first step is to admit to yourself that you are an addict. Experts estimate that more than 90 percent of people who own and run their own business, suffer from addictive behavior. If you're not willing to admit it, there is nothing anyone, including yourself, can do to help, and you'll just have to suffer the psychological withdrawal after you sell. If you will admit addictive behavior, however, you can begin the recovery process of change. It's going to require a change in the way you live, a change in your life–style, and to a very significant extent, a change in your beliefs.

Anger, Fear, and Depression

Anger leads to fear, fear leads to depression. Fear leads to depression, depression leads to anger. Depression leads to anger, anger leads to fear. The three feelings are derivatives of each other. At times, it's difficult to determine which comes first, but they all seem to act together during the sale of a business. You become depressed because you are losing your baby, fearful of the unknown future, and angry at Buyers, your family, professional advisors, and bankers for not viewing your company as the wonderful creation it is. There doesn't seem to be any way to separate these three bad feelings, so let's deal with them all together.

All of us feel angry at times, and usually we're able to let it out without damage to ourselves or anyone else. Exercise, physical work, a change of scenery, sports, a couple of martinis or, if nothing else, pounding our desk and shouting, relieve angry feelings. By identifying the source of our anger as another person, we can often dispose of the feeling by confronting that person head-on, telling him how we feel, and asking him not to repeat whatever it was that made us angry.

During the selling process, however, there generally isn't any one person to point the finger at. It's more of a culmination of events that threaten to cause you to lose control of your power base. You have been able to control events and people, and have everything your own way for a long time. Suddenly, you are losing your power base and your ability to control others. You become afraid, filled with panic, despair, and anger. It is the fear of losing that causes your depression. It is the uncertainty of your ability to fill the power vacuum that creates despair. It is not knowing who or what to lash out at to stop these feelings that can result in such unbridled anger it seems impossible to function.

You feel depressed but you're unable to correlate this despair with your fears and angers. All you know is that very soon you're going to lose your company, to be without a steady source of income, and left with nothing constructive to do with your time. Of course you'll be depressed, it's a very normal reaction. The future is always depressing if you have nothing enjoyable to look forward to.

So what can you do? Recognizing your power addiction must come first. Once you know what causes your anger, you can deal with it through a constructive program of rehabilitation. Having owned and sold a number of companies myself, I have experienced these emotions many times. I finally hit upon a recovery program that works, and that is what I pass on to you now. For a more complete description of power addiction recovery programs, take a look at the *The Battle-Weary Executive*, book that explores methods to deal with executive, emotional dysfunction caused by addicted power behavior.

GUIDELINES TO A BETTER LIFE

A change in your power base causes fear, anger, and depression, so it is change that you must first deal with. It's not enough to merely change your source of income or change occupations or careers. You must also change the way you look at things, the way you regard life, and the way you want to live the rest of your days. This requires a change in attitudes about yourself, your family, your employees, and your customers or clients. The following Guidelines to a Better Life were put together for a talk I presented to a group of small businessmen attending a management conference.

Guidelines to a Better Life

I promise myself, that starting today:

1. I will live each day as if it were the last.

2. I will look to a Higher Power to solve problems I am unable to handle.

3. I will not worry about other people's problems. They can handle them better than I can.

4. I will let events occur in their normal fashion without trying to change things to my way.

5. I will not be afraid to admit I am wrong.

6. I will be honest and open with my family, employees, clients, and others.

7. I will not berate another person if I think he is wrong.

8. If I am angry, fearful, or depressed I will talk to another person about it and tell them how I feel.

9. I will not blame others for my mistakes and errors.

10. I will accept whatever tomorrow brings tomorrow, without fear or prejudice.

Following these guidelines won't solve all of your problems. It won't even cure your addiction. But by basing your life on these standards and actively pursuing changes in attitudes and relationships, you can get started on the road to recovery.

A FOUR–STEP POWER ADDICTION PROGRAM

For years, I have struggled trying to help other people deal with emotional turmoil caused by everyday business frustrations and events. Being an experienced management consultant to small businesses, and an inveterate believer in kindness, caring, compassion, and other efforts that bring people closer together, has brought me into close contact with many people with a variety of emotional ills.

Not being a professional counselor or a psychologist seems to permit people to open up to me when they might not make the effort or spend the money to seek professional help. Whatever the reason, active participation in trying to help others, as well as myself, deal with emotional turmoil has led me to develop this four–step program for those who suffer from power addiction:

Four–Step Program for Happiness

1. Get to know yourself. Spend time alone, practice silence, and communicate with your conscience.

2. Identify the internal and external circumstances causing bad feelings and take actions to deal with them, one brick at a time.

3. Make a prolonged, conscious effort to improve relationships with your spouse, family, friends, and employees. Develop a caring attitude toward others.

4. Plan for financial survival and for a life away from the business.

Know Yourself

To "know yourself" sounds simplistic, and it certainly isn't very profound. Your response is probably, "Of course I know myself. Don't bother me with such platitudes!" OK, I accept that comment. But let me ask three questions, and if you answer them truthfully, you'll see what I mean:

1. How many times yesterday did you take some action or say something that you had a feeling was wrong, would hurt someone, or was done to satisfy your ego? How many times the day before, and the day before that?

2. In the past week, how often, and how much time did you spend alone and in silence—without anyone else around, no radio, no television— just by yourself thinking?

3. How many times in the past week have you let your conscience dictate what you did or said rather than external circumstances or reasoned logic?

There is something deep within all of us giving us wisdom to know what is right and to resolve problems that seem rationally insoluble. We have all experienced deja vu, mental telepathy, unexplained occurrences, or seemingly miraculous recoveries from illness. We have all felt at times that the action we take, the path we follow, or the words we speak are not right. Somehow, unconsciously, we all know the difference between right and wrong. Religious leaders claim this knowledge and these feelings emanate from a Higher Power. Without getting into a lengthy theological discussion, let me refer to this unexplained power and knowledge as your conscience.

Several years ago, I conducted a small seminar on recordkeeping for small businesses. During the morning coffee break, a young lady approached me with a startling observation.

"Mr. Tuller, you've been talking about using bookkeeping tricks to get by with paying less taxes and how we can camouflage deductions that might not be allowed by the IRS. It seems to me that that's cheating. I know everyone does it, but doesn't your conscience bother you to advocate something you know isn't right?"

She stopped me dead in my tracks. My conscience had been bothering me. Although I knew what I was advocating was a perfectly acceptable practice throughout the business world, it was nevertheless, cheating and morally wrong. When the meeting reconvened, I sheepishly acknowledged my error and, much to my surprise, it felt as if a large weight had been lifted from my shoulders. That was the last time I gave that seminar. To this day, I still do not teach bookkeeping or accounting classes that involve taxes.

So listen to your conscience. Don't ignore that small voice deep within telling you what is right and what is wrong. That's part of getting to know yourself. If you don't listen to your conscience you can never really get to know yourself. It's the foundation upon which a caring and compassionate attitude is built, and it's the inner strength you can draw on when things get tough. When anger, fear, and depression take their toll; when you don't know where to turn to relieve the horrible loss of losing your company; when you can't figure out how to cope with a future without power; and, if you are ever in financial trouble and don't know how you'll survive, listening to your conscience will always give you hidden strength and see you through the emotional turmoil to find a way.

There are many ways to do it. Find out what works best for you and then make a practice of doing it every day. It really does work wonders!

Identifying What Causes Bad Feelings

If you can define the problem, you can solve it. You know that already. So obviously, if you can define the source of your anger, fear, depression, despair, self-doubt and all of your other bad feelings, you can certainly put an end to them. Let's go back to our earlier definition of the problem. As a business seller you will experience:

- Loss of your "way of life"
- Feelings of failure
- Fear of the future

When you sell your business, your way of life will change, so, in a sense, this is a loss. As we saw, the reason this loss hits home so hard is that you have become addicted to your business. But is there more to it than merely losing the source of your addiction? Probably, yes. When you sell your business, there will be a vacuum in your life–style. No more getting up at six o'clock to get to the office or plant. No more weekends spent sorting through unopened mail. No spur of the moment decisions to make. No more disputes to arbitrate. Nothing. Sleep as long as you like. Play golf every day. Clean the yard. Tinker with your car. But nothing of importance! Inactivity breeds apathy and such indifference to life can be deadly. Inactivity also gives birth to self-pity—the forerunner of despair.

Once you recognize the dangers of inactivity, start developing something to take the place of your business. Some activity or project, a new social cause to promote, or community volunteer work. Perhaps broaden your education or learn a new skill. Anything, as long as it requires effort, thinking, time, and involvement with people. The following are a few ideas to consider:

1. Run for the local school board.
2. Start a fund-raising drive for a local charity.
3. Enroll in college courses.
4. Start a weekly newsletter for your local business community.
5. Participate in administrative chores for political races—gubernatorial, congressional, mayoral, or presidential.
6. Put together and conduct a seminar on your business specialty.
7. Become active in your college alumni organization—fund raising, luncheon meetings, recruiting.
8. Begin a writing campaign for Amnesty International, write magazine articles, or even your memoirs.

These are just some of the things you might do initially to fill the void while you are developing plans for your new life-style. The main idea is to do something. Keep busy, but be sure you keep busy with productive activities. If they don't contribute something to yourself or other people, the projects won't do any good. What you are really trying to do is provide a substitute activity in place of the addictive business, just like a recovering alcoholic replaces liquor with an activity he can throw himself into.

Given time, your new life–style will take the place of your business. In the meantime, you can feel pretty despondent and miserable if you don't stay busy.

Are You A Failure?

The second reason for all of your bad feelings is that many ex-business owners believe that they have lost their social status by getting out of their business. This preceived loss of social status creates a loss of self-esteem. In reality, you probably have more money now than ever before. You successfully ran your business for many years, and now you will turn it over to someone else to make their fortune. You've accomplished what very few people ever do—you have owned your own business and survived! So why this loss of self-esteem?

If you really do feel the social stigma of failure, however, there are some surefire ways to rebuild who you are and what you are. All it takes is a little courage and determination.

Howard married money so to speak and, although he was a successful lawyer who specialized in bankruptcy law, when he married a lady whose wealthy father was a district judge. Until the marriage, she appeared frequently in the society pages of the Westchester newspapers. When Howard reached his mid-forties he became disenchanted with the legal profession, sold his practice, and took a teaching position at a small local college. His father-in-law was mortified. Nobody in his family had ever left the law. It just wasn't done. Howard must have failed, and a failure had no place in his family! The judge made Howard feel so low he even considered ending it all, but he didn't, and two years later, received an honorarium from the college for outstanding community service. Howard overcame his perceived failure and went on to become one of the truly exceptional teachers in his area.

When I asked Howard how he had overcome his feelings of failure he told me of a list of personal beliefs he had clipped out of the newspaper one day, hung on the wall of his den, and began following, which follow:

Why I Didn't Fail

1. Because I did my best.
2. Because I have helped at least one other person to live a better life.
3. Because I have raised my children to be spiritually strong.
4. Because I have learned that being first is not being best.
5. Because I am spiritually strong, mentally alert, and morally straight.
6. Because I like myself and I have not met anyone else I like better.
7. Because only my God and I know who I am.
8. Because I have tried never to hurt another person.
9. Because many people love me.
10. Because society's judgment of my actions is not a true measure of success or failure, only God has the right to approve or disapprove of my actions.

You have the inherent right to accept or reject society's standards, as long as by rejecting them you do not hurt others. There's no reason for you to believe that getting out is a sign of failure. It is not! Regardless of society's judgment, no one has the authority to call you a failure. Only you can make that determination. Of course, facing your friends or meeting new people when the first line of conversation is, "What do you do?" can be disarming. We all like to label people. He is a doctor, or a lawyer, or a teacher, or he owns a string of service stations, or she is a scientist or homemaker are all convenient and acceptable labels. During the transition period to your new life-style, why not answer the question with, "I manage my investments." I guarantee that will quiet the most insistent labeler around. If you have enough money to have investments, you must be a success, even if you do cut your grass in the middle of the week and wear jeans out to dinner!

Fear of the Future

Fear is the real enemy. Fear of the future can cause more bad feelings than anything else. The reason is obvious. We have all been taught to hope for a better tomorrow. If today is dreary, stick around because tomorrow holds the promise of a brighter future. But what if you see only financial hardship, broken relationships, and inactivity in the future? Take heart. Once you take the first step for a better life after the sale, you'll begin to feel your despondency lifting and a new excitement building for the future. And that first step is to develop a second source of income, something other than your business. Some possibilities you might want to consider include:

1. Developing a securities investment program that yields monthly or quarterly dividend or interest payments.

2. Acquiring rental real estate that provides monthly income.

3. Purchasing an insurance annuity with monthly payment provisions.

4. Investing in qualified, Limited Partnership ventures with potential for annual dividends.

5. Beginning a part–time business for your spouse—bookkeeping, tax preparation, writing, flower shop, computer programming, word processing, travel consultant.

6. Obtaining certification or a license in a new field—real estate sales, stock brokerage, medical technician, teaching, or whatever your background happens to be.

7. Developing a program of seminars in your profession.

8. Teach night school in adult education classes or local colleges.

These are only a few ideas. You can probably come up with another 10 or 20. The only criteria should be something that produces at least some income in the immediate future but doesn't take time away from managing your business. With at least some income coming in, regardless of what life–style you choose after the sale, you will be able to survive financially, and that will mitigate fears of surviving the future.

Re–examining Your Relationships

The third step in the "Four–Step Program To Happiness" is to reexamine your relationships with your spouse, family, and friends and change these relationships wherever necessary. While you have been building your business over the years, devoting most of your thoughts, energies, and time to solving business problems and improving the profitability of the company, chances are high that developing and nurturing your relationships has been a second priority. Many small businessmen and professionals have miserable family lives and few close friends. Their addiction to the business has all but eliminated the possibility of a loving relationship. But now is the time to change that.

The best way to deal with fears, anger, self-doubt and other bad feelings is to get support from other people. As an entrepreneur you have had to fend for yourself for many years. You probably developed your business with your own grit and determination. You might never have felt a need for approval and support from anyone other than yourself. There's a difference now, however. You are no longer going to be in charge. You will no longer have your successful business to prove to yourself and others what a great guy you are. You are going to need some kind of support from someone when the going gets tough, which it will.

So now is a good time—before you actually get out—to begin a change in your relationships with others. A good starting point is your spouse. How long has it been since you actually acknowledged your fears and weaknesses to your wife (or husband)? How many years since you let your spouse into your inner feelings—all of those self-doubts, fears, angers, and self-trepidations? When was the last time you told your spouse that you loved her (him)? Have you ever really let yourself become totally vulnerable before your spouse? For most entrepreneurs the answer is no. Showing your weaknesses to your spouse, letting your hair down, and becoming totally vulnerable, however, can and will make the relationship stronger than ever. Even if you have drifted apart over the years, a full confession now can bring your spouse to your side.

The same thing goes for good friends. They probably think of you as the rock of Gibralter. Never any major problems, concerns, or fears. As long as that's the case, the support and approval they give you will be superficial and meaningless. So let them know how you really feel. How afraid of the future you really are. What a cataclysmic decision selling your business really is. More times than not, you will see a new breed of friendship born. Now that they see you are just like everyone else, not the superman they thought you were, help and support will pour forth. And that's exactly what you need. You need to know that people care about you—that they care whether you are happy or depressed. With a little compassion and love, you can achieve anything, including getting over the blues and going on with your life. I have found the following Ten Commandments of Human Relations to be especially helpful in maintaining a healthy respect and care for others. Why not see if they can't help you.

Ten Commandments of Human Relations

1. Thou shalt listen because only in listening to others can you help.
2. Thou shalt be patient because patience is a virtue.
3. Thou shalt not try to solve other people's problems, yours are enough for one person to handle.

4. Thou shalt ask God to handle problems that are too big for you to cope with because that's his job.

5. Thou shalt be available when a friend calls. He wouldn't be calling if he didn't need you.

6. Thou shalt learn to love yourself and who you are because only then can you love others.

7. Thou shalt be vulnerable in front of your friends so that they know you are human like themselves.

8. Thou shalt never betray a confidence for that is one of the worst of all sins.

9. Thou shalt not lie, because honesty will open the doors of love.

10. Thou shalt only worry about today's problems today, because you can't do anything about tomorrow until it comes.

Planning for a New Life

The fourth step to happiness is to begin a plan for your new life after the sale. Chapter 2 explains how planning for a life after the sale is part of the preparation process to getting out. It is a prerequisite for emotional survival. In order to achieve a fulfilling new life, you must first plan to achieve financial independence and continue to be mentally and physically productive.

Financial independence doesn't mean wealth. It doesn't mean an irresponsible and unnecessary accumulation of money or material possessions. Financial independence means that you will have enough resources to take care of yourself and your family in case you become ill. It means that you do not have to rely on government programs to pay the rent and buy the groceries. It means that you can afford to acquire the basic necessities to allow you to concentrate your mental and emotional efforts in developing a meaningful, caring life without fear of financial hardship. Only through financial independence can you truly exert your creative abilities in new challenges. Developing part–time, income–producing activities independent of your business provides a psychological lift in coping with tomorrow's uncertainties. These activities, together with the wise investment of the proceeds from the sale of your business, should provide you with an adequate financial base from which to develop a new life–style.

Planning for a new tomorrow should start before closing the deal. Examine alternative investment opportunities. Research options in traded securities, real estate, private business, government issues, limited partnerships, collectibles, and the myriad of other possibilities so that when you get the cash, you can put it to immediate use in generating a stream of income.

The second objective is to develop a plan for your new life that is productive and contributes to the welfare of humanity. You have probably never thought of yourself as a person particularly concerned or dedicated to the improvement of your fellow man. You have probably felt that such high-minded objectives are better left to the social workers and do-gooders. Maybe you're right. But I don't believe that anyone can deal effectively with feelings of loss and uncertainty without examining his own motivations relative to humanity. The result of a self-examination must inevitably be a rededication of helping others.

You don't need to be a social worker or a religious leader to live a socially productive life. You don't need to be in medicine, psychology, or other healing sciences to help others mend their bodies, minds, or souls. Nor must you operate a home for wayward children, a half-way house, or shelters for the homeless to make a contribution to society. Ann found her own solution to the question of how to make a contribution.

Ann owned and operated a small pet store in an affluent suburb of Boston. When her husband died, she opted to join the ranks of entrepreneurs and acquired a small, run-down business specializing in fish, turtles, snakes, and other aquatic life. Early in the game, she noted her high-society neighbors' desire for socially acceptable thoroughbred dogs and cats and added them to her offerings. Ann's business grew rapidly, and when she finally decided to sell out, she was known throughout New England as one of the foremost authorities on white Persian cats.

Ann made a good living and a substantial cash profit when she finally sold out. Only 55, she felt a severe loss of incentive and motivation, was depressed about her future, and eventually entered therapy. She felt that life held no meaning for her anymore. That the hypocrisy and false values prevalent in her old life-style were something she couldn't cope with anymore, but she didn't know what to do. Financially secure, she wanted to do something meaningful for a change, something to help others rather than merely transferring wealth from one pocket to another.

Ann's therapist happened to be a believer in the Ten Commandments of Human Relations and together they worked out a plan for Ann to open an animal rescue home in the inner city to care for and place homeless animals. Small grants from local veterinary schools enabled Ann to place these pets in low-income homes free of charge, including free care and feeding for two years after placement. Eventually, she solicited larger grants from her affluent ex-customers and with these funds provided elderly, home-bound people with pets to care for and nurture.

Five years later, Ann died of cancer and was posthumously recognized as a humanitarian who cared enough to do something for others less fortunate. Although a small contribution in terms of solving world problems, Ann made a significant difference in the lives of many and will be remembered and revered for years to come.

Ann had not planned for a life after the sale and spent several months with a therapist trying to cope with her feelings of emptiness. Before her illness, she wrote me a letter postulating that she would have been more confident and secure in her new life had she taken the time to think about it and plan for it prior to the sale of her pet shop. Her life turned out fine, but it might have been even better with a little planning, or so she stated. Some of the questions to be answered in your plan for a new life are:

1. Will my new life–style involve a business relationship or something else?

2. What changes must I make in my personal attitudes?

3. How can I diminish the feelings of inadequacy in trying something new?

4. What will take the place of my business as a support unit?

If you completed the self-analysis profile in Chapter 2, it should have given you some of the answers. The main idea is to at least begin the thinking process early in the game. New careers and new life–styles can be a marvelous way to get a new grip on life, but they can also be devastating if the wrong choices are made. There are many possibilities for both a new career and a new life–style after the close. The next chapter examines some of the ways to prepare yourself and develop common guidelines to select a new career that is right for you.

15

A New Life

Changing Careers After the Sale

"You're never too old to learn new tricks," was Rick's favorite saying. Rick sold his small tool and die shop because he wanted to retire from the rat race of business decisions, but spending six months puttering around the house convinced him to look for a new career. "I thought a career change at age 65 would be impossible, yet it's turned out that teaching at West Brook College was the best move I ever made. Business was fun while it lasted, but the challenge can't compare to helping young people develop their own skills."

Many business owners, particularly those who net a substantial gain on the sale of their business, find returning to the business world repugnant. They are ready to try something new—to meet new challenges; to make a contribution; or to satisfy a life–long dream. Even with the financial security the sale has brought them, they find it difficult to cope with unstructured inactivity. They also prefer to keep their excess cash in sound investments for a rainy day, and seek a new career that can produce at least some income to meet daily living needs.

Limited only by personal desires and objectives, career opportunities for the ex-business owner outside the business community are plentiful. While impossible to examine even a small percentage of available options, career possibilities will be explored in five broad categories:

1. Independent, social services organizations

2. Federal government agencies

3. Teaching

4. Combined teaching, consulting, and writing

5. Semi-retirement

Chapter 1 already discussed the importance of researching and planning for a new career before selling your business, but choosing the right career is also important. A new career should provide at least a modest stream of income and also fit your new life–style. Each alternative has advantages and risks. Psychological, financial, and social criteria must be weighed for each plausible alternative. Is a non-business oriented career compatible with your new goals and objectives? Can it be managed in an environment conducive to furthering your personal and spiritual growth? Will exigencies of the new career force compromises in your personal philosophies? These and many other questions must be carefully examined before committing your resources, time, and effort into developing a new vocation.

PSYCHOLOGICAL CRITERIA

There are three psychological hazards to guard against when choosing a new career:

1. An addictive organization.

2. A stressful environment.

3. Controlling policies.

The last thing you want to do is get into another addictive situation. You've seen how addiction to power can and does promote a whole series of bad feelings. It makes no sense to repeat the addictive conditions of your entrepreneurial saga. Seeking a kinder and gentler career might bring a lot more contentment. It can be just as deadly to work for an addictive organization as to own one.

Addictive organizations exist outside the business world as well as within. But how do you know ahead of time which organizations are addictive? How do you know whether the social service organization, or the university, or the government agency you would like to join does, in fact, foster addictive behavior? The best way to find out is to observe. Observe the workings of the group, its avowed mission, its affiliations, its leadership. As pointed out in *The Battle-Weary Executive,* there are several questions to ask to ferret out such behavior:

1. Does the performance of the organization reflect ignorance of its stated mission for existence?

2. Are communications within the organization predominantly in written form?

3. If an organization has financial, credibility, or personnel problems are the reasons for these problems blamed on external situations?

4. Is there internal strife within the organization that promotes competition between people?

5. Does secrecy play a major role in the internal operations of the organization—secrecy between the organization and the outside world and secrecy within its own membership?

6. Does the organization have a reputation for dishonesty in its dealings with its own membership and/or with the outside community?

No organization is immune to addictive behavior. If the government agency, educational, or social organization you're interested in provides affirmative answers to these questions, chances are it fosters addictive behavior. It only makes sense to do sufficient research to avoid inadvertently walking into one of these situations. Being addicted to power in your own company was bad enough; in an external group it can be even worse.

Running your own business generates a high level of executive stress. Once your out of it, you'll probably want to stay away from another career that has the same pressures. Severe mental and physical symptoms are often associated with stressful situations, and most ex-business owners have had enough of that! However, it's unlikely you'll want to give up the intellectual stimulation of constantly changing conditions and challenging opportunities. Intellectual stimulation in a new career can be extremely rewarding and, even though it can lead to stressful feelings, controlled stress can provide remarkable inspiration.

It's also important to avoid an organization that fosters implicit or explicit control over your actions and thoughts by its policies or practices. Religious organizations, professional governing bodies (such as the AMA, ABA, and AICPA), or any organization or group requiring it's members to conform to a predetermined set of rules and regulations for continued association emphasizes control of the individual, and this you don't need.

Controlling practices are not so easily recognized in a private organization such as a large law practice or accounting firm. However, the same control techniques used in the business world apply to these organizations:

1. Membership in the organization family unit.
2. Dedication to the organization's goals.
3. Requirement to meet your boss's personal objectives.
4. Internal competition.

Avoid any organization exhibiting these characteristics or extolling policies intended to control either individuals within the organization or those whom the organization serves.

"I had no idea what I was getting into," lamented Maggie, a graduate nurse who ran her own business as a medical counselor. "I was sick and tired of the nursing rat race and really wanted to do something to help others for a change instead of being caught up with all the internal politicking in the medical profession. That's why I got out and took the job with the Girl Scouts. But what a disappointment. My boss had her own agenda. She insisted everyone adhere to it. Other people in the organization constantly fought. And the head man ran the office like a military camp, trying to control everyone. This was much worse than I ever saw in nursing!"

FINANCIAL CRITERIA

Before making the decision to change careers, take a hard look at your financial resources and requirements. The following eight steps from *The Battle-Weary Executive* will provide you with an outline to follow:

1. Prepare a written budget of living expenses, eliminating all superfluous expenses.
2. Convert all possible assets to liquid investments.
3. Estimate the minimum income needed by month for the next three years to cover living expenses.
4. Determine what contingency funds could be raised through borrowing in the event of an emergency.
5. Determine as close as possible how much cash will be required to get established in your new career.
6. Estimate as closely as possible, how much time will be required to make the career change.
7. Decide if you will need to relocate and what it will cost.
8. Combine all of the above elements into a monthly financial plan.

A budget of necessary monthly living expenses can be prepared from checkbook expenditures over the past year. The format might be like the one shown in Fig. 15–1. Total necessary expenses will tell you how much cash must be available to survive. Remember, this exercise should be done as if your business was already sold.

To calculate which of your assets could be converted into cash in the event of an emergency, use the format shown in Fig. 15–2. Obviously, you don't plan to sell off all these treasured assets, but just having them listed will give you a psychological boost of confidence. It's amazing how much we accumulate over the years without realizing what these possessions would bring on the open market.

	Monthly Expenses	
	Last Year Actual Average	**Next Year Estimate**
Mortgage/Rent	_____	_____
Real Estate Taxes	_____	_____
Electricity	_____	_____
Fuel Oil	_____	_____
Fuel Gas	_____	_____
Water/Sewer	_____	_____
Telephone	_____	_____
Trash Pick Up	_____	_____
Insurance		
House/Apt.	_____	_____
Auto	_____	_____
Life	_____	_____
Health	_____	_____
Other	_____	_____
Repairs		
House/Apt.	_____	_____
Auto	_____	_____
Other	_____	_____
Medical	_____	_____
Dental	_____	_____
Clothing	_____	_____
Charge Cards		
Visa	_____	_____
Master Card	_____	_____
American Express	_____	_____
Gasoline	_____	_____
Department Stores	_____	_____
Other	_____	_____
Big Ticket Purchases		
Auto	_____	_____
Furniture	_____	_____
Appliances	_____	_____
Other	_____	_____
Total	_____	_____

Fig. 15-1 You need to create a realistic budget for after the sale. A good way to do this is to figure out all of your expenses over the last year using a checklist like this one.

	Conversion Value
Cash Surrender Value of Life Insurance	_____
Bank Accounts and CDs—	
_____	_____
_____	_____
_____	_____
_____	_____
Marketable Securities (Stocks, Bonds, Funds)	
_____	_____
_____	_____
_____	_____
_____	_____
Real Estate Investments	
_____	_____
_____	_____
_____	_____
_____	_____
Second Automobile	_____
Collectibles (Stamps, Coins, etc.)	_____
Other Assets—	
_____	_____
_____	_____
_____	_____
_____	_____
Total Cash Available if Converted	_____

Fig. 15-2. Use these forms to calculate which of your assets can be converted into cash in case of an emergency.

To determine your borrowing power, the procedure is much the same. List your assets that could be used as collateral to secure a loan if you absolutely had to raise cash in a hurry and didn't want to liquidate your investments or prized possessions. My clients use the format shown in Fig. 15–3.

In addition to necessary monthly living expenses, but after you have some idea of what your new career and/or life–style will be, you'll need to include those expenditures necessary to get you started down the new road. Such expenditures might be schooling or training costs, relocation expenses, extra start-up costs, maybe a piece of property, a truck, or a new car. Whatever your choice,

	Market Value	Loan Value
Residence for second mortgage, net of existing mortgage		
Automobiles		
Life Insurance		
Investment real estate		
Marketable securities		
CDs and Money Market Funds		
IRAs		
Keogh Plan funds		
Pension funds		
Annuities		
Royalties		
Collectibles		
Boat, airplane, RV		
Other assets with loan value		
Total Available for Borrowing		

Fig. 15-3. For added peace of mind, determine which of your assets could be used as collateral should you ever need to borrow money.

there will probably be some expenses associated with getting started and clearly, they must be included in your financial plan.

Combining the full eight steps can be accomplished by following the format shown in Fig. 15–4.

SOCIAL ACCEPTABILITY

Your own business was a terrific support mechanism. Whenever you felt confused, angry, uncertain, rejected, inadequate, or just tired you could always feel better going to your office and working among familiar settings and problems. It was a soothing balm, an oasis in the midst of external chaos. Your company became, in a sense, a substitute for the support normally received from

---

Cash Expenditures:

Total monthly living expenses (annualized)   _____

Total costs of starting my new career/life style   _____

    Cash Required for First Year   _____

Annual Cash Income From:

Interest and dividends   _____

Rental property   _____

Other investments   _____

Spouse's job   _____

Pensions and annuities   _____

Other sources   _____

    Cash Income for First Year   _____

    Cash Shortfall or (Overage)   _____

Cash Shortfall from cash received for company: _____

    Borrowings Required for First Year (if any)   _____

    Total Cash Available
(must equal or exceed Cash Required)   _____

Fig. 15-4. Using this format, determine any new expenses you might need for beginning your new career or life-style.

family and friends. There was no need to seek reassurance from others; working in your business was support enough. When you sell, however, this crutch is taken away. Suddenly you do need the support of family and friends.

Therefore, choosing a career that is acceptable to your family and friends should influence your decision, at least to some extent. Buying a country inn in Vermont will certainly meet with disapproval if your spouse loves the lights and glitter of the city. Becoming an activist for disarmament will probably not be welcomed by friends intent on a strong national defense policy. Teaching a course in "Love," as Leo Buscaglia does, is not going to bring much support from family or friends who regard such care and concern as frivolous behavior befitting a second childhood.

Don't get me wrong. There's no reason to worry about the social acceptability of your choice if you are so strong and self–assured that you don't need reassurance from others. Such concern is foolish for those with the self–confidence to make their way independent of what anybody thinks. But for most, recognition by others that you have made the right choice is important. A new career and life–style that is acceptable to friends and family should be an important criteria.

PHILOSOPHICAL CRITERIA

As was pointed out in Chapter 14, part of the solution to coping with the psychological trauma of selling your business is to get to know yourself. What you believe in, what you want to contribute to others, how important the accumulation of wealth is, what your goals and objectives for a new life are, and so on. You developed a set of belief criteria that expresses your personal philosophies of life. Now that it's time to make some decisions about a new career or life–style, these philosophies are even more important.

It's not a question of the goodness or badness of a given career. There are no inherent right or wrong answers in your choice. What is important though is that, whatever you decide to do, the characteristics of the career mesh philosophically with your personal goals and beliefs. If you have a genuine desire to help people, sharing your experiences by teaching a college course might be a viable path to follow, but be sure the college or university you choose extols the same teaching philosophies. If you decide to become active in the political arena, you certainly want to direct your efforts toward a party and an office commensurate with your beliefs. Although this seems obvious, without consciously thinking about your new goals and beliefs after getting out you could blissfully dive into a new career doomed from the beginning because of conflicting philosophies. So much for the criteria for selection. Let's get on with the process of choosing a new career.

HOW TO CHOOSE THE RIGHT CAREER

There is no magic formula for successfully choosing the right career. Everyone is different, and each person has his own abilities, goals, needs and desires. The starting point is to pinpoint your personal characteristics and match them with career opportunities. To do that you need to complete a personal self-assessment such as the one shown in Fig. 15-5 at the end of the chapter.

I have repeatedly used the self-assessment form at the end of this chapter to direct career choices for clients and friends alike. It should also be helpful for you. Clearly, the interpretation and weighing of the answers is left to your discretion. The purpose of the form is to crystallize your thinking about yourself.

Once you complete the self-assessment form, see if the results match up with any of the five career possibilities that follow. If they do, it could save you a lot of time and effort searching further.

Independent Social Services Organizations

While an entrepreneur, it was easy to scorn social service workers as do-good dreamers, unable to cope with the hard realities of the rugged individualism of American business. Now that you are getting out, with new personal attitudes about other people and hopefully, a desire to put something back into the society that has been so good to you over the years, working with a social services group might be just the ticket. The type of groups I'm referring to are independently financed and, except for the Peace Corps., supported through private sources. Independent organizations are generally less addictive than government agencies and more opportunities exist for the ex-business owner. Most of the time they are open and above board, non-controlling and not obsessive about their rules and regulations.

If you like to travel internationally, and have a genuine interest in improving environmental and/or human conditions worldwide, not just in America, one of the following international organizations might be a good fit:

- Greenpeace—dedicated to protecting the world's environment and natural resources.
- Amnesty International—trying to free people unjustly incarcerated for their religious or political beliefs.
- American Freedom from Hunger Foundation—concentrating on solutions to the world food shortage.
- Interfaith Center on Corporate Responsibility—also works to resolve food shortages, especially for children.

If you are interested in any of these causes, or possibly in some other international opportunity, the best sources of information and addresses are your public or university library or the Institute for International Economics in Washington, DC.

The Peace Corps is probably the only government–funded social services organization I can unequivocally recommend. The reason is simple. Active duty in the Peace Corps removes the individual physically and emotionally from the bureaucratic hierarchy. Living and working for two years in a far off, underdeveloped country provides little opportunity to be influenced by bureaucratic addictive behavior in Washington. The Peace Corps is really an excellent opportunity to give something back to humanity.

It might be surprising to many, but the Peace Corps desperately wants people over age 50 to serve on active duty. Contrary to the youth–oriented American culture, in underdeveloped nations served by the Corps, society reveres and looks up to age. A volunteer over age 50 is automatically accepted by the local populace as respected and knowledgeable. Not only will you make a concrete, measurable difference in the world, but you will gain valuable insights into yourself and human nature. For further information, contact the Peace Corps recruiting office in your city.

On the other hand, if you prefer to serve in an organization in your hometown, try the yellow pages of the local telephone directory under the heading "Social Services Organizations." Any large city will probably have 150 to 200 such listings. Some have paid staffs, some are all volunteers. A few examples that might be of interest to you include the:

· YMCA and YWCA
· Action Alliance of Senior Citizens
· Traveler's Aid Society
· Meals on Wheels
· National Council on Alcoholism
· American Cancer Society
· Big Brothers-Big Sisters of America
· Cystic Fibrosis Foundation
· National Committee for the Prevention of Child Abuse

Most local chambers of commerce will gladly provide listings of organizations, addresses, and telephone numbers. The whole idea of social services is to provide help, caring, and other services to needy people, or for socially worthwhile causes. Most organizations will readily accept help from people committed to these beliefs.

Perhaps your work will be voluntary for a while, but with a little ingenuity and foresight, you can usually get a paying job eventually. I can't think of a better way to exercise your caring and compassion toward people than to participate, either voluntarily or through a staff paying job, with a reputable social services organization. Personal satisfaction from helping others with no motivation for accumulating wealth or power can be an uplifting experience unparalleled in the business community.

Federal Government Agencies

There are some distinct advantages to choosing government service as a career:

1. Age is generally not a barrier. The mission of many of these agencies requires extensive practical work experience and this can only come with age. In addition, age discrimination laws are enforced more readily in government agencies than in private industry.

2. In the higher grades, salaries come fairly close to private industry. Therefore, if you need to earn a living wage, you'll find more opportunities here than in social services organizations.

3. Pension and retirement programs are generally competitive and many times better than private plans. Health insurance is always included.

4. Many government positions are significantly less stressful than those in the business world. There is usually such a hierarchy of supervision that buck passing becomes a way of life and if the employee doesn't want to share in stressful decision–making, he can always pass it on to someone else.

5. There are many agencies whose main purpose is to help people. All federal social services agencies purport to have this mission.

There are also some very significant disadvantages to government service.

1. If you need to express your creativity, don't look to government service. Regulations proliferate, extensive limitations are placed on individual judgment, and innovative actions are frowned upon.

2. Many of the best positions are political appointments, and when there is a new election, appointees and staff are readily terminated.

3. After experiencing the freedom of being your own boss, the control exerted over your performance and actions might be intolerable. Internal political maneuvering is probably something you can't put up with either, and in most government agencies, internal politicking is a way of life.

4. Many government agencies are addictive organizations. Control, repression of views, obsession with regulations, dishonesty, and denial characteristics proliferate such as the CIA, the IRS, and the military. On the

other hand, there are several organizations that seem to be pressure–free, such as the National Forest Service, the National Park Service, and certain health services.

There is a tremendous need for qualified executives in all types of government service:

- International agencies—U.S.A.I.D. and the foreign service.
- Enforcement agencies—the FBI, CIA, the Department of the Treasury, and the EPA.
- Social welfare organizations—Social Security Administration, and the Federal Housing Administration.
- Natural resource groups—forest service and Parks and Recreation.

These are merely a sample of government agencies that need talented help. Just be sure to examine the downside risks.

Teaching as a Career

Either full or part time teaching can be a very rewarding experience. While many larger colleges and universities require advanced degrees for tenured professorships, local community colleges are often more than willing to accept an experienced executive into the faculty—particularly if the school offers a business curriculum.

A few more enlightened private secondary schools are also beginning to recognize the value of experience outside the education profession and are willing to hire talented businessmen to conduct special classes on business subjects.

Adult education schools, generally taught in the evening, offer another opportunity to change careers. Although the pay isn't much, the work can be satisfying and can augment other part–time income producing activities.

The best way to get a teaching job is to establish public credibility of your expertise. One way of doing this is to develop the curriculum for a one–day seminar on a subject you are intimately familiar with. Arrange to hold the seminar in a local hotel and advertise for registrants in your local newspaper, or even by carefully selected direct mailings. Use the publicity generated by announcements in the business section of your newspaper to authenticate your expertise. If you don't want to spend the time or money to become a celebrity, however, there are other ways to establish credibility. You can become an authority by:

- writing articles for local newspapers, trade publications, chamber of commerce bulletins, or newsletters;

. public speaking engagements with local civic or educational groups; and

. participating in activities in your local, public school system.

You can also become a supporter by:

. writing letters of commendation to local educational groups and colleges identifying actions they have taken of which you approve;

. volunteering for community fund–raising drives; and

. working with local candidates running for political office.

Whether you become a celebrity, an authority, or a supporter, these activities will improve your public image and give you the credibility essential to attracting teaching positions.

Teaching, Consulting, Writing, and Public Speaking

Another interesting possibility for a new career is a combination of part–time teaching and management consulting. A favorite pursuit of entrepreneurs, relating lessons learned in running a business, can be turned into an income–producing activity. Many ex-businessmen now teaching in our nation's business schools supplement their formal teaching assignments with management consulting engagements selling advice from their years of experience to other small businessmen. Many of these part–time professor/consultants also write about solving specific business problems they are familiar with. Writings might appear as articles for trade publications, business journals, newsletters, and even business books. In fact, the old standard of academia—publish or perish—holds true for part–time professorial positions as well as full–time faculty. One activity breeds the other, and in no time, you could find yourself invited to public speaking engagements as well. There is a natural fit in all four opportunities—teaching, consulting, writing, and public speaking—to transfer your business knowledge to others and smooth the road for beginning or struggling business owners.

You'll never get rich following this path, but it can be very rewarding because you are helping others in a very real, concrete way. Though the income isn't substantial, in many cases, it's enough to live on, and after all, that's really all you need.

Getting started in this combination of careers almost invariably requires establishing a public image as an expert in a particular specialty. Once you begin your teaching and writing activities, your reputation will spread and invitations for consulting and public speaking engagements will eventually come without much solicitation on your part.

HOW TO GET STARTED

Regardless of which new career you choose, it's unlikely any will yield the income you earned as an entrepreneur, but all provide some cash flow, and they certainly promote a life–style significantly different from owning your own business. I've made two mid-life career changes. The first one took a long time to sort out just what I wanted to do, but the second time, having been through it once already, I followed three simple rules which made the change smooth and productive:

1. **Research.** Thoroughly investigate the career possibility that interests you the most. Use library sources, government publications, magazines and books, career counseling, talk to friends, visit colleges and universities, interview people already in that career, anything you can think of to give you a thorough understanding of its specific and unusual characteristics.

2. **Training.** If your career choice requires additional training, such as law school or learning a foreign language, take the appropriate steps to qualify for entrance long before you decide to make the change. This way you won't get hung up trying to do something that can't be done.

3. **Public Image.** Establish your credibility as an expert and develop a strong, public relations image as a person with unique abilities. You won't have much difficulty doing this if you've been successful in your own business. In fact, you probably already have a good public image and don't even know it. Once attained, market this new image in the career of your choice.

None of these steps are especially profound, yet it's surprising how many people expect to jump right into a new career without giving it much thought or planning. This inevitably leads to disappointment. It is important to carefully consider several alternatives before making the jump.

SEMI-RETIREMENT

By this time, you're probably saying, "Why worry about a new career. I've run my business for years and now I'm tired. All I really want to do is retire to the golf course and have some peace and quiet". A perfectly normal reaction, and you are certainly entitled to some relaxation and fun after the selling ordeal. So go ahead, play golf, go fishing, take a cruise, and get rested up. If you're like 90 percent of most ex-entrepreneurs, however, such inactivity won't keep you happy for long.

If you've made enough profit on your sale to retire, or if deferred payment terms will keep the income flowing in future years, you won't need to worry about your financial security. On the other hand, unless you are in poor health, the odds are that, once the vacation wears thin, you'll want to do something productive to keep busy.

Most physically and mentally healthy ex-business owners never completely retire. The same drive and energy that lifted you to unprecedented heights as an entrepreneur preclude vegetating on the golf course or in a fishing boat. You need something to keep yourself productive and prevent mental stagnation. If you have learned the lessons of merciful management, perhaps you'd enjoy an activity that adds to the well being of other people. Some constructive activity is essential to avoid the disorientation that almost invariably results when retirement years are non-productive. Retirement disorientation creates a whole host of unsavory conditions. Among the worst are:

· Boredom

· Loss of interest

· Deteriorating family relationships

· Psychosomatic health problems

Although physical activity is important, without an active mind, the body will soon lose its energy. Fortunately, your mental inspiration should be at a peak after just having successfully sold your business. You have a wealth of experience to draw upon, and now is the time to put it to use.

There are a host of activities to keep you busy and productive during your retirement years. Some touch on your past experience, some are just for fun. Clearly, the choices are limited only by your own imagination. Just to get your little gray cells churning, here are a few ideas.

1. **Buy speculative real estate.** If you have never tried real estate investing, give it a whirl. Residential rental properties, commercial buildings, industrial plant sites, apartment buildings, are all income–producing ventures that will keep you busy managing the property. If you don't want to do it alone, invest in a real estate limited partnership. There are plenty around now that most tax shelters have been obsoleted.

2. **Invent a new product, process, or practice.** Maybe you're not a Ben Franklin, and you don't hold an engineering degree, but you can still design a new bookshelf, create a new salad, or invent a stronger garbage can. Haven't you ever said, "With all the technology nowadays, why can't somebody invent . . . ?" Well, go ahead. There must be some better process or product or method that you can come up with. Whatever it is, it will stimulate your creative processes, and that's good!

3. **Expand a hobby.** Now that you have the time, why not develop those dormant talents for carpentry work, or those suppressed desires for working with ham radios or personal computers. Perhaps you have hidden talents for performing in a musical group, producing a play, or painting. Collecting rare stamps, coins, jewelry, or antiques might be fun. Gentleman farming, although not as popular as it once was, still provides the opportunity to commune with nature while maintaining physical and mental activity. What about getting active in your local Boy Scouts or Girl Scouts. How about a Junior Achievement project? You probably have at least one hobby you've enjoyed over the years, and now is the time to expand it.

4. **Invest in small, start-up companies.** Investment bankers are always looking for private investors to share in the seed money or first–stage financing of promising new companies. This is a risky investment, obviously, but many pan out to be very lucrative. Also, it will give you a new interest and a way to put your past entrepreneurial experience to use.

5. **Become a director of a small company.** With all of your experience, this is certainly something you are qualified for. Many investment bankers welcome retired business executives on boards of companies they have invested in.

6. **Take an extended trip.** Go on a Safari to Kenya or cruise to Argentina on a freighter. Buy a EuroRail pass and tour Europe by train. Join an expedition up the Amazon. Hike the Appalachian Trail. Fly to the Far East and tour China or Nepal. Perhaps, if you are in good health, go to an Outward Bound school for two weeks or take a boat trip. After sitting in an office or walking a plant floor for years, get some fresh air and rejuvenate your mental processes.

7. **Relocate your household.** Sounds too drastic? Perhaps, but it's amazing what a change in scenery can do for you. If you have a house, try a condo. If you live in a condo, try the shore. Move to the country from the city or from the city to the country. Anything to change your perspective.

8. **Write your memoirs.** Even if you don't have any writing talent, you can always talk into a recorder and hire a typist to put it into print. Don't expect to sell the project, but it can be a lot of fun recounting past experiences and people. Plus, this type of project focuses your mind on being creative, and that's important.

9. **Join a SCORE chapter.** SCORE stands for the Service Corps of Retired Executives, a volunteer organization sponsored by the Small Busi-

Fig. 15-5. Personal Self-Assessment Evaluation.

	Like	Don't Like	Good At	Must Have
Job Characteristics				
Working with numbers	___	___	___	___
Working with people	___	___	___	___
Working with computers	___	___	___	___
Working by myself	___	___	___	___
Working with others	___	___	___	___
Working on projects	___	___	___	___
Seeing the result of my efforts	___	___	___	___
Administrative work	___	___	___	___
Managing people	___	___	___	___
Pleasing my boss	___	___	___	___
Moving around (travel)	___	___	___	___
Staying in one place	___	___	___	___
Selling	___	___	___	___
Buying	___	___	___	___
Analyzing	___	___	___	___
Writing	___	___	___	___
Reading	___	___	___	___
Calculating	___	___	___	___
Instructing others	___	___	___	___
Public speaking	___	___	___	___
People Orientation				
Doing the work myself	___	___	___	___
Getting others to do the work	___	___	___	___
Delegating authority	___	___	___	___
Praising or rewarding others	___	___	___	___
Criticizing others	___	___	___	___
Work with young people	___	___	___	___
Work with older people	___	___	___	___
Work with people my own age	___	___	___	___
Work with the handicapped	___	___	___	___
Work with poor people	___	___	___	___
Compensation				
Income over $100,000/yr	___	___	___	___

(Fig. 15-5 continues)

(Fig. 15-5.) continued

	Like	Don't Like	Good At	Must Have
Income $75–$100,000/yr	___	___	___	___
Income $50–$75,000/yr	___	___	___	___
Income $25–$50,000/yr	___	___	___	___
Income up to $25,000/yr	___	___	___	___
Company paid pension plan	___	___	___	___
Company car	___	___	___	___
Group health/life insurance	___	___	___	___
Company stock saving plan	___	___	___	___
Opportunity for advancement	___	___	___	___
Personal Attitudes				
Playing the corporate "game"	___	___	___	___
Winning	___	___	___	___
Seeing others advance	___	___	___	___
High social status	___	___	___	___
Peer acceptance	___	___	___	___
Driving long distances	___	___	___	___
Flying	___	___	___	___
Meeting new people	___	___	___	___
Meeting new challenges	___	___	___	___
Time with my family	___	___	___	___
Working Conditions				
Work standing up	___	___	___	___
Work sitting down	___	___	___	___
Work moving around	___	___	___	___
Working indoors	___	___	___	___
Working outdoors	___	___	___	___
Willing to commute—				
Up to ½ hour	___	___	___	___
Up to 1½ hours	___	___	___	___
Up to 2 hours	___	___	___	___
No limit	___	___	___	___
Drive to work	___	___	___	___
Public Transportation	___	___	___	___
Fly to work	___	___	___	___

ness Administration to counsel mostly start-up entrepreneurs. Some local chapters perform a real service to beginning small businessmen, and your experience would be invaluable to them. Some chapters are worthless, however, so you'll have to check out the chapter in your locale.

Whatever you decide to do, the most important thing is to stay active, both physically and mentally. Be productive, do something constructive, expand to new horizons, let that entrepreneurial spirit continue to thrive, and above all, enjoy your well–earned new life–style. You've worked hard to get there. You've taken a lot of risks. You've probably hurt some people on your way to being a successful businessman, but hopefully you have also helped more. Once your business is sold, you deserve to reap the benefits of a lifetime of hard work. Go to it. Enjoy!

Epilogue

A New Tomorrow— Make it Count

BY THIS TIME I'M SURE YOU ARE TIRED OF HEARING SUCH PHRASES AS merciful management, care and compassion, helping others, and so on. You are also probably perturbed about continual admonishments to stand up and be counted and take an active role in solving some of society's ills. I wouldn't blame you if you were. Nobody likes to be preached at, except perhaps in church, temple, synagogue, or other house of worship. I have taken this approach for three reasons because:

1. Many entrepreneurs and professionals, in the heat of battle, tend to lose sight of the benefits they can derive from socially conscious endeavors.

2. Entrepreneurs and professionals occupy unique positions in American society. They can influence many people, from employees to political groups. Their power, prestige, and money enable them to become leaders in the community.

3. Feelings of failure or loss can devastate even the strongest person, and when this happens, he desperately needs other people for support— family, friends, employees, and customers.

In any walk of life, and especially in the business and professional worlds, a person receives only as much as he gives over a period of time. True, some people hit it lucky and become millionaires with very little effort. Selling the right product or service at the right time, making the right investment, or inventing a new product or process can yield enormous financial gain almost overnight. Most people aren't that fortunate, however, and must struggle to build their nest egg over many years. This requires the help and cooperation of many people, including those in community and political bodies. It is not something a person can master all by himself.

Although it is never a favorite topic, business failure remains a real possibility for many entrepreneurs. One out of every two businesses started from scratch will fail, and at least one-third of business acquisitions turn out to be

263

financial nightmares. More often than not, imbued with overwhelming optimism, a business owner or professional fails to recognize serious financial problems until they are out of hand and reaching calamitous proportions. The psychological impact of potential failure can be enormous, and an owner must rely on the support, advice, caring, and compassion of others. Customers, employees, bankers, and community leaders can very often pull the business through when the owner, by himself, cannot. So from a purely selfish motive, if nothing else, it behooves a person to develop a caring attitude in relationships with others.

For these reasons, I have been a bit preachy. The world of business is not a hard, cold world. It is warm and caring, and a simple exercise in kindness and compassion now, can stave off or diminish financial anguish later on.

THE DARK SIDE OF BUSINESS

There is a second face of business, however, and this face is not all smiles and warmth, it is the dark side. It is the face of cruelty, ruthlessness, and selfish greed. It is the face worn by an increasing number of those in positions of power in the business and financial communities, many corporate manipulators, investment speculators, and government influence–peddlers. Historically, America has been a land of the entrepreneurial spirit, thrilled when the little guy makes it big. Always pulling for the underdog. In recent years, however, there has been a radical change in our underlying social culture. The work ethic has all but disappeared. While the so-called middle class has shrunk, the wealthy have increased in numbers, and the poor have multiplied, reaching new levels of despair. Money has come too easy. Fortunes have been made, and lost, and made again with the stock market breaking all records. Many money brokers who purport to help expand small and midsized businesses have collected billions of dollars simply by manipulating companies for their own account in the thriving business acquisition market.

Fortunately, some financial institutions are socially conscious and make a strong effort to be responsible such as the Chemical Bank of New York's community outreach program. Sadly, other banking conglomerates, including some investment bankers and venture capitalists, instead of committing to active participation in resolving human disparities, have become more interested in amassing huge fortunes for themselves. And at whose expense? The money must come from somewhere. Certainly not from the airlines, or the steel industry, or farmers, or the shoe industry, or the computer industry, or ITT, GE, or General Motors. Where then? Did the government print more money to provide these billions? Did foreign governments, oil sheiks, or South African gold mines supply the cash? No. Most of this money came from entrepreneurs, small businessmen and professionals, gullible individuals, and yours and my tax dollars.

The American free enterprise system is founded on, and supports, businesses that are creative in the development of new products and services and in marketing ingenuity. We have transcended the era of the harder you work, or the smarter you are, the better you do. We have entered a new era where playing the credit game means anything goes, no matter who gets hurt or what harm comes to our national economy.

American business is facing a crisis. Not because of the trade deficit, ineffective import quotas, government regulations, Big Business, or Big Brother. Many individuals, small business owners, and professionals cannot be heard over the roar of Wall Street, and they need help. They need the rest of us to join forces with them and tell these proponents of money mania that enough is enough. How? By refusing to deposit money in socially irresponsible banks. By ignoring offers of loans at usurious interest rates and fees. By withdrawing our investment accounts from gluttonous brokerage houses. By refusing to live on "funny money" credit. And by concentrating on building our businesses and practices with honest, caring people, not with someone else's money.

At the root of this financial and business crisis is the continuous, ambitious striving for wealth and power without any regard for its effect on others. The never ending chase for the buck. The all consuming fervor to be the best. Now don't get me wrong. There are plenty of millionaire entrepreneurs making fortunes honestly and aboveboard. They're entitled to whatever they can earn legitimately. That is what free enterprise is all about. But private wealth alone is not the measure of a long-term healthy economic system. If wealth is accumulated by laying off workers who have been with a company for their lifetime and are too old to find employment elsewhere, cheating the customer by producing inferior goods and services while increasing prices, and lying to employees to keep wage rates down, it cannot last. Such ill-gotten gains will inevitably tumble. Any student of economic history knows that whenever the social needs of a culture have been ignored, it has died, from the Greeks to the U.S.S.R., to several present–day African nations. Every entrepreneur and professional has it within his power to change things. Perhaps he can't stop worldwide famine and suffering, but he certainly can help individuals. If it's one kindness today, maybe reach for two tomorrow. Think of it this way: if you helped two people today, and each of them helped two people tomorrow, and each of those people helped two more people the next day—well, you can see where that would lead. In one month, one billion people would be helped by others. Just think of what a change that would make in our sick, tired world.

A NEW LIFE AWAITS

One final, and personal, anecdote. Discussions of psychological trauma and picking up the pieces of a person's life after the sale are not idle speculation. It is rare when someone can walk away from his business without feeling any qualms or anxiety for the future. When I sold my last business (with my partner), it felt like the world was caving in. Market and economic deterioration forced us to make many layoffs, including scores of older employees. Many were unable to find new employment and were forced to live their remaining years on pension and social security checks. In the end, a work force of over 400 people was decimated to less than 100. Tired and sick at heart, we sold the business to a small group of employees.

All the traumatic feelings described in this book converged: fear of the future, anger, depression, self-doubt, and eventually, overwhelming grief for hurting so many innocent people. Down, but not out, a new career and a new life-style offered a chance for survival. Through the forgiving encouragement of family members, the unflinching support of friends, and a hidden inner strength, I became determined to dedicate the remainder of my life to encouraging a more caring and compassionate relationship between people and to help one person solve one small problem each day. I now know that moral community is not only the answer to feelings of loss and abandonment, but the only solution to a troubled world.

You can help improve the system and you can make a difference, one person at a time, soon, we can swing the pendulum back to where it belongs. Best wishes for a terrific future!

Sample Stock Purchase Agreement

This Agreement is made and entered into as of the _____day of _____, 19XX, between (name of Buyer), hereinafter referred to as the "Buyer," and (name of Seller), hereinafter referred to as the "Seller".

Recitals

1. Seller owns all of the issued and outstanding shares of common stock of (name of the company being sold), a Delaware corporation, hereinafter referred to as the "Company".

2. The Company is engaged in the business of (whatever business it is in), in the State of (State of residence of Company).

3. Seller desires to sell and Buyer desires to purchase all of the subject shares on the terms set forth herein.

NOW THEREFORE, in consideration of the sale and purchase of the subject shares and of the premises and the mutual promises, covenants and conditions hereinafter set forth, the parties hereby agree as follows:

ARTICLE I
Definitions

1.1 "Closing Date" shall mean the date on which the Closing hereunder is held. The Closing shall be at _____AM in the offices of (name of Seller or Buyer lawyer).

1.2 "Intellectual Property" shall mean any patent, copyright, trademark, service mark, brand name or trade name, any registration of the same, and any other proprietary rights, inventions, trade secrets, know-how or processes, and any rights in or to the foregoing.

ARTICLE II
Purchase and Sale

2.1 **Purchase Price.** On the Closing Date, subject to the terms and conditions set forth in this Agreement, Seller agrees to sell and convey to Buyer, and Buyer agrees to purchase the subject shares, for an amount equal to $_____.

2.2 **Payment.** Payment of the purchase price shall be made as follows:

a. Buyer shall deliver to Seller a Promissory Note (the "Note") substantially in the form of Exhibit _____attached hereto in the original principle amount of $_____ .

b. The balance of the Purchase Price shall be paid to Sellers in the form of a wire transfer to a bank account designated by Seller, or by cashier's check.

All payments hereunder are subject to the terms and conditions herein set forth, and will be made by Buyer in reliance upon the representations, warranties, covenants and agreements contained herein.

2.3 Note, Guaranty and Security Interest. The Note shall be personally guaranteed by the Buyer. In addition, the Note shall be secured by a security interest in the assets of the Company. Additionally, the Note shall be secured by all of the common stock issued or to be issued of the Company. These Guaranties and Security Interests are pursuant to a Guaranty and Security Agreement substantially in the form of Exhibit _____attached hereto. Seller agree that the security interest in the assets of the Company shall be subordinated to the interest of the Lender.

2.4 Leases. At the Closing, Buyer shall personally guarantee to Seller the payment of any obligations under any leases which arise from and after the Closing Date.

ARTICLE III
Deliveries

3.1 Seller's Deliveries. On the Closing Date, subject to the terms and conditions set forth in this Agreement, Seller shall make the following deliveries:

(a) Stock certificates representing Subject Shares, endorsed in blank;

(b) Stock record books, minute books, and corporate seals of the Company;

(c) Resignations of the officers and directors of the Company;

(d) All files, records and correspondence of the Company;

(e) All other items or documents necessary or reasonably appropriate hereunder,

3.2 Buyer's Deliveries. On the Closing Date, subject to the terms and conditions set forth in this Agreement, Purchaser shall make the following deliveries:

(a) Payment of the Purchase Price as heretofore provided;

(b) All other items or documents necessary or reasonably appropriate hereunder;

(c) The Note, duly executed by Buyer, together with a Guaranty thereof by Buyer's shareholders;

(d) The Guaranty and Security Agreement, duly executed by the parties thereto, together with the deliveries required thereunder.

ARTICLE IV
Closing

The Closing hereunder shall take place at the offices of Able, Baker and Grey, counsel for Buyer, on the Closing Date, or at such other place as may be mutually agreed upon in writing by the Buyer and the Seller.

ARTICLE V
Representations and Warranties of Seller

Seller represents and warrants to Buyer that, except as specifically set forth in Exhibit ____ annexed herein, the following statements are true and correct as of the Closing Date:

5.1 **Seller.** Seller has full power and authority to sell the Subject Shares and to enter into this Agreement and to carry out the transactions contemplated hereby. This Agreement constitutes a valid and binding obligation of Seller enforceable in accordance with its terms.

5.2 **Ownership.** Seller is the owner of the Subject Shares, free and clear of all claims, liens and encumbrances whatsoever. Seller will convey to Buyer, at the Closing Date, good and marketable title to the Subject Shares free and clear of all claims, liens and encumbrances whatsoever, and upon said conveyance, Buyer will have good and marketable title to the Subject Shares free and clear of all liens, claims and encumbrances whatsoever.

5.3 **Organization and Standing.** The Company (i) is a corporation duly organized and existing and in good standing under the laws of its state of incorporation, (ii) is entitled to own or lease its properties and to carry on its business as and in the places where such properties are now owned. leased or operated, or such business is now conducted, and (iii) is duly qualified as a foreign corporation in good standing in each jurisdiction in which the nature of the business or character of it's properties makes qualification necessary and the failure to qualify would have a material adverse effect on such corporation or would permanently preclude such corporation from enforcing its rights with respect to any material asset. The copies of the Articles of Incorporation, Bylaws, Minute Book, and stock records of the Company, as in effect on the date hereof and previously delivered by the Seller to the Buyer, are true, correct, current and complete.

5.4 **Capitalization.** The authorized capital stock of the Company consists of 1,000 shares of capital stock, of no par value per share. The Subject Shares have been validly issued, are now outstanding, are fully paid and nonassessable and constitute all of the issued and outstanding shares of capital stock of the Company.

5.5 **No Options or Warrants.** There are no outstanding options, warrants, rights or privileges, pre-emptive or contractual, to acquire any shares of the capital stock of the Company.

5.6 **Financial Statements.** The Financial Statements and the Interim Financial Statements which have been presented by Seller to Buyer are true, complete and correct and have been prepared in accordance with generally accepted accounting principles consistently followed throughout the periods indicated. These Statements present fairly the financial position of the Company as of the dates indicated and the results of operations for the periods then ended.

5.7 Liabilities. To the best of Seller's knowledge, except as and to the extent reflected or reserved against in the Company statements, or otherwise disclosed herein, (i) the Company had no material Liabilities or Obligations, and (ii) as of the date of Closing, the Company will not be subject to, and will not have, any Liabilities or Obligations which in the aggregate are material, except as either disclosed in the Interim Statements or as may have arisen in the ordinary course of business of the Company since the date of said Balance Sheet, none of which newly arisen Liabilities or Obligations shall have a material adverse effect upon the Company or its organization, business, properties or financial condition.

5.8 No Violation. Neither the execution and delivery of this Agreement nor compliance with the terms and provisions of this Agreement by Seller or the Company, will: (i) conflict with or result in a breach or violation of any of the terms, conditions or provisions of the articles of incorporation or bylaws of the Company or of the terms and provisions of any indenture or other agreement to which Seller or the Company may be a party or to which any of them may be bound or to which any of the may be subject, or any judgment, order, decree, ruling of any court or governmental authority or any injunction to which either of them is subject.

5.9 Contracts. As used herein "contracts" means any contract, agreement, or understanding, including but not limited to instruments or evidences of indebtedness, leases and licenses. Except as listed in Exhibit _____, the Company is not a party to any written or oral contracts:

(a) for the employment of any officer, director, consultant, or employee;

(b) with any labor union;

(c) for the purchase of any materials or supplies or for the sale of any product or service;

(d) relating to any licenses, distributorships, representatives or leases;

(e) relating to any bonus, pension or profit sharing plan;

(f) if not referenced above which are material to the Company.

5.10 Insurance. As of the Closing Date, The Company will carry the appropriate insurance against loss by fire casualty and other or other such losses as may be customary for the type of business operated and such insurance policies will be turned over to Buyer at Closing Date.

5.11 Litigation. There are no claims, actions, suits, proceedings or investigations pending or threatened against or affecting the Seller or the Company, at law or in equity or admiralty or before or by and federal, state, municipal or other governmental department, commission, board, agency or instrumentality, nor has any such action been pending during the 12 month period preceding the date of this Agreement; and Seller or the Company are not operating under or subject to, or in default with respect to any order, writ, injunction or decree of any court or federal or other governmental department or other instrumentality.

5.12 Compliance With Laws. To the best of Seller's knowledge the company has complied with all laws, regulations and orders including, but not limited to, OSHA, EEOA, and EPA or any similar or equivalent state legislation or rule applicable to its business in any material aspect. All permits, licenses and authorizations required by such regulatory bodies have been obtained and are in effect for the Company.

5.13 No Conflict Of Interest. Except for the normal rights of a stockholder, officer or director, as the case may be, (a) no stockholder, director, officer or employee of the Company has any interest in any property, real or personal, tangible or intangible necessary for or used in the business of the Company; and (b) no stockholder, director, officer or employee has an interest, direct or indirect, in any person or entity which (i) competes with the Company, or, (ii) is a party to any contract, oral or written, with the Company.

5.14 Accounts Receivable. The Company's financial statements and interim statements accurately and fairly reflect the amount of the trade receivables of the Company as of the date of such statements, in accordance with generally accepted accounting principles consistently applied. All trade accounts receivable arise out of sales occurring in the ordinary course of business and Seller has no reason to believe that any person obligated upon such accounts has any right of offset to payment thereof.

5.15 Inventory. The inventory of the Company as reflected on the most recent Interim Statements consists of items of a quality and quantity usable or salable in the normal course of business and which are not obsolete or unusable. Such inventory is valued at the lower of cost or market in accordance with generally accepted accounting principles.

5.16 Intellectual Property. All licenses, trademarks, copyrights, patents, etc. and all other such Intellectual property belonging to or used by the Company in its ordinary course of business are listed in Exhibit _____ attached hereto.

5.17 Labor Controversies. There are no controversies pending or threatened between the Company and any union or any employee. The Company is not subject to any threatened strikes or work stoppages or any organizational efforts by any union or collective bargaining unit not currently representing the employees of the Company.

5.18 Pension and Profit Sharing Plans. The Seller has delivered to Buyer copies of all pension and profit sharing plans or programs and has included in such delivery the most recent Internal Revenue Service determination letter issued in respect of each such plan or program together with all pertinent trustee reports and tax returns for such plans or programs.

5.19 Certain Tax Matters. No election has been made under Section 341 (f) of the Internal Revenue Code to treat the Company as a "consenting corporation" nor is the Company a "personal holding company" as defined under Section 542 of the Code.

5.20 Securities Matters. The shares of the Company are not required to be registered under provisions of Section 5 of the Securities Act of 1933 or any applicable state securities law.

5.21 Conduct of Business. Since the last Interim Statements and until the Closing Date the Company has not undertaken to enact any transactions not in the ordinary course of business other than those transactions which have been listed on Exhibit _____.

5.22 Material Change. Since the date of the last Interim Statement, there have been no adverse changes of a material nature in the condition of the Company, financial or otherwise that is not disclosed in Exhibit _____.

5.23 Tax Returns. The Company has made timely filings of all required Federal and State tax returns. There are no claims pending against the Company for unpaid or disputed tax liabilities and the last year which has been audited by the Internal Revenue Service is 19XX and by the State 19XX.

5.24 Disclosure. No representation or warranty made by the Seller herein contains any untrue statement of a material fact or omits to state a material fact necessary to make such representation or warranty not misleading.

ARTICLE VI
Representations and Warranties by Buyer

Buyer represents and warrants to Seller that the following statements are true and correct on the Closing Date:

6.1 Organization and Standing. Buyer is a corporation duly organized, existing and in good standing under the laws of the State of _____.

6.2 Breach of Statute or Contract: Required Consents. Neither the execution and delivery of this Agreement nor compliance with the terms and provisions of this Agreement by Buyer will: (i) conflict with or result in a breach or violation of any of the terms, conditions or provisions of the articles of incorporation or bylaws of the Buyer or any judgment, order, decree or ruling or any court or governmental authority or of any contract or commitment of which Buyer is a party which is material to the operations or conduct of business of the Buyer; or (ii) require the affirmative consent or approval of any nongovernmental third party (except Buyer's shareholders). Buyer is not in violation of any applicable law, order, rule or regulation promulgated or judgment entered by any federal or state court or governmental authority relating to the operation or conduct of the business of Buyer which might impair the consummation or the transaction contemplated hereby.

6.3 Litigation. Buyer is not a party to or subject to any legal, administrative, arbitration, investigation proceeding or controversy nor are any such actions threatened which might materially affect the financial condition of Buyer.

6.4 Authority. Buyer has full power and authority to enter into this Agreement and to carry out the transactions contemplated hereby, and all corporate and other proceedings required to be taken by Buyer in connection with this Agreement have been duly and validly taken. This Agreement constitutes a valid and binding obligation of Buyer and is enforceable in accordance with its terms.

ARTICLE VII
Conditions Precedent of Buyer

The obligations of Buyer hereunder are subject to the conditions that:

7.1 Representations and Warranties True. The representations and warranties of Seller contained in this Agreement shall be true on the Closing Date.

7.2 Compliance With The Agreement. Seller shall have performed and complied with all agreements and conditions required by this Agreement to be performed or complied with by him prior to or on Closing Date.

7.3 Opinion of Company's Counsel. Buyer shall have received an opinion of counsel to the Company and Seller, dated the Closing Date in the form of Exhibit _____.

7.4 Injunction. On the Closing Date there shall be no effective injunction, writ, restraining order or any order of any kind issued by a court or competent jurisdiction directing that the transaction contemplated herein shall not be consummated as herein provided.

7.5 Casualty. Neither the business of the Company nor any of its property shall have been affected in any material way, prior to Closing Date, by any flood, fire, accident or other casualty or act of God or the public enemy.

7.6 Adverse Development. Between the date of the last Interim Statements and the Closing Date there shall have been no material adverse developments which materially affect the value of the business or the assets or the goodwill of the Company.

7.7 Deliveries. On or before the Closing Date Seller shall have delivered to Buyer all of the materials specified herein.

7.8 Financing. Buyer shall have obtained financing for the transaction from his own sources satisfactory to the Buyer.

ARTICLE VIII
Conditions Precedent of the Seller

The obligations of Seller hereunder are subject to the conditions that:

8.1 Representations and Warranties True. The representations and warranties of Buyer contained in this Agreement shall be true on the Closing Date.

8.2 Compliance With The Agreement. Buyer shall have performed and complied with all agreements and conditions required by this Agreement to be performed or complied with by him prior to or on Closing Date.

8.3 Opinion of Company's Counsel. Seller shall have received an opinion of counsel to the Buyer, dated the Closing Date in the form of Exhibit _____.

8.4 Injunction. On the Closing Date there shall be no effective injunction, writ, restraining order or any order of any king issued by a court or competent jurisdiction directing that the transaction contemplated herein shall not be consummated as herein provided.

8.5 Payment. Payment shall be made as provided herein.

8.6 Deliveries. On or before the Closing Date Buyer shall have delivered to Seller all of the following documents: (i) Certified Articles of Incorporation of Buyer; (ii) Copies of Buyer's Bylaws certified by Buyer's Secretary; (iii) Certificate of Good Standing; (iv) all other deliveries required hereunder.

ARTICLE IX
Indemnification

9.1 By Seller. Seller hereby agrees, notwithstanding the Closing, the delivery of instruments of conveyance, and regardless of any investigation at any time made by or on behalf of any party hereto or of any information any party hereto may have in respect thereof, he will save and hold Buyer and the Company harmless from and against any damage, liability, loss or deficiency arising out of or resulting from and will pay to Buyer and the Company the amount of damages suffered thereby together with any amount which they or any of them may pay or become obligated to pay on account of:

(a) the breach of any warranty or representation by Seller herein or any misstatement of a fact or facts herein made by the Seller;

(b) the failure by Seller to state or disclose a material fact herein necessary to make the facts herein stated or disclosed not misleading;

(c) any failure of the Seller, the Company or its officers or directors to perform or observe any term, provision, covenant or condition hereunder on the part of any of them to be performed or observed, or;

(d) any act performed, transaction entered into, or state of facts suffered to exist by Seller or the Company or its officers or directors in violation of the terms of this Agreement.

9.2 By Buyer. Buyer hereby agrees, notwithstanding the Closing, the delivery of instruments of conveyance, and regardless of any investigation at any time made by or on behalf of any party hereto or of any information any party hereto may have in respect thereof, he will save and hold Seller harmless from and against any damage, liability, loss or deficiency arising out of or resulting from and will pay to Seller the amount of damages suffered thereby together with any amount which he may pay or become obligated to pay on account of:

(a) the breach of any warranty or representation by Buyer herein or any misstatement of a fact or facts herein made by the Buyer;

(b) the failure by Buyer to state or disclose a material fact herein necessary to make the facts herein stated or disclosed not misleading;

(c) any failure of the Buyer, to perform or observe any term, provision, covenant or condition hereunder to be performed or observed, or;

(d) any act performed, transaction entered into, or state of facts suffered to exist by Buyer in violation of the terms of this Agreement.

ARTICLE X
Nature and Survival of Representations

All statements contained in any certificate delivered by or on behalf of Seller or Buyer pursuant to this Agreement or in connection with the transactions contemplated hereby shall be deemed representations and warranties by Seller and Buyer hereunder. All representations and warranties and agreements made by Seller or Buyer in this Agreement or pursuant hereto shall survive the Closing hereunder.

ARTICLE XI
Notices

All notices, requests, demands, and other communications hereunder shall be in writing and shall be deemed to have been duly given if delivered or mailed first class postage prepaid to the following addresses:

(a) To Seller:

(Seller's address)

(b) To Buyer:

(Buyer's address)

or to such other address or to such other person as Buyer and Seller shall have last designated by notice to the other.

ARTICLE XII
Modification

The Agreement contains the entire agreement between the parties hereto with respect to the transactions contemplated herein and shall not be modified or amended except by an instrument in writing signed by or on behalf of all of the parties hereto.

ARTICLE XIII
Expenses

Each of the parties hereto shall pay their own expenses in connection herewith including but not limited to fees for legal, accounting, consulting and other services.

ARTICLE XIV
Assignment

This Agreement shall not be assignable by either party hereto without the prior written consent of the other party.

ARTICLE XV
Law to Govern

This Agreement shall be governed by and construed and enforced in accordance with the laws of the State of _____.

IN WITNESS WHEREOF, the parties hereto have duly executed this Agreement as of the date first above written.

SELLER   BUYER

_____   By _____

                                Its _____

Sample
Getting Out Agreement
Between Shareholders

THIS AGREEMENT, entered into this _____day of _____, 19XX, between (name of shareholder) ("Jones") and (name of second shareholder) ("Smith"), hereinafter referred to as Shareholder or collectively as Shareholders;

Witnesseth:

WHEREAS, XYZ Corp., a Delaware corporation ("Corporation") has authorized and outstanding shares of no par value Common Stock ("Stock"); and,

WHEREAS, the Shareholders are interested in the management of the business of the Corporation and are respectively the owners of the Stock set forth below in Section 1.1; and,

WHEREAS, the parties hereto mutually desire to make provision for the purchase and sale of the Stock upon the occurrence of certain significant events; and to make provision for other significant events involving the transfer and ownership of the Stock;

NOW THEREFORE, the Shareholders mutually hereby agree:

ARTICLE I
Stock Subject to Agreement

1.1 Stock Subject To This Agreement. The following number of shares of Stock are presently held by the Shareholders:

Shareholder	Shares
Jones	100
Smith	100

The terms of this agreement shall apply to all Stock presently held by the Shareholders and any additional Stock acquired by a Shareholder during his lifetime in his own behalf, or by his estate after his death, whether by purchase, Stock dividend or otherwise. It is contemplated that any such additional Stock will be endorsed in accordance with Section 1.2 hereof and identified by a written memorandum executed by the parties and attached hereto, but failure so to endorse and include the additional Stock in a memorandum shall not remove such Stock from the terms of this Agreement.

1.2 Endorsement of Stock Certificates. Each Stock certificate representing shares of Stock now held or hereafter acquired by the Shareholders shall be endorsed substantially as follows:

> "The shares represented by this certificate are subject to the provisions of the Agreement to Purchase Corporate Stock, dated _____, which Agreement is available for inspection at the principal office of the Corporation".

Provided, however, that failure so to endorse any of the Shareholders' Stock certificates shall not invalidate this Agreement. The Corporation shall keep a copy of this Agreement available for inspection by all properly interested parties at the principal office.

1.3 Use of Stock as Collateral. The Shareholders have the right to pledge Stock owned by them as Collateral security for personal indebtedness, even though the certificate of such Stock is endorsed as provided in Section 1.2, but any Stock so pledged shall remain subject to the terms of this Agreement. The mere pledge of Stock shall not be an event which provides the Shareholder the option to purchase or sell Stock pursuant to Article 2 of this Agreement.

1.4 Rights of the Shareholders. The Stock owned by the respective Shareholders subject to this Agreement shall be voted by them, and upon the death of a Shareholder by the legal representative of his estate, until purchase of his Stock pursuant to this Agreement or other permitted transfer or disposition, as the case may be. Any dividends payable on the Stock shall be paid to the respective Shareholders or their respective legal representatives, as the case may be.

ARTICLE II
Purchase and Sale of Stock

2.1 Restrictions of Lifetime Transfers of Stock. (a) A Shareholder shall not, during his lifetime, sell, assign, give, or otherwise transfer or dispose of any shares of Stock without first giving written notice to the non-transferring Shareholder of such intention to sell or make disposition thereof, which notice shall state the Stock proposed to be disposed of, the amount of the consideration offered, if any, and the name of the prospective purchaser or assignee. The date the nontransferring Shareholder receives such notice shall be the Transfer Notice Date. The nontransferring Shareholder may, at his option, purchase all, but not part, of the shares of Stock offered in such notice for a purchase price which is the lower of (i) the price offered as contained in such notice, or (ii) $XXX,XXX, which amount shall be payable within 90 days of the Transfer Notice Date.

2.2 Upon Death. Upon the death of a Shareholder, the Corporation shall purchase all of the shares of Stock owned by the deceased Shareholder on the date of his death for $1,000,000, payable within 30 days of receipt of the proceeds of a $1,000,000 life insurance policy on the life of the deceased Shareholder.

ARTICLE III
Indemnification

3.1 Indemnity. In the event the Stock of a Shareholder is purchase and the Shareholder no longer owns the Stock, the Purchasing Shareholder agrees to assume all obligations of the Selling Shareholder relating to the Selling Shareholder's personal guarantee of certain debt of the Corporation ("Guarantee") and to indemnify and save the Selling Shareholder harmless from any liability on account of the Guarantee. This Section 3.1 is not intended, however, to require the purchasing Shareholder to cause the release of the selling Shareholder from his commitment under the Guarantee.

ARTICLE IV
Amendment and Termination

4.1 Amendment. This Agreement may be amended at any time by written instrument executed by the Shareholders.

4.2 Termination. Notwithstanding any other terms or provisions of this Agreement, this Agreement shall terminate:

(a) Upon the written agreement of the Shareholders.

(b) With respect to any particular Shareholder, upon the disposition by the Shareholder, in accordance with this Agreement, or all of his Stock.

(c) With respect to any Stock transferred as permitted pursuant to Section 2.1, but only with respect to the Stock so transferred.

Provided, however, that regardless of the termination of the Agreement, the rights and obligations of the parties and their successors and assigns shall continue beyond the termination.

ARTICLE V
Miscellaneous Provisions

5.1 Scope of Agreement. This Agreement shall be binding upon and be enforceable by the parties hereto and their respective heirs, legal representatives, successors and assigns, who are obligated to take any action which may be necessary or proper to carry out the purpose and intent hereof; provided, however, that the rights of the Shareholders hereunder are personal to them, their families and representatives and, without the written consent of the parties hereto, or as specifically provided herein, may not be assigned to or be enforceable by any assignee, transferee or other present or future Shareholder of the Corporation.

5.2 Severability. Any provision of this Agreement which is prohibited or held unenforceable by final order of any court or competent jurisdiction shall, within such jurisdiction, be ineffective to the extent of such order without invalidating the remaining provisions of this Agreement or affecting the validity or enforceability of such provision in any other jurisdiction.

5.3 Effective Date. This Agreement is effective as of the day and year first above written.

5.4 Articles and Bylaws of the Corporation. All provisions of the Articles of Incorporation and Bylaws of the Corporation shall remain in full force and effect as to the Shareholders' Stock except to the extent inconsistent with the express provisions of this Agreement, in which event the provisions of this Agreement shall control. The Shareholders agree to cause the Corporation to waive its rights, relating to its "first refusal" option under the Eighth Article of the Corporation's Certificate of Incorporation in the event of an event giving rise to the conditions under Section 2.1 hereof.

5.5 Arbitration. Any dispute arising out of or relating to this Agreement or the breach thereof shall be discussed between the parties hereto in good faith effort to arrive at a mutual settlement of any such controversy. If, notwithstanding, such dispute cannot be thus resolved within a period of 30 days, any party may submit the same for arbitration in the City of Wilmington, State of Delaware, to an arbitrator selected from the panel of the American Arbitration Association in accordance with its rules and regulations. The award shall be made by the decision of the arbitrator and judgment upon the award rendered by the arbitrator may be entered in any court having jurisdiction thereof.

5.6 Notices. All notice herein provided for, if mailed rather than delivered, shall be mailed by certified or registered mail with return receipt requested, addressed to the addressee at his or its last known address.

5.7 Governing Law. This Agreement shall be governed by and construed and enforced in accordance with the laws of the State of Delaware.

IN WITNESS WHEREOF, the Shareholders have executed this Agreement in the manner appropriate to each, the day and year first written above.

_____
Shareholder "Jones"

_____
Shareholder "Smith"

Sample Buy-Back Agreement Between Corporation and Shareholders

THIS AGREEMENT, entered into this _____ day of _____, 19XX, between XYZ Corp. ("Corporation") and (name of shareholder) ("Jones");

WITNESSETH:

WHEREAS, Jones is the owner of 100 shares of Common Stock of the Corporation ("Stock"); and,

WHEREAS, the parties hereto mutually desire to make provisions in the event of the death of Jones for the sale and purchase of his Stock on a fair and equitable basis; and,

WHEREAS, the Corporation is currently the owner and beneficiary of a policy of insurance on the life of Jones in the face amount of $1,000,000, the purpose of such insurance being to fund the purchase of the Stock in the event of Jones' death;

NOW THEREFORE, the Corporation and Jones hereby agree:

ARTICLE I
Stock Subject to Agreement

1.1 Stock Subject to Agreement. The terms of this Agreement shall apply to all Stock presently owned by Jones. In the event that the Corporation shall declare any dividend or other distribution upon its outstanding capital stock payable in capital stock (a stock dividend), or so subdivide its outstanding shares of capital stock into a greater number of share (stock split), or shall combine the outstanding shares of its capital stock into a smaller number of shares (a reverse stock split), then this Agreement shall apply to any Stock acquired by Jones during his lifetime as a result of such stock divided, stock split or reverse stock split. However, this Agreement shall not apply to any Stock acquired by Jones after the date of this Agreement as a result of a purchase of other stock of the corporation by Jones from the Corporation or any other shareholder.

1.2 Endorsement of Stock Certificates. Each stock certificate representing shares of Stock held or hereafter acquired by Jones shall be endorsed substantially as follows:

"The shares represented by this certificate are subject to the provisions of the Agreement to Purchase Corporate Stock, dated _____, which Agreement is available for inspection at the principal office of the Corporation."

Provided, however, that failure so to endorse any of the Stock certificates shall not invalidate this Agreement. The Corporation shall keep a copy of this Agreement available for inspection by all properly interested parties at the principal office.

1.3 Use of Stock as Collateral. Jones shall have the right to pledge Stock owned by him as Collateral security for personal indebtedness, even though the certificate of such Stock is endorsed as provided in Section 1.2, but any Stock so pledged shall remain subject to the terms of this Agreement.

1.4 Transfer of Stock. This Agreement shall without further mention and despite reference to "Stock owned by Jones," be applicable to all Stock as defined in Section 1.2 hereof which is at any time transferred by Jones to any other person or entity.

1.5 Voting and Dividend Rights. The Stock owned by Jones subject to this Agreement shall be voted by him, and, after his death, by the personal representatives of his estate until purchased pursuant to this Agreement. Any dividends payable on the Stock shall be paid to Jones or the personal representatives of his estate, as the case may be.

ARTICLE II
Death of "Jones"

2.1 Death of Jones. In the event of the death of Jones, the Corporation shall purchase and the legal representatives of his estate shall sell, at a price determined by Article III, all but not part of the shares of Stock owned by Jones on the date of his death.

ARTICLE III
Purchase Price and Payment

3.1 Determination of Purchase Price. The purchase price for all of the Stock subject to this Agreement shall be determined as follows:

(a) **Stipulated Value.** The purchase price for the Stock owned by Jones shall be equal to $1,000,000 or such other value as may from time to time be established by resolution adopted by a vote of at least a majority of the entire Board of Directors of the Corporation and agreed to in writing by ONE (such $1,000,000 value or the value later established is herein referred to as the "stipulated value"); provided, however, that if Jones' death occurs more than 18 months from the date of this Agreement, and if no such resolution has been adopted by the Board of Directors and agreed to in writing by Jones within the 18 month period preceding the death of Jones, then the purchase price for such Stock shall be determined in accordance with the following paragraph (b).

(b) **Alternate Value.** Given the conditions of (a) above, then the purchase price of Jones' Stock shall be equal to the stipulated value last established pursuant to paragraph (a) of this Section 3.1 plus or minus, as the case may be, the increase or decrease in the book value per share of the Stock from the last day of the fiscal year immediately preceding the date on which the stipulated value was last determined to the last day of the fiscal year immediately preceding the date of Jones' death, multiplied by the number of shares of Stock owned by Jones which are subject to this Agreement. The book value per share shall be computed by the CPA's regularly retained by the corporation and in accordance with generally accepted accounting principles on a consistent basis and shall include all adjustments, which in the opinion of the CPA's are necessary for a fair statement of the results of operations of the Corporation for the interim period. In determining such book value, there shall be excluded the amount by which the proceeds of any life insurance on the life of Jones which are payable to the Corporation exceed the value of any such insurance policy as carried on the books of the Corporation prior to Jones' death.

3.2 **Payment of Purchase Price.** The payment of the purchase price for any stock purchased under this Agreement shall be made as follows:

(a) **Initial Payment.** In the event of the death of Jones, the Corporation shall pay to the legal representatives of Jones' estate for application upon the purchase price of stock owned by Jones the total net proceeds, if any, of life insurance upon the life of Jones payable to the Corporation up to but not to exceed the total purchase price therefore as determined in accordance with this Article III. Such initial payment shall be made on or before the later of (1) the date upon which the Corporation receives such insurance proceeds as the designated beneficiary and (2) the 30th day following the date on which the accountants determine the value of the Stock (if a stipulated value is not then if effect). If no such insurance on the life of Jones is paid to the Corporation, then there shall be no initial payment, and the entire purchase price shall be paid in the manner provided in the following paragraph (b).

(b) **Balance.** (i) the Corporation shall pay to the legal representatives of Jones' estate that balance of the purchase price (herein called the "Balance") represented by the amount (if any) by which the aggregate price of the Stock exceeds the amount of the initial payment under paragraph (a) above, in not more than 40 consecutive equal quarterly installments of principal, plus accrued interest thereon, commencing on the first day of January next following (1) the date of Jones' death if a stipulated value is then in effect, or (2) the date on which the valuation of the Stock is determined pursuant to Section 3.1 hereof if no stipulated value is in effect at the time of Jones' death. The amount of the unpaid balance outstanding from time to time shall bear interest at the rate of 9% per annum which shall be payable semiannually with installments of principal, and such interest shall accrue from (1) the date which is 30 days from the date of Jones' death if a stipulated value is then in effect or (2) the date on which the value of the Stock is determined pursuant to Section 3.1 hereof if no stipulated value is in effect at the time of Jones' death, and,

(ii) The obligation to pay the balance and interest due thereon shall be evidenced by a duly executed promissory note payable to the order of the party or parties from whom the Stock is purchased, containing the aforesaid terms and such other terms as are customary for such instruments, including the right of prepayment, in whole or in part, without penalty, from time to time.

(c) **Allocation of Purchase Price.** If the Stock purchased under this Agreement includes Stock owned by anyone other than Jones as a result of transfers made by Jones during his lifetime, a pro rata share of the initial payment and installments of the balance shall be made to such person in the same proportion as the purchase price for the Stock held by them bears to the total purchase price of all Stock so transferred.

3.3 Transfer of Stock. At such time as the first payment is made for the purchase of Stock pursuant to Section 3.2 hereof, the seller of the Stock so purchased shall deliver the stock certificates representing such Stock, properly endorsed for transfer in blank, to the Corporation for cancellation.

ARTICLE IV
Amendment and Termination

4.1 Amendment. This Agreement may be amended at any time by written instrument executed by the Corporation and Jones.

4.2 Termination. Notwithstanding any other terms or provisions of this Agreement, this Agreement shall terminate:

(a) Upon the written agreement of the Corporation and Jones.

(b) Upon the bankruptcy, insolvency or dissolution of the Corporation occurring during the lifetime of Jones, or,

(c) Upon the disposition of all of his Stock to persons other than his wife, children or other issue.

ARTICLE V
Miscellaneous Provisions

5.1 Scope of Agreement. This Agreement shall be binding upon and be enforceable by the parties hereto and their respective heirs, legal representatives, successors and assigns, who are obligated to take any action which may be necessary or proper to carry out the purpose and intent hereof.

5.2 Effective Date. This Agreement is effective as of the day and year first above written.

5.3 Life Insurance Policies. The Corporation shall not at any time without the express written consent of Jones, cancel, transfer or fail to pay the premium upon the policy or policies it owns on the life of Jones as of the date of this Agreement.

5.4 Governing Law. This Agreement shall be governed by and construed and enforced in accordance with the laws of the State of Delaware.

IN WITNESS WHEREOF, the Corporation and ONE have executed this Agreement in the manner appropriate to each, the day and year first written above.

_____   _____
(Corporation name)   Shareholder "Jones"

By _____

Its _____

Bibliography

Acquisitions, Mergers, Sales, Buyouts & Takeovers: A Handbook with Forms, Charles A. Sharf, et. al., Prentice-Hall, 1985.

Anatomy of a Bankruptcy: A Lending Primer for Commercial Bankers, Ronald C. Spurga, Ballinger Publications, 1987.

Bankruptcy and Creditor's Rights, Douglas Boshkoff, Josephson-Kluwer Legal Education Centers, Inc., 1986.

Bankruptcy: A Concise Guide for Creditors and Debtors, W. Homer Drake, Jr. and Richard B. Herzog, Arco Publishing, Inc., 1983.

Business Opportunities from Corporate Bankruptcies, R. Morrison, Wiley & Sons, 1985.

Buying and Selling a Business, Robert F. Klueger, Wiley & Sons, 1988.

Buying and Selling a Small Business, Verne A. Bunn, Arno Press, 1979.

Buying and Selling a Small Business, Michael M. Coltman, ISC Press, 1983.

Buying, Selling & Merging Businesses, Jere D. McGaffey, American Law Institute, 1979.

Buying, Selling, Starting a Business, Ray L. Gustafson, GHC Press, 1982.

Cases, Problems and Materials on Bankruptcy, Baird, Douglas & Jackson, Little, Brown & Co., 1985.

Corporate Financial Distress: A Complete Guide to Predicting, Avoiding and Dealing with Bankruptcy, Edward I. Altman, Wiley & Sons, 1983.

Estate Planning Made Easy, Herbert F. Starr, TAB Books, Inc., 1984.

Everything You Always Wanted to Know About Mergers, Acquisitions and Divestitures but Didn't Know Whom to Ask, Roger Kuppinger, R. Kuppinger, 1986.

Federal Tax Aspects of Bankruptcy, C. Richard McQueen, Shepards-McGraw, 1984.

Get Rich—Stay Rich: Making It, Keeping It, Passing It Along Under the New Tax Laws, Charles Plotnick & Stephan Leimberg, Stein & Day, 1984.

Guide to International Venture Capital, The Editors of *Venture* magazine, Simon & Schuster, 1985.

Handbook of Estate Planning, Larry D. Crumbly, Dow Jones-Irwin, 1988.

Herzog's Bankruptcy Forms and Practice, Asa S. Herzog, et. al., Boardman, Clank Co., Ltd., 1984.

How to Profitably Sell or Buy a Company or Business, F. Gordon Douglas, Van Nostrand Reinhold Co., 1981.

How to Save Your Business: Winning Ways to Put Any Financially Troubled Business Together Again, Arnold S. Goldstein, Enterprise Publishing, Inc., 1983.

How to Start, Expand and Sell a Business, James C. Comiskey, Venture Prospectives Press, 1985.

How to Survive & Succeed in a Small Financial Planning Practice, Andrew M. Rich, Reston Division of Simon and Schuster, 1984.

Legacy of Love: How to Make Life Easier for Those You Leave Behind, Elmo A. Petterle, Shelter Publications, Inc., 1986.

"Profitable Acquisitions: Guidelines for Buying and Selling Companies for Businessmen and Financiers," Thomas H. Hopkins, McTaggart Press, 1984.

Ravish & Repair, Zachary Steele, Vantage Press, Inc., 1987.

The Action-Step Plan to Avoiding Business Bankruptcy: Am I Going Under?, Emery Toncre, Prentice-Hall, 1984.

The Battle-Weary Executives: A Blueprint for New Beginnings, Lawrence W. Tuller, Dow Jones-Irwin, 1990.

The Complete Guide to a Successful Leveraged Buyout, Allen Michel & Israel Shaked, Dow Jones-Irwin, 1987.

The Complete Guide to Buying and Selling a Business, Arnold S. Goldstein, New American Library, 1986.

The Five Deadly Mistakes that Lead to Bankruptcy! A Successful Business Handbook for Today's Men & Women, Gene L. Corder, Redcor Book Publishing Co., 1981.

The Logic and Limits of Bankruptcy Law, Thomas Jackson, Harvard University Press, 1986.

The Mergers and Acquisitions Handbook, M. Rock, McGraw-Hill, 1987.

Buying In: A Complete Guide to Acquiring a Business or Professional Practice, Lawrence W. Tuller, TAB Books, Inc., 1990.

Valuation of Privately Owned Business, Steven M. Reisinger, Acquisition Planning, Inc., 1981.

What Every Executive Should Know About Chapter 11, Benjamin Weintraub, National Association of Credit Management, 1985.

When You Buy or Sell a Company, Paul B. Baron, Center for Business Information, 1986.

Why Companies Fail: Strategies for Detecting, Avoiding and Profiting from Bankruptcy, Harlan D. Platt, Lexington Books, 1985.

Sources

INVESTMENT BANKERS AND VENTURE CAPITAL FIRMS

Acquivest Group, Inc.
1 Newtown Executive Park, Suite 204
Newton, MA 01262

Advest, Incorporated
6 Central Row
Hartford, CT 06103

Allied Bancshares Capital Corporation
1000 Louisiana
Houston, TX 77002

Allied Capital Corporation
1625 I Street, NW., Suite 603
Washington, DC 20006

Allstate Insurance Co.
Allstate Plaza E-2
Northbrook, IL 60062

Amervest Corporation
10 Commercial Wharf West
Boston, MA 02110

Amev Capital Corp.
1 World Trade Center, 50th Floor
New York, NY 10048

Asset Capital & Management Corp.
608 Ferry Blvd.
Stratford, CT 06497

Atlantic American Capital, Ltd.
Lincoln Center, Suite 851
5401 W. Kennedy Blvd.
Tampa, FL 33609

Atlantic Venture Partners
P.O. Box 1493
Richmond, VA 23212

Bancboston Capital Corp.
100 Federal Street
Boston, MA 02110

Bankamerica Capital Corporation
555 California St.
42nd Floor
San Francisco, CA 94104

Bear Sterns & Company
Investment Banking Division
55 Water St.
New York, NY 10041

Blake Investment Group
1101 30th Street, NW, Suite 101
Washington, DC 20007

BNE Associates
Bank of New England
60 State St.
Boston, MA 02109

Bradford Associates
22 Chambers St.
Princeton, NJ 08540

BT Capital Corporation
280 Park Avenue, 10th Floor W.
New York, NY 10017

Butler Capital Corp.
767 Fifth Avenue, Sixth Floor
New York, NY 10153

Cable, Howse & Cozado
999 Third Avenue, Sute 4300
Seattle, WA 98104

Capital Corporation of America
225 So. 15th Street, Suite 920
Philadelphia, PA 19102

Carl Marks & Co., Inc.
77 Water St.
New York, NY 10005

Charles Dethan Group
51 E. 67th Street
New York, NY 10021

Charterhouse Group International, Inc.
535 Madison Avenue
New York, NY 10022

Chase Manhattan Capital Markets
   Corp.
1 Chase Manhattan Plaza—3rd Floor
New York, NY 10081

Citicorp Venture Capital, Ltd.
Citicorp Center, 153 E. 53rd Street,
   28th Floor
New York, NY 10043

Clarion Capital Corporation
1801 E. 12th Street, Suite 201
Cleveland, OH 44114

Connecticut National Bank
Investment Banking Division
1604 Walnut Street
Philadelphia, PA 19103

Continental Illinois Venture Corporation
231 So. LaSalle Street
Chicago, IL 60697

Dain Bosworth, Inc.
100 Dain Tower
Minneapolis, MN 55402

Dillon Reed & Company, Inc.
535 Madison Avenue
New York, NY 10022

DJS Group
745 Park Avenue, 21st Floor
New York, NY 10155

Drexel Burnham Lambert, Inc.
55 Broad Street
New York, NY 10004

E. F. Hutton LBO, Inc.
1 Battery Park Plaza
New York, NY 10004

EAB Venture Corporation
90 Park Avenue
New York, NY 10016

Fidelity Bank
Investment Banking Division, Sixth
   Floor
Broad & Walnut
Philadelphia, PA 19109

First Chicago Venture Capital Corp.
1 First National Plaza, Suite 2628
Chicago, IL 60670

First Connecticut SBIC
177 State Street
Bridgeport, CT 06604

First Dallas Financial Co.
3302 Southland Center
Dallas, TX 75201

First Dallas Group, LTD.
300 Campbell Center, 8350 N. Central
   Expressway
Dallas, TX 75206

First Interstate Capital Corp.
515 So. Figueroa St.
Los Angeles, CA 90071

Fleet Growth Industries, Inc.
111 Westminster St.
Providence, RI 02903

Foothil Capital Corporation
2049 Century Park East
Los Angeles, CA 90067

Fostin Capital Corporation
681 Anderson Drive
Pittsburgh, PA 15220

Founders Ventures, Inc.
477 Madison Avenue
New York, NY 10022

Frontenac Capital Corp.
208 So. LaSalle Street, Suite 1900
Chicago, IL 60604

General Electric Venture Capital Corp.
3135 Easton Turnpike
Fairfield, CT 06431

Gibbons, Green, Van Amerongen
600 Madison Avenue
New York, NY 10022

Golder, Thoma & Cressey
120 So. LaSalle St.
Chicago, IL 60603

Hambrecht & Quist
235 Montgomery St.
San Francisco, CA 94104

Hambro International Venture Fund
17 E. 71st Street
New York, NY 10021

Herbert Young Securities, Inc.
98 Cuttermill Road
Great Neck, NY 11021

Hillman Ventures, Inc.
2000 Grant Bldg.
Pittsburgh, PA 15219

Howard, Lawson & Co., Inc.
2 Penn Center Plaza
Philadelphia, PA, 19102

Interfirst Venture Corporation
P.O. Box 83644
Dallas, TX 75283

ITC Capital Corporation
1290 Avenue of the Americas
New York, NY 10104

James River Capital Associates
9 So. 12th Street
Richmond, VA 23219

*John Hancock Venture Capital
   Management, Inc.*
John Hancock Place, 57th Floor
Boston, MA 02117

Keeley Management Company
2 Radnor Corporate Center
Radnor, PA 19087

Kidder Peabody & Company
Investment Banking Division
Mellon Bank Center
Philadelphia, PA 19102

Lepero de Neuflize & Company
345 Park Avenue
New York, NY 10154

*Manufacturers Hanover Venture Capital
   Corp.*
140 E. 45th Street
New York, NY 10017

Maryland National Bank
Investment Banking Group
P.O. Box 987
Baltimore, MD 21203

Mellon Bank, Corporate Finance Group
Mellon Bank Center
Philadelphia, PA 19102

Menlo Venture
3000 Sand Hill Road
Menlo Park, CA 94025

Midland Capital Corporation
950 Third Avenue
New York, NY 10022

M Venture Corporation
P.O. Box 662090
1704 Main St.
Dallas, TX 75266

Narragansett Capital
40 Westminster St.
Providence, RI 02903

Norwest Venture Capital Management,
Inc.
1730 Midwest Plaza Bldg.
801 Nicollet Mall
Minneapolis, MN 55402

Oxford Partners
Soundview Plaza
1266 Main Street
Stamford, CT 06902

Paine Webber Venture Management
Company
100 Federal St.
Boston, MA 02110

Pennwood Capital Corporation
645 Madison Avenue
New York, NY 10022

Philadelphia Capital Advisors
Philadelphia National Bank Bldg.
Broad & Chestnut Streets
Philadelphia, PA 19107

Phillips J. Hook & Associates, Inc.
5600 Roswell Road, Suite 300
Atlanta, GA 30342

PNC Venture Capital Group
Fifth Avenue & Woods Streets
Pittsburgh, PA 15222

PRU Capital, Incorporated
1 Seaport Plaza, 31st Floor
199 Water Street
New York, NY 10292

Quincy Partners
P.O. Box 154
Glen Head, NY 11545

Regional Financial Enterprises, Inc.
51 Pine St.
New Canaan, CT 06840

Rosenfeld & Company
625 SW Washington St.
Portland, OR 97205

Rothschild, Incorporated
Rockefeller Plaza
New York, NY 10020

Rust Ventures LP
114 W. Seventh St.
Suite 1300
Austin, TX 78701

Salomon Brothers, Inc.
1 New York Plaza
New York, NY 10004

Security Pacific Capital Corp.
4000 MacArthur Blvd.
Suite 950
Newport Beach, CA 92660

Seidler AMDEC Securities, Inc.
515 So. Figueroa St.
Los Angeles, CA 90071

Smith, Barney, Harris, Upham &
Company, Inc.
1345 Avenue of the Americas
New York, NY 10105

Sprout Capital Group
140 Broadway
New York, NY 10025

Summit Ventures
1 Boston Place
Boston, MA 02108

TA Associates
45 Milk Street
Boston, MA 02109

TDH Capital
259 Radnor–Chester Road
Radnor, PA 19087

Tucker Anthony and RL Day, Inc.
120 Broadway
New York, NY 10271

Union Venture Corporation
445 So. Figueroa St.
Los Angeles, CA 90071

UV Capital
9 So. 12th St.
Richmond, VA 23219

Ventue Lending Associates
767 Fifth Avenue
New York, NY 10153

Warburg, Pincus Ventures, Inc.
466 Lexington Avenue
New York, NY 10017

Wells Fargo Equity Corporation
1 Embarcadero Center
San Francisco, CA 94111

Welsh, Carson, Anderson & Stowe
45 Wall Street, 16th Floor
New York, NY 10005

William Blair Venture Partners
135 So. LaSalle Street, 29th Floor
Chicago, IL 60603

ASSET BASED LENDERS

Congress Financial Corporation
American City Bldg.
Columbia, MD 21044

General Electric Credit Corporation
Eastern Corporate Finance Dept.
3003 Summer Steet
Stamford, CT 06905

Glenfed Capital Corporation
Carnegie Center
Princeton, NJ 08540

ITT Capital Corporation
1400 North Central Center Life Tower
St. Paul, MN 55101

Security Pacific Business Credit, Inc.
45 So. Hudson Avenue
Pasadena, CA 91101

Trefoil Capital
Fidelity Bank Bldg.
Broad & Walnut Streets
Philadelphia, PA 19109

Glossary

buyer paper—A promissory note from the buyer or an executed contractual agreement identifying specific amounts to be paid by the Buyer to the Seller on specific dates.

equity—Refers to an ownership share of the business, usually evidenced by common stock or preferred stock certificates. Liquidation proceeds are distributed to equity holders only after all secured and unsecured creditors are satisfied.

mezzanine debt—Refers to short- or intermediate-term debt that is repaid after primary position lenders and secondary position lenders, but before unsecured creditors upon liquidation. Mezzanine lenders might be in a secondary position against these short-term assets.

non-compete covenant—States that for a specified number of years the Seller will not enter into any activity that would hinder or detract from the business being sold. Usually, no longer than three years.

operating line—Short-term debt for use as working capital. Usually secured by accounts receivable, inventory, or both. Always in a primary position against these short-term assets.

primary position or primary debt—Refers to the position of the lender in the order of repayment upon liquidation. Lenders with a primary position will be repaid first.

secondary position or secondary debt—Refers to the position of the lender in the event of liquidation. Secondary position lenders are paid from the liquidation proceeds after the primary lenders are satisfied.

secured debt—Loans made using the assets of the business as collateral that can be used to repay the loan in the event of default.

unsecured debt—Loans made without any collateral except the promise to repay, such as a promissory note or vendor trade credit.

Index